D0556265

Qualitative Inquiry
and Social Justice

In memoriam

Richard A. Atalese
Egon Guba
Joe L. Kincheloe
Steiner Kvale

Qualitative Inquiry and Social Justice

Toward a Politics of Hope

Norman K. Denzin
Michael D. Giardina
Editors

Left
Coast
Press
Inc.

Walnut Creek, California

LEFT COAST PRESS, INC.
1630 North Main Street, #400
Walnut Creek, CA 94596
http://www.LCoastPress.com

ISBN 978-1-59874-422-4 hardcover
ISBN 978-1-59874-423-1 paperback

Library of Congress Cataloguing-in-Publication information available

Printed in the United States of America

⊗™ The paper used in this publication meets the minimum requirements of
American National Standard for Information Sciences—Permanence of Paper
for Printed Library Materials, ANSI/NISO Z39.48–1992.

Printed on post-consumer recycled paper.

09 10 11 12 13   5 4 3 2 1

Contents

Section II: Qualitative Inquiry in Post-Disaster America

Section III: Human Rights and Radical Performance

Coda

||| International Congress of Qualitative Inquiry

The International Congress of Qualitative Inquiry has been hosted each May since 2005 by the International Center for Qualitative Inquiry at the University of Illinois, Urbana-Champaign. This volume, as well as three proceeding volumes, is a product of plenary sessions from these international congresses. All of these volumes are available from Left Coast Press, Inc.

Qualitative Inquiry and Social Justice
Edited by Norman K. Denzin and Michael D. Giardina
2009, based on the 2008 Congress
ISBN 978-1-59874-422-4 hardcover, 978-1-59874-423-1 paperback

Qualitative Inquiry and the Politics of Evidence
Edited by Norman K. Denzin and Michael D. Giardina
2008, based on the 2007 Congress
ISBN 978-1-59874-321-0 hardcover, 978-1-59874-322-7 paperback

Ethical Futures in Qualitative Research
Edited by Norman K. Denzin and Michael D. Giardina
2007, based on the 2006 Congress
ISBN 978-1-59874-140-7 hardcover, 978-1-59874-141-4 paperback

Qualitative Inquiry and the Conservative Challenge
Edited by Norman K. Denzin and Michael D. Giardina
2006, based on the 2005 Congress
ISBN 978-1-59874-045-5 hardcover, 978-1-59874-046-2 paperback

Another product of the Congress is the refereed quarterly journal of the Institute. *International Review of Qualitative Research* is a peer-reviewed journal that encourages the use of critical, experimental and traditional forms of qualitative inquiry in the interests of social justice. We seek works that are both academically sound and partisan, works that offer knowledge-based radical critiques of social settings and institutions while promoting human dignity, human rights, and just societies around the globe. Submissions to the journal are judged by the effective use of critical qualitative research methodologies and practices for understanding and advocacy in policy arenas, as well as clarity of writing and willingness to experiment with new and traditional forms of presentation. Linked to the annual Congress for Qualitative Inquiry, much of the journal's content will be drawn from presentations and themes developed from these international meetings. The journal is also published by Left Coast Press, Inc.

International Review of Qualitative Research

Editor: Norman K. Denzin
Quarterly in May, August, November, February
ISSN 1940-8447

To find more information on these publications, or to order, go to

www.LCoastPress.com

Acknowledgments

We thank Mitch Allen at Left Coast Press for his continued enthusiastic support of our endeavors. We also thank Carole Bernard for her editorial expertise and patience with us throughout the production process and Hannah Jennings for the production design of the volume.

Many of the chapters contained in this book were presented as plenary or keynote addresses at the Fourth International Congress of Qualitative Inquiry, held at the University of Illinois, Urbana-Champaign, in May 2008. We thank the Department of Advertising, the Institute of Communications Research, the College of Media, and the International Institute for Qualitative Inquiry for continued support of the Congress, as well as those campus units that contributed time, funds, and/or volunteers to the effort.

The Congress, and by extension this book, would not have materialized without the tireless efforts of Himika Bhattacharya (diplomatic liaison), Christina Ceisel (logistics and planning), David Haskell (travel), Li Xiong (communications guru), Yiye Liu (webmistress), and James Salvo (the glue who continues to hold the whole thing together). For information on future congresses, please visit http://www.icqi.org.

Norman K. Denzin
Michael D. Giardina
Champaign, Illinois
December 2008

Introduction

Qualitative Inquiry and Social Justice

Toward a Politics of Hope[1]

Norman K. Denzin and
Michael D. Giardina
University of Illinois

*Democratic teaching encourages students to develop initiative
and imagination, the capacity to name the world, to identify
the obstacles to their full humanity, and the courage to act
upon whatever the known demands.*

—William Ayers, 2009

*While the Bush administration may have been uninterested in
critical ideas, debate and dialogue, it was almost rabid about
destroying the economic, political and educational conditions
that make them possible.*

—Henry Giroux, 2008

*Justice constitutes an article of faith expressed through deep
feelings that move people to action.*

—Patricia Hill Collins, 1998

Do we participate in a politics of cynicism or a politics of hope?

—Barack Obama, 2004

I. Proem

What is the role of critical qualitative research in a historical present when the need for social justice has never been greater? This
is a historical present that cries out for emancipatory visions, for
visions that inspire transformative inquiries, and for inquiries that

can provide the moral authority to move people to struggle and resist oppression. The pursuit of social justice within a transformative paradigm challenges prevailing forms of human oppression and injustice. This paradigm is firmly rooted in a human rights agenda. It requires an ethical framework that is rights- and social justice based. It requires an awareness of "the need to redress inequalities by giving precedence … to the voices of the least advantaged groups in society" (Mertens, Holmes, & Harris, 2009, p. 89). Such a paradigm addresses the wholesale failure of a government to respond to a natural disaster such as Hurricane Katrina or on-going wars of aggression waged in our name in Iraq. Or to the ravages of neoliberal capitalism. Or to the blatant disregard for science and education on the part of the Bush administration. Or even to the public displays of racism during the 2008 U.S. presidential election (especially at campaign rallies featuring Republican vice-presidential nominee Sarah Palin).

This is the context within which qualitative researchers reside. Living as we are in a globalized, post-9/11/01 world, both of us recognize that being a U.S. citizen is to be a "enmeshed in the facts of U.S. foreign policy, world trade, civil society and war" (Madison & Hamera, 2006, p. xx). Thus, we share in the shame of Abu Ghraib, of the response to Katrina, of the last eight years of a ruinous administration seemingly hell-bent on dismantling all that we hold true. From "flags in the window" (Denzin, 2007) to the "globalization of dissent" (Denzin & Giardina, 2006a), we have spent the last eight years writing and researching against this regime of theoconservative fundamentalism and neoliberal capitalism: Never before has there been a greater need for a militant utopianism that can help us imagine a world free of conflict, terror, and death; a world that is caring, loving, and truly compassionate; a world that honors healing. Postmodern democracy cannot succeed unless critical qualitative scholars adopt methodologies that transcend the limitations and constraints of a lingering politically and racially conservative postpositivism. This framework attaches itself to state-organized auditing systems and regulatory mechanisms like the No Child Left Behind (NCLB) Act of 2001. These links and these historical educational connections must be broken.

To these ends, we contend that the most important events of the last decade follow from the attacks and events following 9/11/01, including the wars in Iraq and Afghanistan, the global "war on terror," and the institutionalization of a new surveillance regime that affects every traveling body entering or leaving the United States (see especially Denzin & Giardina, 2006a). Critical qualitative inquiry must locate itself in these historical spaces, which now encompass surveillance regimes in virtually every educational setting—school, college, daycare—if it is to live up to its promise. More specifically, we seek forms of qualitative inquiry that make a difference in everyday lives by promoting human dignity and social justice. Critical performance pedagogy, spectacle pedagogy, critical minstrelsy theory (Elam, 2001; Sotiropoulos, 2006), and ethno- and performance drama (Mienczakowski, 2001; Saldana, 2005) are just some forms of such research that advance this agenda by exposing and critiquing the pedagogies of terror and discrimination that operate in daily life (Garoian & Gaudelius, 2008, p. 126; Madison, 2005; Madison & Hamera, 2006, pp. xx–xxi; see also Smith, 2004 and Kaufman, 2001). Simultaneously, we seek morally informed disciplines and interventions that will help people recover meaning in the shadows of a post-9/11/01 world, a world after George W. Bush: If the landmark election of Barack Obama as the 44th president of the United States is any indication, there is a deep desire to transcend and overcome the psychological despair fostered by wars, economic disaster, and divisive sexual and cultural politics.

As global citizens, we have lived through eight long years of cynicism, fraud, and deceit; a time for change is at hand.[2] Our project is clear. We are no longer called to just *interpret* the world, which was the mandate of traditional ethnography. Today, we are called to *change* the world and to change it in ways that resist injustice while celebrating freedom and full, inclusive, participatory democracy. *Such is the mandate of this volume.*

Multiple views, all tangled up in war:

This feels like a battleground to me. I want research done within all of the qualitative research paradigms to be considered legitimate. ... Let us engage in the paradigm wars. Let us defend ourselves against those who would impose their modern notions of science on us by exposing the flaws in what they call scientifically-based research. Let us mount a strong offense ... if we do not fight back, qualitative research could become self-absorbed, fragmented and ineffectual. And the neo-conservative dream of a return to scientific modernity will have become true. (Hatch, 2006, pp. 406–407)

I would like to think that we in educational research had our 'paradigm wars' almost two decades ago ... but the recent ... debates regarding what is and is not ... good science requires students to have some background in the "science wars." (Lather, 2006a, pp. 47–48)

The metaphor of paradigm wars ... is undoubtedly overdrawn. Describing the discussions and altercations of the past decade or two as wars paints the matter as more confrontational than necessary. (Guba & Lincoln, 1994, p. 116)

Although much of the controversy has focused on the "paradigm wars" ... each camp [quantitative, qualitative] has also criticized the other's methods of study, the rigor of its procedures, and the validity of its outcomes. The field of mixed methodology, which we call the "third methodological moment," has evolved as a result of these discussions and controversies and as a pragmatic way of using the strengths of both approaches. (Teddlie & Tashakkori, 2003a, p. ix)

Fruitful dialog is now possible. (Guba, 1990b, p. 370)

Hatch and Lather want to revisit the paradigm wars of the 1970s and 1980s. Teddlie and Tashakkori cast an approving eye back on the wars, noting that much good came of them. Guba and Lincoln feel the metaphor was overdrawn. Guba calls for dialog.We are mid-way between two extremes, searching for a new middle, moving in several different directions at the same time. We are in a third "methodological moment"[3] (Teddlie and Tashakkori, 2003a, p. ix), a time of disruptions, emerging confluences (Guba & Lincoln, 2005; Lather, 2004, 2006a, 2006b).

Mixed methodologies and calls for scientifically based research are in the ascendancy. The evidence-based research movement, with its fixed standards and guidelines for conducting and evaluating qualitative inquiry, seeks total domination: One shoe fits everyone (Denzin & Giardina, 2006b; Morse, 2006; St. Pierre, 2006). The heart of the matter turns on issues surrounding the politics and ethics of evidence and the value of qualitative work in addressing matters of equity and social justice.

But this is like old wine in old bottles, 1980s and 1990s battles in a new century, a New Paradigm War. The terms have "shifted from 'paradigm debate' and paradigm proliferation to a heavy-handed governmental incursion into 'Scientific Research in Education' (a.k.a., SBR) as the gold standard for contemporary educational research" (Wright and Lather, 2006, p. 2). How did we get to this place? How were we silenced? To answer these questions, the qualitative inquiry community must ask itself how it lost its seat at the bargaining table in the first place. How did we snatch defeat from the jaws of victory? We need to mount a resistance against those who would impose a single "gold standard" on what we do.

At the end of the first decade of the 21st century, let us reengage the paradigm disputes of the last three decades (Donmoyer, 2006; Gage, 1989).[4] Let us extend the call for expanding paradigms, breaking boundaries, opening up new spaces, exploring new discourses and new ways of connecting people, methodologies, and institutional sites (Dillard, 2006; Lather, 2006a; Nespor, 2006, p. 124; Wright, 2006). Let us challenge and move beyond postpositivism's complicity with the reactionary racial politics of neoliberalism. Let us do more than just challenge federal laws like NCLB. *Let us imagine new ways of doing what we do.* Let us renew our efforts to decolonize the academy, to honor the voices of those who have been silenced by dominant paradigms. But let us do so from within the framework of a dialog, a conversation that will move us to new, more informed and more sophisticated empowerment paradigms" (Guba, 1990a, p. 27).

After Guba, we call for a new paradigm dialog.[5] This dialog—which anticipates a postparadigm moment—honors inclusion, a coloring of epistemologies (Scheurich and Young,

1997). It rests on standpoint and decolonizing epistemologies. It establishes links between paradigms, sexuality, gender, and ethnicity. It moves forward under a spirit of cooperation and collaboration.

Taking our lead from Hatch, we will briefly review the 1980s paradigm conflicts. We seek a nonmilitary metaphor, something more peaceful, less combative than war.[6] We quickly shift from the 1980s to the present, taking up multiple forms of paradigm discourse in the third methodological moment. We then reengage Hatch and his critique of the SBR backlash against interpretive inquiry and return to Guba's 1990 call for dialog and collaboration across paradigms and interpretive communities. The Introduction concludes with an overview of the chapters contained in this book.

II. The New Paradigm Dialogs and Critical Qualitative Research

Paradigms are more than nested assumptions about ontology, epistemology, methodology, and ethics. They are products of "tensions and conflicts that stretch outside the university to state bureaucracies, pressure groups, big corporations, community groups" (Nespor, 2006, p. 123). They are more than "incommensurably bounded positions ... they are relationally constituted... and proliferate or shift not only when authors bend ideas ... but as opponents ... allies ... situations and events ... change" (Nespor, 2006, p. 123). Paradigms are human constructions. They define the shifting worldview of the researcher-as-bricoleur.

The new paradigm disputes are embedded in the mixed-methods movement, as that movement reenacts arguments from the 1980s and 1990s (see below). According to Gage (1989), and elaborating Teddlie and Tashakkori (2003b, p. 7–8), the paradigm wars of the 1980s resulted in the demise—or, at least, the serious crippling—of quantitative research in education, a victim of attacks from anti-naturalists, interpretivists, and critical theorists. Ethnographic studies flourished. The cultural appropriateness of schooling, critical pedagogy, and critical theorists and feminists analyses fostered struggles for power and cultural capital for the poor, non-Whites, women, and gays (Gage, 1989).

Guba's (1990a) *Paradigm Dialog* signaled an end to the 1980s wars, at least for the constructivists. In the *Paradigm Dialog*, post-positivists, constructivists, and critical theorists talked to one another, working through issues connected to ethics, field studies, praxis, criteria, knowledge accumulation, truth, significance, graduate training, values, and politics. We were, for a moment, one big happy family. Positivism was dead. Long live multiplicity.

By the mid-1980s, "qualitative research had begun to be widely used and widely accepted" (Donmoyer, 2006, p. 18). It was evident that many "champions of qualitative methodology did indeed operate from a fundamentally different worldview than the one more traditional researchers embraced, and this new worldview could not be simply appropriated into traditional thinking" (Donmoyer, 2006, p. 23).

By the early 1990s, there was an explosion of published works on qualitative research, and handbooks and new journals appeared. Qualitative inquiry flourished, as did work in critical, feminist, poststructural, performance, and queer theory paradigms. Increased discourse between and across paradigms seemed to mark a confluence of understandings concerning inquiry, politics, and scholarship. Guba and Lincoln could write in 2005 that "the number of qualitative texts, research papers, workshops, and training materials has exploded. Indeed it would be difficult to miss the distinct turn of the social sciences toward more interpretive, postmodern and criticalist practices and theorizing" (p. 191). Qualitative researchers were comfortably in charge of their own destiny. Perhaps they became too complacent; after all, they had their own journals and special interest groups. Sage Publications led the way (see Staller, Block, & Horner, 2008). But all was not quiet on the Western Front.

Multiple Wars, Multiple Histories

Actually, there has been more than one war. Beneath the surface, there have been at least three paradigm wars: the postpositivist war against positivism (1970–1990); the wars between competing postpositivist, constructivist, and critical theory paradigms

(1990–2005); and the current war between evidence-based methodologists, and the mixed-methods, interpretive, and critical theory schools (2005–present).[7] Each war has turned on a questioning of paradigm assumptions. Each war has reconfigured the relationship between paradigm, methodology epistemology, and ethics.

A dialectic, of sorts, seems to operate: yin and yang, a merger of binaries, opposite sides of the same coin, paradigms and methods. Side One, paradigm discourse drives methodology. Side Two, methodological models drive paradigm discourse. In between the two extremes is an excluded middle, the space of politics and moral discourse. Each war has occurred alongside each other and policed moves to embrace or ignore the politics of inquiry, the moral discourses of empowerment agendas. A ghostly haunting embedded in the legacies and skeletons of postpositivism and state-sponsored methodologies hovers in the background.

War Number One

Teddlie and Tashakkori's history is helpful here. They expand the time frame of the 1980s war. Although locating mixed-methodology in the third methodological movement, they contend that the "Golden Age" (1950–1970) was marked by the debunking of positivism, the emergence of postpositivism, and the development of designs that used mixed quantitative and qualitative methods. Full-scale conflict developed throughout the 1970–1990 period, the time of the first "paradigm war." Constructivism and posposi-tivism were in the ascendancy. End of positivism.

War Number Two

The discrediting of positivism led to vigorous debates and wars between paradigms. This was the time of paradigm war number two, which involved debates over which paradigm was more revolutionary or more empowering. A flourishing of new 'isms" and other labels emerged: constructivism, naturalism, interpretivism, multiple versions of critical theory, critical pedagogy, queer, critical race theory, LatCrit, feminism, poststructuralism, postcolonial, and decolonizing paradigms (see Lather, 2007, pp. 64–65. All received paradigms were challenged. Theorists argued for the superiority of *their* paradigm.[8] Special interest groups committed to particular paradigms appeared; some had their own journals.[9]

War Number Three

Pragmatism and the compatibility thesis emerged in the post-1990 period (see Howe, 1988; Maxcy, 2003). Under a soft pragmatic paradigm, quantitative and qualitative methods became compatible, and researchers could use both in their empirical inquiries (Teddlie & Tashakkori, 2003b, p. 7). Proponents made appeals to a "what works" pragmatic argument, contending that "no incompatibility between quantitative and qualitative methods exists at either the level of practice or that of epistemology ... there are thus no good reasons for educational researchers to fear forging ahead with 'what works'" (Howe, 1988, p. 16). Of course, what works is more than an *empirical* question. It involves the politics of evidence. This is the space that evidence-based research entered, the battleground of war number three.[10]

Wagging the Dog: Paradigmatic and Mixed-Methods Themes

The second paradigm war validated the use of mixed-methods designs. No one could refute the argument that the use of more than one method produced stronger inferences, answered research questions that other methodologies could not, and allowed greater diversity of findings (Creswell & Clark, 2007, p. 18; Teddlie & Tashakkori, 2003b, pp. 14–15). Foot in the door, the mixed-methods movement spawned at least six different variations on a common theme. The methods tail was wagging the dog. Paradigms were being reconfigured to fit methodological presuppositions.

Teddlie and Tashakkori carefully outline at least six different positions on how paradigms can be used in the development of mixed-methods research (2003b, p. 17): (1) the aparadigmatic stance; (2) the incompatibility thesis; (3) the complimentary thesis; (4) the single paradigm thesis; (5) the dialectical thesis; and (6) the multiple paradigm thesis (pp. 17–23). This is familiar territory, variations on common themes. Methods have no paradigmatic implications, are incompatible and cannot be combined, are complimentary and can be combined, or can be combined under a single, dialectical, or multiple framework.

Thus has the discourse thickened. We have moved from value- and theory-laden inquiry, through the incompatibility and complimentary theses, from triangulation to a call for mixed-methods designs. Now a new set of paradigmatic models redefining mixed methods research compete for attention.

Resurgent Postpositivism and NCLB

An additional legacy of the first two paradigm wars was a ready-made institutional apparatus that privileged a resurgent post-positivism, involving experimentalism, mixed methodologies, and "governmental incursion into the spaces of research methods" (Lather, 2006a, p. 35). Lather (2004) calls this the alphabet soup of postpositivist acronyms: CC (Cochrane Collaboration), C2 (Campbell Collaboration), AIR (American Institutes for Research), WWC (What Works Clearinghouse), SBR (scientifically based research), IES (Institute of Education Science), and NRC (National Research Council) (see http://ies.ed.gov/ncee/wwc/).

These institutional structures converged when neoliberalism, postpositivism, and the audit-accountability culture took aim on education and schooling. The interrelationships between these structures are complex and by no means well understood. The financial-auditing mechanism has been substantively and technically linked with the methodology of accountability (Biesta, 2004; MacLure, 2006, p. 730; Skrla & Scheurich, 2004). Champions of neoliberalism added one more piece to their puzzle when they understood that with a knowledge-based economy there was a need to produce better-educated workers for the global economy. IES, NCLB, SBR, CC, C2, and WWC worked hand in glove—a new age was on us, we were blind-sided by a New Paradigm dispute, and didn't even know it! Researchers were obliged "to comply—to submit to a 'methodological fundamentalism'" (MacLure, 2006, p. 730). The watchwords were: audits, efficiency, high-stakes assessment, test-based accountability, and SBR. It was only a matter of time before this apparatus would take aim at qualitative research and create protocols for evaluating qualitative research studies (see Briggs, 2006; National CASP Collaboration, 2006; also AERA, 2006; Bell, 2006; Morse, 2006).

III. The Third Moment and the New Paradigm Dialogs

Teddlie and Tashakkori (2003a, p. ix) use the term "third methodological moment" to describe an epistemological position that evolved out of the discussions and controversies associated with the 1980s paradigm wars. The third moment mediates quantitative and qualitative disputes by finding a third, or middle ground. Extending Teddlie and Tashakkori, we argue that there are, in fact, two distinct versions of the third moment: the mixed-methods version and a somewhat more radical position. This is the version that endorses paradigm proliferation, a version anchored in the critical interpretive social science tradition. It involves the incorporation of increasingly diverse standpoints, the coloring of epistemologies and the proliferation of colors, the subversion of dominant paradigms, the rejection of norms of objectivity, and the pursuit of progressive politics (Dillard, 2006, p. 64; Donmoyer, 2006; Lather, 2006a; Nespor, 2006, p. 124).

Mixed- and Emergent Methods Discourse

In the first version of the third moment, the incompatibility and incommensurability theses are rejected. On the surface this seems somewhat akin to mixing apples and oranges. When the field went from one to multiple epistemological paradigms, popular belief held that methods and paradigms could not be combined. This ushered in the emergence of many different paradigms and methodologies. But, as already noted, conflict followed. It was only a matter of time before critical theorists, feminists, and critical race theorists were fighting. It was no longer just a conflict between positivism and nonpositivism. Beneath the surface, a wider conflict was brewing, one that spread to all perspectives. The language of multiple paradigms prevailed. Some called for a truce; let a thousand different flowers bloom.

Ironically, as this discourse evolved, the complementary strengths thesis emerged, and is now accepted by many in the mixed-methods community (Morse, 2003). Here is where history starts to be rewritten. That is, multiple paradigms can be used in the same mixed-methods inquiry (Teddlie & Tashakkori, 2003b, p. 23). At the same time, the mixed- or multiple-methods approach gained acceptance. This seemed to extend the triangulation arguments of the 1970s (Dixon et al., 2006). Thus, the demise of the single theoretical and/or methodological paradigm was celebrated (Teddlie & Tashakkori, 2003b, p. 24).

The recognition that all methods are hybrid, emergent, interactive productions extended the mixed-methods paradigm discourse (Hesse-Biber & Leavy, 2008, pp. 2–3). Emergent methods innovatively combine quantitative and qualitative mixed-methods strategies. The complex intersections between epistemology, methodology, and specific inquiry techniques are stressed. Pragmatics, multiple interpretive practices, and bricolage are paramount (Denzin & Lincoln, 2005, p. 4). The critical researcher, the bricoleur, the jack-of-all-trades, produces a bricolage based on the use of many different interpretive practices and methodological tools.

For the mixed- and emergent methods advocates, the residues of the first paradigm war are positive and negative. The demise of the incompatibility and incommensurability theses, as applied to methods and paradigms, was "a major catalyst in the development of the mixed methods as a distinct third methodological moment" (Teddlie & Tashakkori, 2003b, p. 24). Regrettably, for the mixed-methods movement, a lingering negative legacy of the 1980s wars is the tendency of students and graduate programs to still consider themselves as QUALS or QUANS. On this, though, some feel "we need to get rid of that distinction" (Schwandt, 2000, p. 210).

Presumably, once this is done, only technical and pedagogical problems remain; that is: How do we implement this new paradigm in our research and in our classrooms (Eisenhart, 2006; Eisenhart & DeHaan, 2005)? The mixed-methods discourse introduced complex discussions involving design typologies, logistics, validity, data, standards, inferences, and findings that can be generalized from studies that combine quantitative (QUAN) and qualitative (QUAL) methodologies.[11]

The new moment requires multiple investigators with competencies in more than one method or paradigm. The problem of dual competency can be solved with a team approach, or with a model that presumes minimal competency in both quantitative and qualitative design (Teddlie & Tashakkori, 2003b, pp. 44–45). Teddlie and Tashakkori recommend "methodological bilingualism" (p. 45). Eisenhart and DeHaan (2005) outline a multi-tiered, interdisdisciplinary educational curriculum that focuses on different cultures and models of science. Students receive instruction in multiple paradigms, methodologies, and concrete inquiry practices. An interpretive approach to scientific inquiry is emphasized. This is a subversive approach to SBR.

For some, it is a short step from methodological bilingualism to SBR, from discussions of design, inference, data quality, and transferability, to inquiries that privilege QUAN over QUAL. But it is not this simple.

Phases in the Paradigm Discourse

In the 1980s paradigm wars, qualitative research took its rightful place in the interpretive community. Qualitative inquiry flourished in this moment, which lasted slightly over two decades (1980–2000). But by the end of the 1990s, SBR emerged as a force, poised to erase the majority of the gains won in phase one. With a wave of Harry Potter's postpositivist wand, the key assumptions of the interpretive moment were demolished. It was if we were back in the 1980s, fighting that old war all over again. The incompatibility and incommensurability theses were back on the table: There is science, and there is non-science.

As SBR was gaining strength, so, too, was the mixed-methods movement (Clark & Creswell, 2008; Creswell & Clark, 2007; Teddlie and Tashakkori, 2003a). Overlapping with the paradigm wars, the mixed-methods movement has evolved through four phases: a formative phase (1950s–1980s), the paradigm debate phase (1970s–1980s), the procedural development period (1990s), and the emerging recent interest period (2000–present). The current moment is exemplified in "public and federal funding, journals, disciplines and special workshops" (Creswell & Clark, 2007, p. 18) and an increased involvement with the SBR movement.

Mixed-methods advocates said it that was more complicated than SBR advocates would have us believe. Mixed-methods critics like Morse (2006) contested the basic assumptions of SBR, including the fact that random clinical trial (RCT) conditions are not replicable in day-to-day clinical care. Morse noted that an exercise of disciplinary power underlies any concept of evidence. SBR had no monopoly over the word "evidence." Indeed, their model of evidence is inadequate for critical, qualitative health care research (p. 80).

Howe (2004) criticized the neoclassical and mixed-methods versions of experimentalism that have been central to the SBR paradigm. Neoclassical experimentalism represents a dogmatic adherence to quantitative methods. Mixed-methods experimentalism fails to understand the deeper roots of qualitative methods. Both models take a technocratic approach to the role of participants in the research process. Howe offers an alternative democratic framework, what he calls mixed-methods interpretivism. This model reverses the primacy of quantitative methods, assigning them an auxiliary role. Mixed-methods interpretivism emphasizes understanding persons on their own terms. It engages stakeholders' participation through the principles of inclusion and dialog. The principle of inclusion has a democratic dimension, ensuring that insofar as it is possible, all relevant voices are heard. The principle of dialog insists that stakeholders be involved in the give and take of conversations involving how and why certain things work and ought to work. Critical dialog involves bringing expert knowledge to bear on a situation.

Regrettably, despite these resistances, the language and discourse of the mixed-methods group was co-opted by the SBR, CC, C2, and NRC movements. That is, experimental, nonexperimental, QUAN and QUAL mixed-methods designs were one answer to the demand for SBR. Soft qualitative research procedures—interviewing, observation—could be folded into RCT protocols (Bell, 2006; Briggs, 2006). These QUAL methods would provide data on context, even as the randomized experimental model turned research into a commodity, or a result. This "scientific result" could be easily compared with other forms of scientific research (Nespor, 2006, p. 118). The story of SBR reveals how the state has become both producer and consumer of only one form of scientific knowledge (Nespor, 2006, p. 119).

Another Discursive Formation

· The field is on the edge of a new paradigm dialog, a third formation existing alongside SBR and mixed-methods discourses. This is the space primarily filled by non-mixed-methods interpretive researchers, the empowerment discourses: critical constructionists, feminists, critical pedagogy and performance studies, oral historians, critical race theory, interpretive interactionists, etc. These are scholars in a different space. They seldom use terms like "validity" or "reliability." For some, a minimalist approach to theory is endorsed. A disruptive politics of representation is the focus, as are methods that disrupt and disturb the smooth surfaces of SBR. Scholars are crafting works that move persons and communities to action, "coupling research with activism and addressing specific situated problems" (Nespor, 2006, p. 123).

Indeed, it is clear that scholars are working in at least three directions at the same time. On the one hand, they are critically engaging and critiquing the SBR movement. They are emphasizing the political and moral consequences of the narrow views of science that are embedded in the movement (Hatch, 2006; Preissle, 2006; St. Pierre & Roulston, 2006). Some advocate a kind of "militant particularism" (Nespor, 2006, p. 122) that privileges meanings and understandings constructed at the local level. They are asking questions about the politics of evidence, about how work can be done for social justice purposes (Denzin & Giardina, 2008). They are struggling to advance the causes of qualitative inquiry in a time of global crisis.

A second group of scholars celebrate and reread paradigm proliferation and the profusion of interpretive communities, even the proliferation of uncertainty (Donmoyer, 2006; Lather, 2006a; MacLure, 2006, p. 732). They do not necessarily endorse the incompatibility-incommensurability theses that are so important for the mixed-methods community. They understand that each community has differing interpretive criteria (Creswell, 2007, p. 24). This discourse functions as a firewall of sorts against the narrow view of nonpositivism held by SBR authors.

A third group of scholars are resisting the implementation of narrow views of ethics, human subject review boards, institutional review boards (IRBs), informed consent, and biomedical models of inquiry (see Canella & Lincoln, 2004; Christians, 2005; Ryan & Hood, 2004). Many campus-level IRBs attempt to manage or redefine qualitative research. This has the effect of interfering with academic freedom, as well as shaping questions concerning design, informed consent, and the researcher-subject relationship.

Two tendencies must be avoided. Some overreact and claim an ethically superior stance to the IRB and SBR apparatuses. Others claim the identity of victim. The dangers of these two versions of ethicisim are self-evident. On the one hand, there is uncritical romanticizing of qualitative inquiry as well as a refusal to seriously engage critics (Brinkmann & Kvale, 2008; Kvale, 2008). On the other, a productive engagement with these competing discourses is shut down. There is no dialog. The opportunity to teach others in the opposing camps is wasted. Nobody wins, nobody learns.

Current turmoil in this version of a third moment repeats thirty-year-old arguments, but progress *has* been made. Moral and epistemological discourses now go on side-by side. A vastly superior mixed-method discourse exists today. The mid-century multi-methods arguments of Campbell and Stanley seem naive. Race, ethnicity, gender, sexuality, class, the research rights of indigenous peoples, whiteness, and queer studies are taken-for-granted topics today. These conversations were not taking place in the 1980s.

IV. Hatch Redux

The above formations in place, we return to Hatch. His argument moves through four steps: (1) neoconservatism and postmodernism; (2) postmodern paralysis; (3) fighting back; and (4) reengaging the paradigm wars. We detail the first three below.

Neoconservatism and the Postmodern Backlash

For Hatch, the efforts to redefine educational research are part of a larger "backlash against what neoconservatives see as the negative consequences of postmodernity" (2006, p. 403). Postmodernity and the postmodern—what some call the postcritical moment—are complex formations (Caputo, 1997; Kvale, 2008;). The postmodern is that which follows the modern. It represents a historical period, extending from World War II to the present. It has been called the cultural logic of late capitalism, a cultural logic focused on the hyperreal, on the commodity and the commodification of experience. Postmodernism represents a turn away from positivism in the social sciences. This leads to an intense preoccupation with the logics and apparatuses of representation, and legitimation, including a critique of scientific reason. In its poststructural versions, it represents a radical reconceptualization of language, and theories of representation. At the level of practice, it represents an attempt to formulate empowerment agendas that would give voice to silenced persons. This involves the development of a politics of resistance that would contest the repressive features of postmodern culture. Methodologically, it urges radical experimentations with new ways of writing and performing culture and personal experience.

Thus did postmodernism insert itself into the first and second paradigm wars. It provided the theoretical ammunition for critics of positivism. However, this ammunition was soon taken up by the neoconservatives. They turned postmodernism back against itself, creating what Hatch calls the postmodern backlash.[12]

To wit:

SBR is a well-orchestrated attempt to return to modern ways of thinking about "knowledge, knowing and research methods" (Hatch, 2006, p. 404). In the language of the paradigm wars, this is a return to positivism, experimental designs, randomized samples, statistical tests, a new gold standard. Methodological conservatism is a form of backlash; it blurs into and supports conservative political ideology and high modernism (Cannella & Lincoln, 2004; Lincoln & Cannella, 2004, p. 6). The political and methodological Right object to postmodernism's challenges to universal truth. They object to the privileging of discovery over verification. They reject the emphasis on context and subjective meaning. They refuse to engage the arguments concerning the theory- and value-ladenness of facts. They disallow the interactive nature of inquiry and the impossibility of objectivity (see Guba & Lincoln, 1994, pp. 106–107).

Methodological fundamentalism operates as a regulatory discourse. It is inscribed in federal regulations and laws (e.g., in the United States with respect to the NCLB Act of 2001). It distinguishes "good" from "bad" science, celebrating especially biomedical models of inquiry. In certain formations of NCLB there is a tendency to blame and punish children, parents, schools, and teachers. Methodological fundamentalists misread and distort postmodern/poststructural theories. They deploy a narrow model of science, a model that valorizes only one version of truth, or scientific evidence. They use research assessment exercises to enforce only one version of quality. It attempts to improve quality by "control, management, and audit rather than debate" (Torrance, 2006, p. 145). This undermines "the democratic politics that inspire our educational system" (St. Pierre, 2004, p. 137).

The convergence that Hatch sees between methodological and political conservatism is nuanced. There are many postpositivists who are not conservative. A sad irony is at work. In this version of the third moment, progressive postpositivists have seen portions of their discourse put to conservative methodological and political purposes. Postpositivism has been placed in the SBR blender, folded into and through the SBR mix (see Torrance, 2006).

The conservative and SBR criticisms of the critical and constructivist (postmodern) paradigms have created divisions within the qualitative research community. Rather than endorsing many different forms of inquiry, SBR has helped *marginalize* critical qualitative inquiry, especially within certain funding discourses. The imposition of experimental criteria on qualitative inquiry has created a rush to produce our own standards (Morse, 2006). The mixed-methods group (Creswell, 2007) has been most helpful, for they have painstakingly catalogued interpretive criteria (see also Lather 2007, pp. 164–165). We have not made productive use of these discourses. They partially answer the charge that there are "no agreed upon standards regarding what constitutes quality in qualitative ... research" (Cabinet Office, 2003, p. 10; see also Torrance, 2006, p. 239). Still, it is as if we were starting in a vacuum, when in fact this not the case at all.

Indeed, Whose Version of Quality?[13]

The backlash to the postmodern turn pivots on positivist criticisms of quality. These criticisms must be confronted head-on. And what better way than through critical pedagogy and the call to decolonize positivist methodologists. Thus do we seek a merger of indigenous and critical methodologies. One of us (Denzin, 2008b, 2009) calls this critical indigenous pedagogy (CIP). Obviously, the concept of quality takes on a different meaning in this discourse.

Contrary to SBR, critical pedagogy inquiry is anchored in the self-definitions and identities that arise out of the researcher's participation in a moral community. The purpose of research is not to produce new knowledge, per se, but to "uncover "and construct truths that can be used for the pursuit of peace and social justice. Dialog is the key to conducting quality research and assessing knowledge claims; that is, inquiry must be dialogical. Knowledge is assessed in terms of its relevance for concrete experience within everyday life. A decolonized epistemology privileges the voices of indigenous persons.

Inquiry grounded in critical indigenous pedagogy should meet multiple criteria. It must be ethical, performative, healing, transformative, decolonizing, and participatory. It must be committed to dialog, community, self-determination, and cultural autonomy. It must meet peoples' perceived needs. It resists efforts to confine inquiry to a single paradigm or interpretive strategy. It seeks to be unruly, disruptive, critical, and dedicated to the goals of justice and equity.

At this level, critical indigenous qualitative research is always already political. The researcher must consider how his or her research benefits, as well as promotes, self-determination for research participants (Bishop, 2005, p. 129). The work must represent indigenous persons honestly, without distortion or stereotype. The research should honor indigenous knowledge, customs, and rituals. It should not be judged in terms of neocolonial paradigms. Finally, researchers should be accountable to indigenous persons. They, not Western scholars, should have first access to research findings and control over the distribution of knowledge.

In this way, quality becomes a matter of democratic discourse—it is a quality of inquiry that empowers. Now, to postmodern paralysis.

Postmodern Paralysis

Hatch places some of the blame for the backlash on the interpretive community itself, on those who speak about the end of ethnography, the crisis of representation, and the postmodern, performance, and autoethnographic turn in qualitative inquiry. He fears that many who fought on the front lines of 1980s paradigm wars now feel trapped between "retrenched positivist forces on the one hand and stinging poststructuralist critiques on the other" (2006, p. 405). This debate, he contends, creates paralysis. People are writing and theorizing about research but not doing it. Students are not being taught how to do actual qualitative research. Few "data-based studies" (p. 406) are being conducted. Hatch worries that "the next generation of qualitative researchers well have been prepared to theorize, deconstruct, and critique but have no clue how to design a study, collect data and generate findings from a thoughtful analysis" (p. 406).

We disagree. In many North American and European journals, scholars working across a wide range of paradigms and methodologies are publishing excellent qualitative research. This work is informed by the postmodern turn. At the same time, it speaks to issues involved in schooling, health care, immigration, the justice system, the family, child care, and literacy, to name just a few areas of social policy concern.14 In other words, we do not believe we are witnessing a postmodern paralysis. We are in a transformative moment, moving between and across paradigms and interpretive frameworks, seeking a new politics of representation. But the facts of a backlash cannot be ignored. To fight back, we need to better educate our students and our critics. There is a danger in responding to the critics. A response can be read as validating the critics' criticisms. This can be unproductive, leading each side to claim it has been misread.

Fighting Back

Acknowledging that the current situation feels like a battleground, Hatch wants research done within all the qualitative paradigms to be considered legitimate (2006, p. 406). He does not want "knowledge and how it is created to be in the hands of those who happen to hold political power" (p. 406). He does not want to take a giant step back to the pre-1980s paradigm wars. He wants a strong line of defense in order to reestablish qualitative inquiry as a valuable and "respected form of inquiry" (p. 406). On this we agree.

He outlines several ways to fight back: (1) publishing well-designed qualitative research in high quality journals; (2) increased support for new scholars doing qualitative research; (3) lobbying journals and editors to publish more qualitative work; (4) defending our territory by "exposing the flaws, faulty logic, shaking assumptions, and sheer banality that characterizes many of the arguments in the SBR movement" (p. 406); (5) rejecting SBR criteria for evaluating our work; (6) critiquing SBR studies that are held up as models for the field; and (7) refusing to accept SBR's concepts of science and knowledge and proper inquiry.

Whose Science, Whose Research?

A brief commentary on Hatch's recommendations is in order. They divide into two groupings: support of qualitative work and criticisms of SBR initiatives. There is an on-going need for exemplars or models of the newer forms of qualitative inquiry. There are ample examples in our journals, and students need to be directed to them. New scholars who produce high quality work must be rewarded in terms of grants, tenure, and salary. They should not be forced to publish only in mainstream journals. Quality work in specialized journals should be recognized.

It is easy to expose, as the discussion above indicates, the flaws and faulty logic in the SBR literature, the criteria of quality, and the concepts of science and knowledge that are embedded in this literature cannot be accepted. We need to proliferate, as the discussion above indicates, new criteria. Additionally, we cannot allow the new positivist SBR camp to claim control over the word science, just as we must reclaim control over what we mean by research (Erickson & Gutierrez, 2002, p. 22). Eisenhart (2006) proposes a model of qualitative science that is interpretive, after Geertz (1973), and practical, after Flyvbjerg (2001). Erickson and Gutierrez (2002) point to social studies of science inquiries that "document the ways in which actual scientists' practice differs from that of its idealized characterizations ... real scientists in their daily work are anything but disinterested and canonically rational" (p. 22).

A development of these interpretive alternatives to positivist experimental science could help improve the status of qualitative inquiry in the current political environment. Likewise, queer, feminist, indigenous, and postcolonial models of science open up additional spaces for resisting the narrow, hegemonic SBR framework.

We endorse Hatch's conclusions. "If we do not fight back, qualitative research in education could become self-absorbed, fragmented and ineffectual. And the neo-conservative dream of a return to modernity will have come true" (p. 407). We will have lost.

Forming Alliances

We need to find new strategic and tactical ways to work with one another in the new paradigm dialog. This means that dialogs need to be formed between the poststructural, mixed-methods, and SBR advocates, as well as spokespersons for the NRC, CC, and C2. These three main interpretive communities need to develop ways of communicating with and learning from one another. This means we must expand the size of our tent; indeed, we need a bigger tent! We cannot afford to fight with one another. Mixed-methods scholars have carefully studied the many different branches of the poststructural tree (Creswell, 2007). The same cannot be said for the poststructuralists (but see Lather, 2007, pp. 164–165). Nor can we allow the arguments from the SBR community to divide us: We must learn from the paradigm conflicts of the 1980s to not overreach, to not engage in polemics, to not become too self-satisfied. We need to develop and work with our own concepts of science, knowledge, and quality inquiry. We need to remind the resurgent postpositivists that their criterion of good work applies only to work within their paradigm, not ours.

Over the course of the last two decades, poststructuralists have fought hard to claim an interpretive space for critical inquiry. They have questioned norms of objectivity, while emphasizing complexity, and the performance turn. They have focused on the importance of subjective interpretive processes, arguing that inquiry is always already moral and political (see Lather, 2006a, pp. 48–52). These understandings, like obdurate structures, ought not be compromised. They are knots in our interpretive handkerchief. They intersect with, interrupt, and reinforce the four major premises of the 1980s paradigm war; namely the incompatibility, incommensurability, value-ladenness of inquiry, and theory-ladenness of facts theses.

Further, we cannot just erase the differences between QUAN and QUAL inquiry, QUAN and QUAL departments, and their graduate training programs. Specialization in discourses is still a requirement. Qualitative inquiry is a huge field, not easily mastered by taking one or two overview courses (see Eisenhart & DeHaan, 2005). A minimal competency model, methodological bilingualism, seems superficial, perhaps even unworkable. We need multi-track models, with majors and minors in the ethics, politics, paradigms, methodologies, strategies, and analytics of qualitative inquiry.

V. Carrying on the New Paradigm Dialogs

Let us turn to the themes outlined in Guba's 1990 essay, "Carrying on the Dialog" (1990b). This work enumerates ten emergent themes and three agenda items from the 1989 "Alternative Paradigm Conference."[15] We believe these themes and agenda items can guide us today. We expand (somewhat) his list, phrasing them as injunctions, or theses:

Thesis 1: There needs to be a greater openness to alternative paradigm critiques.

Thesis 2: There needs to be decline in confrontationalism by alternative paradigm proponents.

Thesis 3: Paths for fruitful dialog between and across paradigms need to be explored.

Thesis 4: There needs to be a greater openness to alternative paradigm critiques.

Thesis 5: There needs to be a greater openness to and celebration of the proliferation, intermingling, and confluence of paradigms (Guba & Lincoln, 2005, p. 192).

Thesis 6: Dominant paradigms should be subverted. Scholars should be encouraged to embrace a militant particularism, individual paradigms that embody, and reframe inquiry "as a healing process, as a process of being in the service of social justice and social change" (Dillard, 2006, p. 65).

Thesis 7: Simplistic representations of the newer (and older) paradigms need to be avoided. This will help address confusion.

Thesis 8: Complexity and interconnectedness, not simplicity, are ineluctable (Guba, 1990b, p. 373).

Thesis 9: The commensurabilty and incompatibility theses, as they apply to paradigms and methods, need to be revisited. What is gained and what is lost with these two theses?

Thesis 10: The incompatibility of cross-paradigm quality of inquiry criteria (validity, rigor, trustworthiness, catalyst to action, love, fairness) must be honored.

Thesis 11: A change in paradigmatic postures involves a personal odyssey; that is, we each have a personal history with our preferred paradigm and this needs to be honored.

Thesis 12: The three main interpretive communities (poststructural, mix-methods, SBR) must learn how to cooperate and work with one another. This is because paradigm dominance involves control over faculty appointments, tenure, training, funding, publication, status, and legitimation (Guba, 1990b, p. 374).

Thesis 13: There is a need for conferences that will allow scholars from competing paradigms to see one another face to face and to interact. The Annual International

Congress of Qualitative Inquiry is one attempt to address this need (see http://qi2009.org).

Thesis 14: The complexity of the field of qualitative research needs to be honored. Polarization and elitism need to be avoided. Multiple language communities need to be represented in conferences and congresses. Dialog between persons and interpretive communities is critical.

Into the Future

Three agenda items emerged from the 1989 conference. We move them forward, into the present, to 2009. They offer a framework for action and collaboration. It is time to stop fighting. To repeat: We need to form strategic and tactical alliances. We need to form interactive networks across interpretive communities.

The Intellectual Agenda: The global community of qualitative inquiry needs annual events where it can deal with the problems and issues that they confront at this historical moment. These events should be international, national, regional, and local. They can be held in conjunction with "universities, school systems, health care systems, juvenile justice systems, and the like" (Guba, 1990b, p. 376).[16]

The Advocacy Agenda: The community needs to develop "systematic contacts with political figures, the media ... the professional press and with practitioners such as teachers, health workers, social workers, [and] government functionaries" (Guba, 1990b, p. 376). Advocacy includes: (1) showing how qualitative work addresses issues of social policy; (2) critiquing federally mandated ethical guidelines for human subject research; and (3) critiquing outdated, positivist modes of science and research.

The Operational Agenda: Qualitative researchers are encouraged to engage in self-learning, and self-criticism, to resocialize themselves, if necessary. Their goals should include building productive relationships with professional associations, journals, policymakers and funders (Guba, 1990b, p. 376). Representatives from many different professional associations (AERA, AEA, ASA, APA, AAA) need to be brought together.

We add an additional item.

The Ethical Agenda: The qualitative inquiry community needs an empowerment code of ethics that cross-cuts disciplines, honors indigenous voices, implements the values of love, care, compassion, community, spirituality, praxis, and social justice.

VI. The Chapters

With the above in mind, *Qualitative Inquiry and Social Justice: Toward a Politics of Hope* aggressively inserts itself into the competing paradigms and contextual transformations at play in the historical present. To this end, the volume is organized around three sections: (1) ethics, evidence, and social justice; (2) qualitative inquiry in post-disaster America; and (3) human rights and radical performance.

To begin Section I, Gaile S. Cannella and Yvonna S. Lincoln ("Deploying Qualitative Inquiry for Critical Social Purposes") explore why, in their view, much of the critical/critical theorist work that has been done has not always resulted in any form of increased social justice. Asking questions such as "How do we deploy qualitative methods for critical historical, social justice, and policy purposes?" and "How do we effect a wider dissemination of critical studies into the broader civic debate?" they examine the extent to which the atmosphere of the academy, neoconservative political forces, and neoliberal capitalism have deemphasized certain forms of knowledge production. In so doing, they engage with debates concerning evidence-based research and the corporatization of knowledge, especially as manifested within government agencies and fields such as medicine, education, and business. They conclude with a call for strategic and persistent critical transformations oriented toward social justice and radical, progressive democracy at the center of qualitative research.

Frederick Erickson ("Four Points Concerning Policy-Oriented Qualitative Research") follows and speaks specifically about the need for engaging more directly policy discourse and policy audiences. He outlines four possible avenues of opportunity—explanation of relative frequency in reporting of findings;

the policy relevance of detailed case study research (particularly as it concerns context and local knowledges); the need for prudential social inquiry; and a critique of scientism within policy discourse—for more positively inserting qualitative research into the policy arena. Like Cannella and Lincoln in the preceding chapter, Erickson similarly interrogates the politics of evidence-based research and practice, especially as related to the discourse of new public management. He concludes by setting the stage for future interventions in this area.

In Chapter 3, Michele J. McIntosh and Janice M. Morse ("Institutional Review Boards and the Ethics of Emotion") offer a critical perspective on the ethics of emotion as it relates to "risk" and IRBs. Utilizing a discussion of unstructured interviews as a point of entry, they give a critical overview of IRB mandates, keying in on emotional distress and questions surrounding its place in such interviews. They further extend this discussion by asking, "Is emotional distress harm?" interrogating in the process emotional valence and polarity, the context and consequences of emotional distress, and the ethical responsibilities of the researcher when conducting such research. They conclude by formulating an ethics of emotion in conducting qualitative research.

The section closes with Joseph A. Maxwell's chapter ("Evidence: A Critical Realist Perspective for Qualitative Research"), which argues that critical realism can make important contributions to the critique of evidence-based research, contributions that are particularly relevant to—and supportive of—qualitative research. Working through arguments outlined by philosophers such as Andrew Abbott and Peter Achinstein, Maxwell argues for a dialogical, postmodern approach to evidence in qualitative research, "one that embraces contrary perspectives such as realism and constructivism, and uses these to gain a better understanding of the phenomena we study."

Section II serves as the volume's metaphorical middle-eight, with three chapters directly engaging with social justice in and around a post-disaster context—specifically, that of Hurricane Katrina, which decimated New Orleans, Louisiana, in 2005. Gloria Ladson-Billings's chapter ("Education Research in the Public Interest") opens the section and weaves together a narrative of New Orleans (pre- and post-Katrina) with a discussion of its (mis-)educational legacies, poverty, and racial climate. She argues that, for education research to matter, it must not merely be about data points and effect size and career advancement, but about what kind of real difference such work can make in the lives of real people.

In a similar vein, Michael D. Giardina and Laura H. Vaughan's chapter ("Performing Pedagogies of Hope in Post-Katrina America") deploys a performative account of the immediate on-the-ground aftermath of Katrina, laced with critical commentary of the political environment that gave rise and contributed to the "politics of disposability" (Giroux, 2006) concerning the citizens of New Orleans. Moving back and forth in he-said, she-said style, the authors highlight the race- and class-based imperatives that contributed to the disaster as well as pointing toward future directions for critical scholarship to respond to such traumas.

Taking up qualitative research in post-disaster contexts more generally, Gaile S. Cannella and Michelle S. Perez ("Power-Shifting at the Speed of Light: Critical Qualitative Research Post-Disaster") close the section by focusing most specifically on the shock doctrine (see Klein, 2008) effects and shifting power maneuvers at play in disaster-related contexts. In so doing, they pull back the veil of neoliberalism that hung over the privatization of schooling in the aftermath of Katrina. Additionally, they forcefully contend that critical scholars now more than ever must fully participate in a form of egalitarian activism and social justice if we are to realize our full potential as agents of change.

Section III begins with D. Soyini Madison's chapter ("Dangerous Ethnography"), which illustrates the complex dynamics and contextual politics of researcher positionality, power, privilege, and safety during the conduct of ethnographic research in locales deemed quite literally dangerous.

Relatedly, Karen A. Stewart, Aaron Hess, Sarah J. Tracy, and H. L. Goodall, Jr. ("Risky Research: Investigating the 'Perils' of Ethnography") offer four vignettes in their chapter that together and in isolation expand the concept of "risk" to include not only physical and mental challenges faced by the researcher

but also the ethical, institutional, paradigmatic, methodological, epistemological, and reception challenges ethnographers face
throughout the whole of their research process. The authors draw
on personal experiences conducting research in 911 call centers,
aboard cruise ships, as part of drug safety advocate groups, and
taking public photography as data as well as being considered the
agent of risk in institutional settings.

Cynthia Dillard's chapter ("Racializing Ethics and Bearing
Witness to Memory in Research") directs our attention to the role
of racial and cultural memory as situated in the research/teach-
ing endeavor, and how this impacts the researcher's identity and
subjectivity. She argues that the usefulness of such memories is
in their power to transform consciousness (in the Freirien sense),
moving, as she says, "through and maybe beyond race to a more
equitable and subjective identity as spiritual beings."

Keeping with the theme of personal transformation and
human rights, Jean Halley's lyrical chapter ("The Death of a
Cow") explores the death of beef cows and contrasts such deaths
with the death of her childhood cat and the sadness in her childhood. She looks at the violence of such deaths, yes, but also at
the ways that deaths are a move from one state to another, not
only for the dying, but for all those involved in and surrounding
death. Through her writing style, she tries to capture the feel,
the atmosphere, and the experience of these changes. Thus is the
social history of beef ranching intertwined with both personal
and political narratives on the production of life and death.

The section concludes with Ian Stronach's philosophical
meditation ("Rethinking Words, Concepts, Stories, and Theories:
Sensing a New World?"), which diverges into two critical ambitions at once and the same: a politico-philosophical excursion
into the co-construction of contemporary meaning, and a sidereal
interrogation of tensions unfurled in the connections and discon-
nections between words like global, local, social, individual, freedom, liberty, justice, and so forth.

The volume closes with a Coda based on a panel discussion
organized by Carolyn Ellis on mentoring relationships and their
importance for creating a future community of scholars within
qualitative inquiry.

VII. By Way of a Conclusion

Qualitative Inquiry and Social Justice: Toward a Politics of Hope marks the fourth[17] entry in our series on qualitative research in the historical present. Each of these four volumes has found its genesis in and come out of our parallel involvement with organizing the annual International Congress of Qualitative Inquiry at the University of Illinois, Urbana-Champaign. The first, titled *Qualitative Inquiry and the Conservative Challenge: Confronting Methodological Fundamentalism* (2006), sought to actively contest the right-wing/neoconservative-dominated direction of regulatory policy governing scientific inquiry. Such regulatory efforts—primarily those obsessed with enforcing scientifically based, biomedical models of research—raise fundamental philosophical, epistemological, and ontological issues for scholarship and freedom of speech in the academy.

Our second volume, *Ethical Futures in Qualitative Research: Decolonizing the Politics of Knowledge* (2007), charted a radical path for a future in which ethical considerations transcend the Belmont Principles (which focus almost exclusively on the problems associated with betrayal, deception, and harm), calling for a collaborative, performative social science research model that makes the researcher responsible not to a removed discipline or institution, but to those he or she studies. In so doing, personal accountability, the value of expressiveness, the capacity for empathy, and the sharing of emotionality are stressed. As such, scholars were directed to take up moral projects that decolonize, honor, and reclaim (indigenous) cultural practices, where healing leads to multiple forms of transformation and the personal and social levels, and where these collective actions can help persons realize a radical politics of possibility, hope, love, care, and equality for all humanity.

In our third volume *Qualitative Inquiry and the Politics of Evidence* (2008), our authors challenged the very ground on which evidence has been given cultural and canonical purchase: What is truth? What is evidence? What counts as evidence? How is evidence evaluated? How can evidence—or facts—be "fixed" to fit policy? What kind of evidence-based research should inform this process? How is evidence to be represented? How is evidence to be discounted or judged to be unreliable, false, or incorrect?

And here, with our fourth volume, our authors take on and advocate for a more activist-minded role for scholarship and research in the academy, of making a space for critical, humane discourses that create sacred and spiritual spaces for persons and their moral communities—spaces where people can express and give meaning to the world around them. It is a project organized around moral clarity and political intervention (i.e., a focus on the personal and the biographical, the launching of critical discourse at the level of the media and the ideological, the fostering of a critical international conversation that helps us develop a contextual theory of radical politics and social justice and democracy, and the enacting of critical interpretive methodologies that can help us make sense of life in an age of the hyperreal, the simulacra, TV wars, staged media events, and the like). Such a project, then, embraces a public intellectualism on the order of Noam Chomsky's 1967 article "The Responsibility of Intellectuals," in which he argues that we (i.e., all of us) have a moral and professional obligation to speak the truth, expose lies, and see events in their historical perspective (see also Denzin & Giardina, 2006a).

Taken together, all four volumes work in tandem to address a fundamental question: How are we as qualitative researchers to move forward in this new paradigm? That is, qualitative researchers belong to a global community. The recent SBR disputes and conflicts in the United States are also being felt around the world. The interpretive community needs to draw together into one large community so we can share our problems and experiences with these new discourses. Scholars who share the values of excellence, leadership, and advocacy need venues to engage in debate, frame public policy discourse, and disseminate research findings. We need a community that honors and celebrates paradigm, and methodological diversity, and showcases scholarship from around world. As fellow travelers, we need research agendas that advance human rights and social justice through qualitative research. If we can do this, the rewards will be "plentiful and the opportunity for professional [and societal] impact unsurpassed" (Guba, 1990b, p. 378).

There is reason to hope that the era of President Barack Obama will usher in a new era of critical inquiry. The time seems to have arrived for a new conversation about paradigms, race, methods and leadership. We need a roadmap and an agenda to carry us through the third moment and into the next decade—a call to arms, if you will.

Hope is peaceful and nonviolent. Hope is grounded in concrete performative practices, in struggles and interventions that espouse the sacred values of love, care, community, trust, and well-being (Freire, 1999, p. 9). Hope, as a form of pedagogy, confronts and interrogates cynicism, the belief that change is not possible, or is too costly. Hope works from rage to love. It articulates a progressive politics that rejects "conservative, neoliberal postmodernity" (Friere, 1999, p. 10). Hope rejects terrorism and the spectacles of fear and terror that have become part of daily life since 9/11/01. Hope rejects the claim that peace comes at any cost.

This volume is one step in that direction.

Notes

1. Earlier versions of this chapter appeared in Denzin (2008, 2009, ch. 13), and continue arguments outlined in Denzin & Giardina (2006a, 2006b, 2007, 2008).

2. This Introduction was written a few weeks after the election of Sen. Barack Obama (D-IL) as the 44th president of the United States.

3. Teddlie and Tashakkori call the field of mixed methodology the third methodological movement (2003a, p. ix). They have four moments in their history (1900–1950, 1950–1970, 1970–1990, 1990–present. They insert this model and their third moment/movement within and alongside Denzin and Lincoln's first five major moments in the history of qualitative research: 1900–1950, 1950–1970, 1970–1986, 1986–1990, 1990–.

4. Following Guba, a paradigm is a basic set of beliefs that guides action. Inquiry paradigms (positivism, postpositivism, constructivism, structuralism, poststructuralism, etc.) can be differentiated in terms of ontology, epistemology, methodology, and ethics (Guba, 1990a, pp. 17–18).

5. This is Guba's spelling.

6. Less militaristic terms would include dispute, fracas, conflict, and engagement. More peaceful terms would focus, as Guba (1990b) did, on dialog, discourse, conversation, collaboration.

7. In sociology and anthropology, fierce disputes and wars over quantitative and qualitative paradigms flared up in the 1920s, and extended through the immediate post–World War II period (see Vidich & Lyman, 1994, pp. 38–41).

8. Conflict broke out between the many different empowerment pedagogies: feminist, anti-racist, radical, Freirean, liberation theology, postmodernists, poststructuralists, cultural studies, etc. (see the chapters in Guba & Lincoln, 2005; Luke & Gore, 1992; McLaren & Kincheloe, 2007).

9. The second paradigm war also involved disputes "between individuals convinced of the 'paradigm purity'" of their own position (Teddlie & Tashakkori, 2003b, p. 7). Purists resurrected the incommensurability an incompatibility theses from the first war. They extended and repeated the argument that quantitative and qualitative methods, that postpositivism and the other "isms" cannot be combined because of the differences between their underlying paradigm assumptions. On the methodological front, the incompatibility thesis was challenged by those who invoked triangulation as a way of combining multiple methods to study the same phenomenon (Teddlie & Tashakkori, 2003b, p. 7). Thus was ushered in a new round of arguments and debates over paradigm superiority.

10. Importantly for our purposes here, the seeds of war number three in North America can be found in "the current upheaval and argument about 'scientific' research in the scholarly world of education" (Clark & Scheurich, 2008; Scheurich & Clark, 2006, p. 401). These seeds began before No Child Left Behind (NCLB) and Reading First Acts. Thus, although it is too easy to blame NCLB for the mess we are in today, the turmoil did not *start* here: The first two paradigm wars clearly created the conditions of emergence for the current conflict.

11. This is a gloss on a complex discourse. The mixed-methods community is by no means defined by a single set of assumptions, beliefs, or practices.

12. Stronach (this volume) observes that much postmodern discourse has been fueled by over-arching ideologies of accountability, there are right- and left-wing versions of postmodernism. The SBR movement responds negatively to postmodernism, by imposing an ideology of postmodern accountability.

13. The next four paragraphs rework comments in Denzin and Lincoln (2008, pp. 4–5).

14. Monograph series sponsored by such university presses as New York University, Minnesota, and Duke, and such commercial publishers as AltaMira, Left Coast Press, Oxford, Routledge, and Sage are also publishing qualitative work in these newer traditions

15. This, of course, is the conference recorded in Guba (1990a).

16. On May 7, 2005, on the last day of the First International Congress of Qualitative Inquiry, the International Association of Qualitative Inquiry (IAQI) was founded in Urbana, Illinois. IAQI is the first international association solely dedicated to the scholarly promotion, representation, and global development of qualitative research. At present, IAQI has 2,500 delegates representing sixty-five nations worldwide. It has established professional affiliations with more than fifty collaborating sites in Oceana, Africa, North and South America, the Caribbean, Europe, the Middle East, Japan, Korea, and China (see http://qi2009.org). The IAQI Newsletter appears quarterly, as does a new journal published by Left Coast Press, *The International Review of Qualitative Research.*

17. Or this is the fifth, if you count our contextually related volume *Contesting Empire, Globalizing Dissent: Cultural Studies after 9/11* (Denzin & Giardina, 2006a).

References

American Education Research Association (AERA). (2006). Standards for Reporting on Empirical Social Science Research in AERA publications. Available online at www: aera.net/opportunities/?id = 1480 (accessed February 6, 2007).

Ayers, W. (2009). Obama and education reform. The Huffington Post. Available online at http://www.huffingtonpost.com/bill-ayers/obama-and-education-refor_b_154857.html (accessed January 5, 2009).

Bell, V. (2006). The Cochrane Qualitative Methods Group. Available online at http://www.lancs.ac.uk/fass/ihr/research/publich/cochrane.htm (accessed March 13, 2007).

Biesta, G. J. (2004). Education, accountability, and the ethical demand: Can the democratic potential of accountability be regained? *Educational Theory*, 54(3), 233–250.

Bishop, R. (2005). Freeing ourselves from neo-colonial domination in research: A Kaupapa Maori approach to creating knowledge. In N. K. Denzin & Y. S. Lincoln (Eds.), *Handbook of qualitative research*, 3rd ed., pp. 109–138. Thousand Oaks, CA: Sage.

Briggs, J. (2006). Cochrane Qualitative Research Methods Group. The Cochrane Collaboration. Available online at http://www.joannabriggs.eduau/cqrmg/role.html (accessed March 12, 2007).

Brinkmann, S. & Kvale, S. (2008). Ethics in qualitative psychological research. In C. Willig & W. Stainton-Rogers (Eds.), *Handbook of qualitative research in psychology*, pp. 261–279. London: Sage.

Cabinet Office. (2003). *Quality in qualitative evaluation: A framework for assessing research evidence* (full report). London: Cabinet Office.

Cannella, G. S. & Lincoln, Y. S. (2004). Dangerous discourses II: Comprehending and countering the redeployment of discourses (and resources) in the generation of liberatory inquiry. *Qualitative Inquiry*, 10(2), 165–174.

Caputo, J. (1997). Dreaming of the innumerable: Derrida, Cornell, and the dance of gender. In E. Feder, M. Rawlinson and E. Zakin (Eds.), *Derrida and feminism: Recasting the question of woman*, pp. 141–160. New York: Routledge.

Christians, C. (2005). Ethics and politics in qualitative research. In N. K. Denzin and Y. S. Lincoln (Eds.), *Handbook of qualitative research*, 3rd ed., pp. 139–164. Thousand Oaks, CA: Sage.

Clark, C. & Scheurich, J. (2008). The state of qualitative research in the early twenty-first century—take 2. *International Journal of Qualitative Studies in Education*, 21(4), 313–314.

Clark, V. L. Plano & Creswell, J. W. (Eds.). (2008). *The mixed methods reader.* Thousand Oaks, CA: Sage.

Collins, P. H. (1998). *Fighting words: Black women and the search for social justice.* Minneapolis: University of Minnesota Press.

Creswell, J. W. (2007). *Qualitative inquiry & research design: Choosing among five approaches*, 2nd ed. Thousand Oaks, CA: Sage.

Creswell, J. W. & Plano Clark, V. L. (2007). *Designing and conducting mixed methods research.* Thousand Oaks, CA: Sage.

Denzin, N. K. (2007). The secret Downing Street memo, the one percent doctrine, and the politics of truth: A performance text. *Symbolic Interaction*, 30(4), 447–464.

Denzin, N. K. (2008). The new paradigm dialogs and qualitative inquiry. *The International Journal of Qualitative Studies in Education*, 21(4), 315–325.

Denzin, N. K. (2009). *Qualitative inquiry under fire: Toward a new paradigm dialogue.* Walnut Creek, CA: Left Coast Press.

Denzin, N. K. & Giardina, M. D. (2006a). Introduction: Cultural studies after 9/11. In N. K. Denzin & M. D. Giardina (Eds.), *Contesting empire, globalizing dissent: Cultural studies after 9/11*, pp. 1–22. Boulder, CO: Paradigm.

Denzin, N. K. & Giardina, M. D. (Eds.). (2006b). *Qualitative inquiry and the conservative challenge: Contesting methodological fundamentalism.* Walnut Creek, CA: Left Coast Press.

Denzin, N. K. & Giardina, M. D. (2007). Introduction: Ethical futures in qualitative research. In N. K. Denzin & M. D. Giardina (Eds.), *Ethical futures in qualitative research: Decolonizing the politics of knowledge*, pp. 9–44. Walnut Creek, CA: Left Coast Press.

Denzin, N. K. & Giardina, M. D. (2008). Introduction: The elephant in the living room, OR advancing the conversation about the politics of evidence. In N. K. Denzin & M. D. Giardina (Eds.), *Qualitative inquiry and the politics of evidence*, pp. 9–52. Walnut Creek, CA: Left Coast Press.

Denzin, N. K. & Lincoln, Y. S. (2005). Introduction: The discipline and practice of qualitative research. In N. K. Denzin & Y. S. Lincoln (Eds.), *The handbook of qualitative research*, 3rd ed., pp. 1–32. Thousand Oaks, CA: Sage.

Denzin, N. L. & Lincoln, Y. S. (2008). Critical methodologies and indigenous inquiry. In N. K. Denzin, Y. S. Lincoln, & L.T. Smith (Eds.), *Handbook of critical and indigenous methodologies*, pp. 1–20. Thousand Oaks, CA: Sage.

Dillard, C. B. (2006). When the music changes, so should the dance: Cultural and spiritual considerations in paradigm "proliferation." *International Journal of Qualitative Studies in Education*, 19(6), 59–76.

Dixon-Woods, M., Bonas, S., Booth, A., Jones, D. R., Miller, T., Sutton, A. J., Shaw, R. L., Smith, J. A., & Young, B. (2006). How can systematic reviews incorporate qualitative research? A critical perspective. *Qualitative Research*, 6(1), 27–44.

Donmoyer, R. (2006). Take my paradigm ... Please! The legacy of Kuhn's construct in educational research. *International Journal of Qualitative Studies in Education*, 19(6), 11–34.

Eisenhart, M. (2006). Qualitative science in experimental time. *International Journal of Qualitative Studies in Education*, 19(6), 697–707.

Eisenhart, M. & DeHaan, R. L. (2005). Doctoral preparation of scientifically based education research. *Educational Researcher*, 34(4), 3–14.

Elam, Harry Jr. (2001). The device of race. In H. J. Elam, Jr., and D. Krasner (Eds.), *African American performance and theatre history: A critical reader*, pp. 3–16. New York: Oxford University Press.

Erickson, F. & Gutierrez, K. (2002). Culture, rigor, and science in educational research. *Educational Researcher*, 31(8), 21–24.

Flyvbjerg, B. (2001). *Making social science matter*. Cambridge: Cambridge University Press.

Freire, P. (1999). *Pedagogy of hope* (trans. R. R. Barr). New York: Continuum (orig. pub. 1992).

Gage, N. L. (1989). The paradigm wars and their aftermath: A "historical" sketch of research and teaching since 1989. *Educational Researcher*, 18(7), 4–10.

Garoian, C. R. & Gaudelius, Y. M. (2008). *Spectacle pedagogy: Art, politics and visual culture*. Albany: State University of New York Press.

Geertz, C (1973). *Interpreting cultures.* New York: Basic Books.

Giroux, H. (2006). *Stormy weather: Katrina and the politics of disposability.* Boulder, CO: Paradigm.Guba, E. (1990a). The alternative paradigm dialog. In E. Guba (Ed.), *The paradigm dialog,* pp. 17–30. Newbury Park, CA: Sage.

Giroux, H. (2008). Obama and the promise of education. Journal of Education Controversy Blog. Available online at http://journalofeducationalcontroversy.blogspot.com/2008/11/democracy-and-obama-presidency.html (accessed November 18, 2008).

Guba, E. (1990a). The alternative paradigm dialog. In E. Guba (Ed.), *The paradigm dialog,* pp. 17–30. Newbury Park, CA: Sage.

Guba, E. (1990b). Carrying on the dialog. In E. Guba (Ed.), *The paradigm dialog,* pp. 368–378. Thousand Oaks, CA: Sage.

Guba, E. & Lincoln, Y. S. 1994. Competing paradigms in qualitative research. In N. K. Denzin and Y. S. Lincoln (Eds.), *Handbook of qualitative research,* pp. 105–117. Thousand Oaks, CA: Sage.

Guba, E. & Lincoln, Y. S. 2005. Paradigmatic controversies, and emerging confluences. In N. K. Denzin & Y. S. Lincoln (Eds.), *Handbook of qualitative research,* 3rd ed., pp. 191–216. Thousand Oaks, CA: Sage.

Hatch, A. (2006). Qualitative studies in the era of scientifically-based research: Musings of a former QSE editor. *International Journal of Qualitative Studies in Education,* 19, 4: 403–409.

Hesse-Biber, S. N. & Leavy, P. (2008). Introduction. In S. N. Hesse-Buiber & P. Leavy (Eds.), *Handbook of emergent methods,* pp. 1–15. New York: Guilford Press.

Howe, K. R. (1988). Against the quantitative-qualitative incompatibility thesis or dogmas die hard. *Educational Researcher,* 17(8), 10–16.

Howe, K. R. (2004). A critique of experimentalism. *Qualitative Inquiry,* 10(1), 42–61.

Kaufman, M. (2001). *The Laramie Project.* New York: Vintage Books.

Klein, N. (2008). *The shock doctrine: The rise of disaster capitalism.* New York: Picador.

Kvale, S. (2008). Qualitative inquiry between scientistic evidendialism, ethical subjectivism and the free market. *International Review of Qualitative Research,* 1(1), 5–18.

Lather, P. (2004). This is your father's paradigm: Government intrusion and the case of qualitative research in education. *Qualitative Inquiry,* 10, 1: 15–34.

Lather, P. (2006a). Paradigm proliferation as a good thing to think with: Teaching research in education as a wild profusion. *International Journal of Qualitative Studies in Education,* 19(6), 35–57.

Lather, P. (2006b). Foucauldian scientificity: Rethinking the nexus of qualitative research and educational policy analysis. *International Journal of Qualitative Studies in Education*, 19(6), 783–791.

Lather, P. (2007). *Getting lost: Feminist efforts toward a double(d) science.* Albany: State University of New York Press.

Lincoln, Y. S. & Cannella, G. S. (2004). Dangerous discourses: Methodological conservatism and governmental regimes of truth. *Qualitative Inquiry*, 10(1), 5–14.

Luke, C. & Gore, J. (Eds.). (1992). *Feminists and critical pedagogy.* New York: Routledge.

MacLure, M. (2006). The bone in the throat: Some uncertain thoughts on baroque method. *International Journal of Qualitative Studies in Education*, 19(6), 729–745.

Madison, D. S. (2005). *Critical ethnography.* Thousand Oaks, CA: Sage.

Madison, D. S., & Hamera, J. (2006). Performance studies at the intersection. In D. S. Madison and J. Hamera (Eds.), *The Sage handbook of performance studies*, pp. xi–xxv. Thousand Oaks: Sage.

Maxcy, S. J. (2003). Pragmatic threads in mixed methods research in the social sciences: The search for multiple modes of inquiry and the end of the philosophy of formalism. In A. Tashakkori & C. Teddlie (Eds.), *Handbook of mixed-methods in social and behavioral research*, pp. 51–89. Thousand Oaks, CA: Sage.

McLaren, P. & Kincheloe, J. L. (Eds.). (2007). *Critical pedagogy: Where are we now?* New York: Peter Lang.

Mertens, D, Holmes, H. M., & Harris, R. L. (2009). Transformative research and ethics. In D. M. Mertens & P. E. Ginsberg (Eds.), *The handbook of social research ethics*, pp. 85–101. Thousand Oaks, CA: Sage.

Mienczakowski, J. (2001). Ethnodrama: Performed research—limitations and potential. In P. Atkinson, A. Coffey, S. Delamont, J. Lofland and L. Lofl (Eds.), *Handbook of ethnography*, pp. 468-476. London: Sage.

Morse, J. M. (2003). Principles of mixed methods and multimethod research designs. In A. Tashakkori & C. Teddlie (Eds.), *Handbook of mixed-methods in social and behavioral research*, pp. 189–208. Thousand Oaks, CA: Sage.

Morse, J. M. (2006). The politics of evidence. In N. K. Denzin & M. D. Giardina (Eds.), *Qualitative inquiry and the conservative challenge*, pp. 79–92. Walnut Creek, CA: Left Coast Press.

National CASP Collaboration. (2006). 10 questions to help you make sense of qualitative research, critical appraisal skills program (CASP). Milton Keyenes Primary Care Trust (The Cochrane Collaboration. Available online at http://www.joannabriggs.edu.au/cqrmg/role.html) (accessed February 20, 2009).

Nespor, J. (2006). Methodological inquiry: The uses and spaces of paradigm proliferation. *International Journal of Qualitative Studies in Education*, 19(6), 115–128.

Obama, B. (2004). Democratic National Convention keynote address. Boston, July 27. Available online at http://obamaspeeches.com/002-Keynote-Address-at-the-2004-Democratic-National-Convention-Obama-Speech.htm (accessed January 10, 2009).

Preisle, J. (2006). Envisioning qualitative inquiry: A view across four decades. *International Journal of Qualitative Studies in Education*, 19(6), 685–696.

Ryan, K. E. & Hood, L. (2004). Guarding the castle and opening the gates. *Qualitative Inquiry*, 10(1), 79–95.

Saldana, J. (2005). *Ethnography: An anthology of reality theatre*. Walnut Creek, CA: AltaMira.

Scheurich, J. J. & Clark, M. C. (2006). Qualitative studies in education at the beginning of the twenty-first century. *International Journal of Qualitative Studies in Education*, 19(4), 401.

Scheurich, J. J. & Young, M. (1997). Coloring epistemologies: Are our research epistemologies racially biased? *Educational Researcher*, 26(4), 4–16.

Schwandt, T. A. (2000). Three epistemological stances for qualitative inquiry: Interpretivism, hermeneutics and social constructivism. In N. K. Denzin and Y. S. Lincoln (Eds.), *Handbook of qualitative research*, 2nd ed., pp. 189–214. Thousand Oaks, CA: Sage.

Skrla, L. & Scheurich, J. J. (Eds.). (2004). *Educational equity and accountability: High schools and high stakes*. New York: Routledge Falmer.

Smith. A. D. (2004). *House arrest and piano: Two plays*. New York: Anchor Books

Sotiropoulos, K. 2006. *Staging race: Black performers in turn of the century America*. Cambridge, MA: Harvard University Press.

Staller, K. M., Block, E., & Horner, P. S. (2008). History of methods in social science research. In S. N. Hesse-Biber & P. Leavy (Eds.), *Handbook of emergent methods*, pp. 25–54. New York: Guilford Press.

St. Pierre, E. A. (2004). Refusing alternatives: A science of contestation. *Qualitative Inquiry* 10(1), 130–139.

St. Pierre, E. A. (2006). Scientifically based research in education: Epistemology and ethics. *Adult Education Quarterly*, 56(3), 239–266

St. Pierre, E. A. & Roulston, K. (2006). The state of qualitative inquiry: A contested science. *International Journal of Qualitative Studies in Education*, 19(6), 673–684.

Teddlie, C. & Tashakkori, A. (2003a). Preface. In A Tashakkori & C. Teddlie (Eds.), *Handbook of mixed-methods in social and behavioral research*, pp. ix–xv. Thousand Oaks, CA: Sage.

Teddlie, C. & Tashakkori, A. (2003b). Major issues and controversies in the use of mixed methods in the social and behavioral sciences. In A. Tashakkori & C. Teddlie (Eds.), *Handbook of mixed-methods in social and behavioral research*, pp. 3–50. Thousand Oaks, CA: Sage.

Torrance, H. (2006). Research quality and research governance in the United Kingdom: From methodology to management. In N. K. Denzin & M. D. Giardina (Eds.), *Qualitative inquiry and the conservative challenge*, pp. 127–148. Walnut Creek, CA: Left Coast Press.

Vidich, A. J. & Lyman, S. M. (1994). Qualitative methods: Their history in sociology and anthropology. In N. K. Denzin & Y. S. Lincoln (Eds.), *Handbook of qualitative research*, pp. 23–59. Thousand Oaks, CA: Sage.

Wright, H. K. (2006). Are we (t)here yet? Qualitative research in education's profuse and contested present. *International Journal of Qualitative Studies in Education*, 19(6): 793–802.

Wright, H. K. & Lather, P. (2006). Special issue: Paradigm proliferation in educational research. *International Journal of Qualitative Studies in Education*, 19(6), 1–11.

Section I

Ethics, Evidence, and Social Justice

Chapter 1 ||| Deploying Qualitative Methods for Critical Social Purposes

Gaile S. Cannella
Tulane University

Yvonna S. Lincoln
Texas A&M University

Twenty years ago, in her now-famous *Harvard Educational Review* article, Elizabeth Ellsworth (1989) questioned the assumption that critical perspectives or critical research were either empowering or transformative. She argued that critical theory was embedded within patriarchal forms of reason, Enlightenment logic, and male domination, such that the attempted adoption of a critical lens can easily create the illusion of justice while actually reinscribing old forms of power.

Beyond Ellsworth's criticisms, it is also clear now that critical inquiry cannot be described utilizing traditional research language like models, predetermined linear methods, or any forms of unquestioned methodologies (Richardson, 2000). Indeed, even several of the foundational terms of critical theory—divided consciousness, false consciousness—imply a singular truth to which adherents must pledge allegiance, lest they be charged with failing to see or own this singular truth. Further, some critical perspectives would challenge the notion of a singular truth while remaining concerned about power and oppression. Although many contemporary researchers claim to use critical qualitative research methods (and we are among those), these inquiry practices often do not transform, or even appear to challenge, the dominant or mainstream constructions.

Our intent here is to explore why much of the critical/critical theorist work has not always resulted in any form of increased social justice. We echo Ellsworth's question: Why does this not feel empowering? Our own questions, however, go further and we explore the issues of how we filter research through a critical lens. How do we deploy qualitative methods (which are by and large far less linear than conventional experimental and quantitative methods) for critical historical, social justice, and policy purposes? How can we be more explicit about critical methodologies and make both our methodologies and our analyses clearer and more accessible to a larger set of publics? How do we construct an environment that values a critical perspective? Is it possible to construct critical research that does not simultaneously create new forms of oppressive power for itself, or for its practitioners? What does a critical perspective mean for research issues and questions, for frames that construct data collection and analyses, and forms of interpretation and re-presentation? How do we effect a wider dissemination of critical studies such that we prompt a broader civic debate around our analyses?

The Criticism Inherent in Critical Perspectives

One of the major, but unexplored, issues surrounding critical perspectives is what, precisely, is meant by them. Thus, we are offering a preliminary definition of how we are using the term "critical perspectives." By critical perspectives, we mean any research that recognizes power—that seeks in its analyses to plumb the archaeology of taken-for-granted perspectives to understand how unjust and oppressive social conditions came to be reified as historical "givens." These taken-for-granted perspectives might include, for example, unequal educational opportunity, racism, the acceptance of an inevitability of poverty, the relegation of women to second-class political and economic status, the systematic devaluation of homemaking and childrearing as productive economic activity and romanticized views of children and childhood that actually create forms of oppression for those who are younger (Cannella, 1997), and the like.

The foundational questions to critical work are: Who/what is helped/privileged/legitimated? Who/what is harmed/oppressed/disqualified? In addition to poststructural analyses and postmodern challenges to the domination of grand narratives, the range of feminist perspectives, and queer theory and its critique of forms of normalization, as well as anti-colonialist assessments of empire, are included in our broad definition. Such research, in addition to searching out the historical origins of socially and politically reified social arrangements, also seeks to understand how victims of such social arrangements come to accept and even collaborate in maintaining oppressive aspects of the system.

Further, critical perspectives seek to illuminate the hidden structures of power deployed in the construction and maintenance of its own power, and the disempowerment of others (e.g., groups, knowledges, ways of being, perspectives). Frequently, these power structures (whether hidden or obvious) are/can be tied to late capitalism and more currently, neoliberalism and its counterpart, invasive hypercapitalism. Neoliberalism, with its political roots in globalization and the discourse of "free" markets (however inequitably these markets actually function), serves as an economic backdrop to the redistribution of wealth in the guise of liberal political theory. The real power of neoliberalism has been to create corporate states and individuals who are more powerful and more wealthy than many nations, but further, to facilitate corporate power (Said, 1979) that is not restricted by national boundaries, and, finally, to concentrate wealth in an ever-smaller set of hands. As capital has been created, so has more extensive and dire impoverishment, both at home and abroad.

Critical perspectives also inquire deeply into the usages of language and the circulation of discourses that are used to shape all of social life, from advertising to decisions regarding the candidate for whom we should vote. Primarily, however, critical researchers are interested in the "language games" that maintain power relations, that appear to prevent transformative action, and that insistently shape a dulled, misled, and/or false public consciousness. Language gives form to ideologies and prompts action, and consequently, is deeply complicit in power relations and class struggles.

Next, critical perspectives are profoundly engaged with issues of race, gender, and socioeconomic level as major shapers as well as components of historically reified structures of oppression. Often, a given scholar's focus will be on one of the three, but increasingly, consciousness of how various forms of oppression and privilege intersect (Collins, 2000) results in a focus on the interactive nature, and institutionalization, of power, oppression, and injustice. An example would be the hybrid condition of injustice suffered by individuals based on race, economic status or class, and the particular political destitution of women. More recently, scholars have also been deconstructing whiteness, the invisible advantage assumed because of it, and the oppressions suffered by the intersecting of societal power structures based on gender, sexual orientation, and economic status.

Finally, along with race, class, and gender, indigenous scholars virtually always approach relations between themselves and imperialist forms of power from the perspective of colonialism, neocolonialism, and postcolonialism. Relations shaped by conquest and occupation inevitably demand critical interrogation, for the lasting vestiges of cultural, linguistic and spiritual destruction alter forever the cultural landscape of an indigenous people (Gandhi, 1998; Spivak, 1999).

Why Are Critical Perspectives Not Empowering?

One might well ask, as critical perspectives are profoundly engaged with powerful issues of our time, why does so little critical research becomes a part of civic debate? Why does so little important work make it to the editorial pages of newspapers, or into venues routinely perused by intellectuals and engaged citizens, such as the *Atlantic Monthly* or *Harper's*, but is instead aimed at the even smaller audiences captured by such publications as *Daedalus* or *Tikkun?* Certainly, the lack of wider public discussion surrounding such research is one reason why most of such work has not yet resulted in any measurable increase in social justice or has had any real visible transformative effect on social policy or education.

Critical perspectives have already acknowledged the role of the research "construct" in the generation and perpetuation of power for particular groups, especially knowledge and cultural workers such as academics (Greenwood & Levin, 2000; Knorr-Cetina & Mulkay, 1983). Indeed, knowledge production—traditionally the province of the scholarly profession—has finally seen its flowering in the information age and the information society. However, even when we recognize this research/power complicity, we must still, as academic knowledge generators and producers, conduct research, both because of the influence that it holds within dominant discourses and, more selfishly, because that is what we are hired to do in certain kinds of institutions. Critically inclined academics, however, continue to struggle with how to rethink our fields in ways that generate critically oriented questions and methods, even while addressing issues such as voice, representation, and the avoidance of new forms of oppressive power. Although qualitative methods and alternative paradigm inquiry offer possibilities for the generation of epistemologies and methodologies that insist on the examination of themselves, even qualitative inquiry creates power for—and all too frequently, a focus on—the researcher her- or himself. Thus, we are caught in the paradox of attempting to investigate and deconstruct power relations even as we are ourselves engaged in a project that creates and re-creates power accruing primarily to us.

We believe that three issues can be identified that contribute to the continued marginalization of critical theorizing and critical pedagogy. One is endogenous to critical theories themselves, whereas two others are exogenous, but each can be addressed by the community of critical knowledge workers. First, we discuss things that academics do to keep their work from being read by broader audiences. These practices are both tied to training and to the insolated environment that is the academy. Second, we believe that there are political forces, particularly on the political right, that have a large stake in quelling serious critiques of schooling practices, critical research, and critical researchers (Horowitz, 2006). Conservative forces within and external to the academy mount rigorous efforts at systemic and systematic disqualification of critical qualitative research and those who produce it; the most serious effort thus far have been to "capture" federal resources sufficiently to deny funding to qualitative and critical researchers, while mandating that "what works" is primarily or solely randomized experiments (Mosteller & Boruch, 2002; National Research Council, 2002). Third, we believe the effects of neoliberal and hypercapitalism have created additional social problems (e.g., increasing poverty of some segments of Western society, demands for goods and services that outstrip the global ability to produce or deliver them, unquestioned nationalisms), which, in turn, have led to a deemphasis on certain forms of academic knowledge production. We will deal with each of those in turn.

"Repressive Myths," Difficult Language, and Writing Complexities

When Ellsworth (1989) speaks of "repressive myths" associated with critical theorizing and critical pedagogy, she refers to forms of language that "operate at a high level of abstraction" (p. 300), the overall effect of which is to reinscribe certain forms of oppression within the classroom. In part, this occurs because

> when educational researchers advocating critical pedagogy fail to provide a clear statement of their political agendas, the effect is to hide the fact that as critical pedagogues, they are in fact seeking to appropriate public resources (classrooms, school supplies, teacher/professor salaries, academic requirements and degrees) to further various "progressive political agendas that they believe to be for the public good—and therefore deserving of public resources. ... As a result, the critical education "movement" has failed to develop a clear articulation for its existence, its goals, priorities, risks, or potentials. (p. 301)

Some of the foregoing criticism has since been answered by the critical community, but some critical theorizing remains connected to patriarchy and rationalist abstraction. Ellsworth found, in her media course, that concepts borrowed from the critical pedagogy literature were singularly unhelpful in uncovering the experiences of racism and other "isms" brought to her classroom. She recognized that she and her students needed to move away from the regulating aspects of rationalism, which "operate[s] in ways that set up as its opposite an irrational Other,"[1] as it "has become a vehicle for regulating conflict and the power to speak" (p. 301), silencing some voices and marginalizing others.

Rationalistic argumentation, however, is not the only issue the critical educationists face. The issues of abstraction, of difficult languages, and of "complicated writing styles" make the work of many critical researchers appear less transparent than it might be and creates a smaller audience than the ideas warrant. At times, we have been guilty of the same charge, so we abstain from adopting some sort of literary high ground here. Indeed, at times, the material we undertake to deconstruct and demystify demands a complex political and philosophical treatment, circling as it does around abstruse social and democratic theory. Nevertheless, as Lather (1996) makes clear, language itself possesses a "politics," wherein "clear speech is part of a discursive system, a network of power that has material *effects*" and thus, "sometimes we need a density that fits the thought being expressed" (p. 3). Additionally, St. Pierre (2000) reminds us that the "burden of intelligibility" lies with the reader/receiver as well as with the writer/constructor. She asks: "How does one learn to hear and 'understand' a statement made within a different structure of intelligibility?" (p. 25). We argue, however, that Lather's analysis regarding the deskilling effects of "clear and concise plain prose" and its relationship to a pervasive anti-intellectualism in American society, although true, does not mitigate the necessity of making our theories and arguments more accessible to a broader set of audiences to further public scrutiny and debate about these ideas.

Consequently, although we strongly hold to the premise that sound theorizing is both academically necessary and epistemologically moral, and that there indeed might be some "violence of clarity," a kind of "non-innocence" in plain prose, it is also clear that many who would like to understand the foundational elements of what is being argued either cannot, or will not, struggle with our terminologies and languages. The requirement that thinking differently necessitates speaking differently becomes a barrier. Rather than being the rational argument makers, we are unfortunately cast in the mold of being Ellsworth's "irrational Other." Thus, in part, the problem of critical pedagogues and theorists is partially one of our own making and partially one of difficult circumstance. When dominant understandings are so thoroughly embedded within truth orientations, critical language and abstract terminologies sometimes ensure that ideas will not be received by a patient audience that has learned to expect answers to generalizable solutions.

There are, however, greater reasons why so little critical qualitative research makes it into the public realm of debate. One of these is linked to the backlashes against feminisms and other traditionally marginalized knowledges. As Patricia Hill Collins (2000) explains in her discussion of black feminist thought, as critical work and resistance become evident related to intersecting oppressions, new forms of power are generated to silence/ignore the traditionally oppressed, and to reinscribe/reinstate power for those who have been traditionally privileged.

Reinscribing Oppressive Forms of Knowledge: Attacking Diversity and Discrediting Critique

As we and others have written, the civil rights successes of the 1960s resulted in new possibilities for academia and the acceptance of the voices and knowledges of those who have been traditionally marginalized. In academia, women and gender studies, ethnic studies, and diverse research philosophies and methodologies emerged and gained credibility. Yet, there were those who were not happy with these gains across society in general and in academia specifically. For example, as women made gains in the workplace and elsewhere, actions were taken to resubjugate them/us (Faludi, 1991). As women made gains in traditional domains of academia, there was/is a backlash against their leadership styles, their research topics, their publication outlets, and so on.

In society in general, a movement was specifically designed and funded to (re)inscribe a monocultural conservative agenda in the media, the judiciary, and in academia. Foundations and think tanks were created that funded a range of broad-based societal activities, including particular forms of literature used to discredit feminisms, qualitative research methods, and constructs like affirmative action and multiculturalism. Most are familiar with these activities by now because of the past eight years of a U.S. government administration that has been entirely supported by this monocultural agenda. However, most (even academics) do not notice the ways that this activity has entirely transformed the expectations for intellectual engagement; for example, when an academic discussion is conducted via the media, most listeners are not aware that three out of four of the panel members are employed by "right of center" foundations or think tanks.

An Example of Narrowed Scholarship: Privileging Evidence-Based Research

Specific academic activities have ranged from publications designed to discredit feminist, critical, postmodern, and post-colonial voices—to funding for students whose purposes would be to build careers using the narrowed academic agenda—to the redeployment of public grant funding privileging monocultural practices (Lincoln & Cannella, 2004). Contemporarily, a major example is the discourse of evidence-based research infused throughout government agencies and invading academic fields like medicine, education, and business within nation states and globally. Constructs like controlled experiments, replicability, efficiency, validity, and generalizability are again imposed as superior, more sophisticated, and representing quality (Cannella, 2008). All the language is present, from designs that use "randomized experiments"—to quantitative orientations like "correlational," "disciplined," and "rigorous"—reference terms used as legitimation like "medicine" and "technology" as academic fields of power, the degrading of the field of education, calls for what our "children deserve"—to actions that would redeploy "funding." This discourse is not simply found in academic journals, but is used in testimony of academics before Congress as illustrated in the words of Jeffrey Pfeffer in March 2007: "Organizations ... ought to base policies NOT on casual benchmarking, on ideology or belief ... but instead should implement evidence-based management." He goes on to promote notions like high performance culture, gold standard, and "what we know" (Evidence-Based Management, 2007).

Critiques have come from a range of perspectives. Two articles in different fields demonstrate this further. In the *Journal of Management Studies*, Morrell (2007) uses Russian Formalism to illustrate the ways that the evidence-based systematic review technique is used to defamiliarize the conventional notion of systematic and the ways that the term "transparency" is reinvented to reinforce assumptions and values within the evidence based discourse. Further, credibility is generated by invoking a powerful discipline like medicine, as well as calls for thoroughness and rigor, while referring to practices like narrative as older or obsolete. The discourse methods privilege a perspective in which critique of the evidence-based construct is not permitted. In *Social Theory & Health* (2008), Wall uses feminist poststructural analyses to demonstrate how the discourse of evidence-based research positions and labels nurses as subjects of humanist individualism who are blamed for rejecting research and interpreted as "laggards," yet are excluded from the very game that would control them. Further, feminine and nursing ways of knowing, like esthetics, personal, and ethical knowledges are excluded. As Wall states: "What passes for objective research is a search for what elites want knowledge about" (p. 49). And, in contemporary times, those elites want knowledge to be about efficiency, measurement, objectives/outcomes/benchmarks, profiteering, and corporate capitalism. Other critiques of evidence-based research call attention to a lip service that is paid to qualitative methods while practices are put forward that would exclude its possibilities (Freshwater & Rolfe, 2004), the ways that postmodern (or other such) critiques reveal the choices, subjectivities, and genres through which particular authors/researchers choose to function (Eaglestone, 2001), and the limits of evidence-based perspectives even in the legitimating "power" field of medicine (e.g., the interplay between observation and theory even in critical realist work, the subjectivity even within "randomized trials," the denial of individual patient circumstances and variations, and the limitation of patient rights within the assumptions of evidence-based research, [Cohen, Stavri, & Hersh, 2004]).

Critiques and deconstructions have occurred, yet evidence-based research discourses are alive, expanding, and most likely invading locations that would surprise us all. A recent Google search resulted in 35,500,000 sites, with over 14,000,000 of those devoted to the U.S. government and evidence-based research/practice. Examples of the actual funded entities related to the sites abound, such as the U.S. Department of Health & Human Services, Agency for Healthcare Research and Quality, and Evidence-Based Practice Centers. In October 2007, a third wave of fourteen centers in the U.S. and Canada were funded to "review all relevant scientific literature on clinical, behavioral, and organization and financing topics to produce evidence reports and technology assessments." Funded centers include the ECRI Institute, RTI International, Minnesota and Oregon Evidence-Based Practice Centers, and the Blue Cross and Blue Shield Association, as well as U.S. and Canadian universities like Duke, Johns Hopkins, and Vanderbilt (Canadian examples include the University of Alberta and the University of Ottawa).

In the United States, the Council for Excellence in Government (2008) has created alliances like the Coalition for Evidence-Based Policy with corporate partners like the Annenberg, Bill and Melinda Gates, Ford, and William T. Grant Foundations, as well as Geico, Goldman Sachs, Google, Johnson & Johnson, and Microsoft, just to name a few. The coalition's mission is to "promote government policymaking based on rigorous evidence." Conducting activities like the April 2008 workshop "How to Read Findings to Distinguish Evidence-Based Programs from Everything Else" and deploying funding like $10,000,000 to a HHS evidence-based home visitation program, the coalition claims (through an independent evaluation conducted by the William T. Grant Foundation) to have been "instrumental in transforming a theoretical advocacy of evidence-based policy among certain (federal) agencies into an operational reality."

One could go on and on with examples, but we would rather note that the discourse is invasive, often hidden from the public eye (and even the gaze of many politicians) through legislation embedded within hundreds of pages of text. The discourse (and its agents) literally restructures public agencies and redeploys research funds to support itself. Further, it creates ties with, and gives a greater voice to, the financially elite of society. The obvious next step, in addition to the controlling and discrediting of a range of people, perspectives, and ways of being, is to further produce and support the discourse through neoliberal, hypercapitalist, free-market profiteering that commodifies and industrializes everything; this "next step" is much less of a next step than corresponding insidious function.

Examples of this also abound, like Evidence Based Research, Inc., with headquarters located in Vienna, Virginia. Organized in two divisions, Military Studies and Decision Systems, the company sells its ability to address problems all around the globe, ranging "from creating systems to measure political and economic reform ... to designing improved systems for decision-making ... (to) improving the ability of coalition forces to provide disaster relief and peacekeeping services" (Evidence Based Research, Inc., 2008). Does anyone hear (read) further construction of the "military-industrial complex" using evidence-based discourses here? But there are many other examples that we can find familiar in our own fields—like the selling of school "turnaround specialist" programs for "evidence-based failing" schools (read evidence and failing as industry created test scores, by the way). And, again, we could go on and on.

Challenges to postpositivist science (or critical realism) are certainly *prohibited* (excluded), while the *ritual* of experimental science is certainly reinscribed. Critical perspectives (and critical research) are certainly silenced. Further, the discourse on evidence-based research creates an elite group who become so because of their willingness to accept and use the discourse— those who would invoke validity, generalizability, replicability, and intervention are given the *right to speak and act*. The notion of evidence is used to reinforce the reinscribed *appeal to reason*, the will to truth that creates the claim to reason versus folly, labeling those who would be discredited as half truths, without intellect, as relativist or nonsensical. Evidence-based research further constructs, and is constructed by, a range of *disciplinary technologies* that are broad based, from appeals to surviving illness (for everyone, as in medicine) to publishing in "upper-tier" journals (as representing quality and intellectual sophistication), to specific area technologies like evidence-based research that would raise achievement test scores. This discourse can literally erase critical and qualitative research methods as well as critical voices of those who have been traditionally placed in the margins (whether as people of color, women, children/students, nurses, patients, or anyone who would challenge positivist evidence-based science).

Perhaps the main, and interconnected, reason for the almost

invisibility of critical qualitative research in attempts to transform inequitable societal conditions is the corporatization of knowledge. As illustrated in our discussion of the ways that the discourse of evidence-based knowledge is used to redeploy resources and control fields of understanding, a neoliberal hypercapitalism has invaded all aspects of scholarship, values that influence decision-making and administration. Although this invasion is certainly monocultural and masculinist, it certainly goes beyond the imposition of these particular ideologies because of the importance played by resources and finances in societies dominated by capitalism. A major example in the corporatization of knowledge is the construction of the contemporary corporate university

Corporatization of Knowledge

Colleges and universities have always been more closely connected to capitalism and the business community than many of us would like, but recent discourse practices that have supported decreases in percentages of public taxes designated for higher education have resulted in an increased openness to neoliberal capitalism as a means of survival. As a fundamentalist hypercapitalism has invaded (and, we would add, has been strategically infused into) all of society (in the United States and probably globally), so, too, has higher education been transformed. Even historically cultural knowledge is now being commodified, patented, labeled as "wonderfully entrepreneurial," and sold for a profit. Further, a hypercapitalist perspective has been/is being used to interpret all of life, whether to explain human action as self-benefiting, knowledge as valuable because of market possibilities, or "saving" the environment as a profitable venture (Cannella & Miller, 2008). And the list goes on.

This corporate fundamentalism is probably the most profound influence on higher education today. University presidents are hired to function like CEOs; deans are employed as fundraisers; faculty "stars" are recruited with large salaries that increase pay inequities in their fields, yet, the general faculty workforce is becoming increasingly female, temporary, and low paid. This larger group of faculty has little voice in the governance of the institution.

In 1969, over 96% of academic faculty was in tenure-track appointments: Currently, less than 40% of faculty members are (Washburn, 2005). Even if the newly constituted workforce is talented and informed, it is not protected by freedoms of scholarship that would counter CEO administrators or customers who are not satisfied. The reconstituted workforce is expected to go easy on customers and teach whatever content is predetermined (by those with power—whether financial, legislative, or administrative). Research superstars are employed with tenure for exorbitant amounts of money and often named to chaired positions funded by wealthy donors; less than 50% of the remaining faculty is employed in tenured or tenure-track positions. The workforce has become one in which faculty votes concerning academic issues can potentially be carried by low-paid academic workers who have no choice but to be controlled by the administrators who hire them. Salaries are increasingly inequitable across the range of individuals employed to teach, with the larger group of temporary, low-paid workers being women. Inequity and corporatized power abound.

If this corporatization of the workforce continues as retirements occur of those who are tenured, the voices of faculty who have actually been the determiners of both research and curricular content will be silenced. Examples of this academic erasure can be easily found generally, but especially in colleges/schools that do not have alumni donors who can be used to "leverage" (a business term) power. Overall, attempts by administrators to require program faculty to determine curricular benchmarks (another business terminology) and to prove the quality of research, while on the surface appearing justifiable, actually fosters a perspective that assumes faculty incompetence and need for regulation. Some administrators have even imposed curricular content on entire universities without faculty governance by creating required courses for all students (like freshman courses literally constructed and imposed on all programs by university presidents). Faculty of public institutions of higher education have been forced by administrators to accept partnerships with private charter school corporations, to offer graduate programs strictly designed to generate revenue, and to offer online courses and programs using social content that is not appropriate for learning at a distance, just to name a few.

Those who are rewarded as faculty appear to be those who "buy into" the corporate entrepreneurial function. Short- or long-term profit is privileged over education gains. Professors are commodities to be traded, as the institution gives up those who are less likely to generate money for those who are proven grant writers or inventors whose work can be patented and sold for great profits (Andrews, 2006; Mohanty, 2004). Professors are expected to be entrepreneurs by constructing courses, workshops, conferences, and academic programs that generate profits, as well as obtaining grants. Further, as with capitalism in general, this entrepreneurial perspective demonstrates a remasculinizing of academia (Baez, 2008) in that the privileging of competition and the call for training a particular type of worker is also focused on the fields that have not accepted notions of hypercapitalism, entrenprenurialism, and competition. For example, teacher education (a traditionally female-gendered field) is blamed for all the problems in education (although those problems are constructed from a neoliberal, market perspective); yet, business schools are not held responsible for the fate of the U.S. economy (Saltman, 2007).

This context privileges knowledge that can be converted into profit—either as a direct commodity for financial gain, as the knowledge that is preferred by an outside donor, or as the knowledge that would attain grants redeployed for positivist and masculinist purposes like evidence-based research knowledge. Fields that do not result in a profit or that would actually challenge free-market perspective are certainly placed in the margin, if not entirely erased. Critical forms of research and knowledges fall into this category.

Coda: Can We Create Critical Transformations?

We believe that qualitative methods can be used for critical social purposes. However, academics will most likely need to be strategic and persistent in this endeavor:

First, knowledge of what's happening in society is necessary to understand the discourses that dominate; many of us have not been aware of the agendas and actions that surround us and, further, have not engaged in informed critique. In "Meeting across the Paradigmatic Divide," Moss (2007) uses the work of Mouffe (2000), which focuses on agonistic pluralism to suggest that we construct an agonistic politics that searches for common ground, continually fosters engagement with diverse paradigms, and values pluralism in democracy.

Second, researchers will need to determine if there are, in unexpected locations, specific investigations/circumstances in which qualitative methods have been successful in addressing critical social purposes. As research would no longer accept the objectivity of positivist science, research would no longer be appropriately located in the "objective," protected ivory tower. Research conceptualizations, practices, and researchers themselves would be inextricably interconnected to human communities (e.g., locally, academically, nationally, racially). Therefore, in addition to research purposes, researchers would serve as informed reflexive community members, as well as scholars who conduct research as informed by human community relations. Rather than statistical technicians, scholars could be expected to spend time exploring the range of interconnected societal structures that impact individuals and communities.

Third, *revolutionary* critical social sciences (e.g., feminisms, postcolonial perspectives) will need to be strategically placed at the center of academic research discussions, conceptualizations, and practices. Successful strategies will necessitate networking, collaborative planning, and persistent support for each other (Mohanty, 2004). Research conceptualizations, purposes, and practices would be grounded in critical ethical challenges to social (therefore science) systems, supports for egalitarian struggle, and revolutionary ethical awareness and activism from within the context of community. Research would be relational (often as related to community) and grounded within critique of systems, egalitarian struggle, and revolutionary ethics.

Revolutionary critical inquiry could ask questions (and take actions) similar to the following that challenge social (and therefore science) systems:

How are particular groups represented in discourses practices and social systems?

What knowledges are silenced, made invisible, or literally erased?

What are examples of oppressions (and/or new exclusions) that are being made to sound equitable through various discourses?

How do elite groups define values, constructs, and rhetoric in ways that maintain matrices of power?

Research that supported egalitarian struggles for social justice would ask questions such as:

How are particular discourses infused into the public imaginary? (e.g., media, parenting, medicine)?

How are power relations constructed and managed through?

Perhaps most important for us as researchers is the development of a nonviolent revolutionary ethical consciousness. As researchers who are concerned about equity and regulation, we would ask how we construct research practices that facilitate our becoming aware of societal issues, rhetoric, and practices that would continue forms of marginalization or that would construct new forms of inequity and oppression.

Fourth, and finally, critical work is likely not possible without the construction of alliances within/between academia and the public that would place at the forefront concern for equity and justice. Scholarship in higher education must actively work to counter corporatization of knowledge from within by challenging controlling, narrow discourses of accountability, quality, and excellence. Further, to inquire into the regulatory and equity issues that are most important to a range of communities, both inside and outside of academia, and to construct new ways to share those inquiries, we must be involved with them. Networks, collaborations, and strategic forms of dissemination are necessary that address foundationally issues like: enlarging the public's understanding of the research imaginary, generating unthought discursive spaces, and public critique of the ways that groups are privileged and silenced by various forms of research, science, and academic practice.

Note

1. For an interesting note on this same topic, see the brief discussion of rationalism and arationalism, in Lincoln (1985).

References

Andrews, J. G. (2006). How we can resist corporatization. *Academe.* Available online at http://www.aaup.org/publications/Academe/2006/06mjandrtabl. htm (accessed May 27, 2006).

Baez, B. (2008). Men in crisis? Race, gender, and the remasculinization of higher education. Paper presented at the American Educational Research Association Meeting, March 25–27. New York.

Cannella, G. S. (1997). *Deconstructing early childhood education: Social justice and revolution.* New York: Peter Lang.

Cannella, G. S. & Miller, L. (2008). Constructing corporatist science: Reconstituting the soul of American higher education. *Cultural Studies ↔ Critical Methodologies,* 8(1), 24–38.

Cohen, A. M., Stavri, P. Z., & Hersh, W. R. (2004). Criticisms of evidence-based medicine. *Evidence-based Cardiovascular Medicine,* 8, 197–198,

Collins, P. H. (2000). *Black feminist thought: Knowledge, consciousness, and the politics of empowerment.* New York: Routledge.

Council for Excellence in Government. (2008). Coalition for Evidence-Based Policy. Available online at http://www.excelgov.org/index. php?keyword=a432fbc34d71c7 (accessed on May 8, 2008).

Eaglestone, R. (2001). *Postmodernism and holocaust denial.* Duxford, U.K.: Icon Books.

Ellsworth, E. (1989). Why doesn't this feel empowering? Working through the repressive myths of critical pedagogy. *Harvard Educational Review,* 59(3), 297–324.

Evidence-Based Management. (2007). Jeffry Pheffer testifies to Congress about evidence-based practices. Available online at http://www.evidence-basedmanagement.com/research_practice/commentary/pfeffer_ congressional_testimony (accessed April 28, 2007).

Evidence Based Research, Inc. (2008). Available online at http://www.ebrinc. com/html/about_organization.html (accessed May 5, 2008). Faludi, S. (1991). *Backlash: The undeclared war against American women.* New York: Anchor Books, Doubleday.

Freshwater, D. & Rolfe, G. (2004). *Deconstructing evidence-based practice.* Abingdon, Oxford, U.K.: Routledge.

Gandhi, L. (1998). *Postcolonial theory: A critical introduction*. New York: Columbia University Press.

Greenwood, D. J. & Levin, M. (2000). Reconstructing the relationships between universities and society through action research. In N. K. Denzin & Y. S. Lincoln (Eds.), *Handbook of qualitative research*, 2nd ed., pp. 85–106. Thousand Oaks, CA: Sage.

Horowitz, D. (2006). *The professors: The 101 most dangerous academics in America*. Washington, DC: Regnery Publishing.

Knorr-Cetina, K. & Mulkay, M. (Eds.). (1983). *Science observed: Perspectives on the social study of science*. London: Sage.

Lather, P. (1996). Troubling clarity: The politics of accessible language. *Harvard Educational Review*, 66, 3. Available online at http://www.edreview.org/harvard/1996/fa96/f96lath.htm (accessed May 6, 2008).

Lincoln, Y. S. (1985). Epilogue: Dictionaries for languages not yet spoken. In Y. S. Lincoln (Ed.), *Organizational theory and inquiry: The paradigm revolution*, pp. 221–228. Thousand Oaks, CA: Sage.

Lincoln, Y. S. & Cannella, G. S. (2004). Qualitative research, power, and the radical right. *Qualitative Inquiry*, 10(2), 175–201.

Mohanty, C. T. (2004). *Feminism without borders: Decolonizing theory, practicing solidarity*. Durham, NC: Duke University Press.

Morrell, K. (2007). The narrative of "evidenced based" management: A polemic. *Journal of Management Studies*, 45(3), 614–635.

Moss, P. (2007). Meetings across the paradigmatic divide. *Educational Philosophy and Theory*, 39(3), 239–245.

Mosteller, F. & Boruch, R. (2002). *Evidence matters: Randomized trials in education research*. Washington, DC: Brookings Institution Press.

Mouffe, C. (2000). *The democratic paradox*. London: Verso.

National Research Council (2002). *Scientific research in education* (Committee on Scientific Principles for Education Research, R. Shavelson & L. Town, (Eds.). Center for Education, Division of Behavioral and social Sciences and Education). Washington, DC: National Academy Press.

Richardson, L. (2000). Writing: A method of inquiry. In N. K. Denzin & Y. S. Lincoln (Eds.), *Handbook of qualitative research*, 2nd ed., pp. 923–948. Thousand Oaks, CA: Sage.

Said, E. (1979). *Orientalism*. New York: Vintage Books.

Saltman, (2007). *Capitalizing on disaster: Breaking and taking public schools*. Boulder, CO: Paradigm.

Spivak, G. C. (1999). *A critique of postcolonial reason: Toward a history of the vanishing present*. Cambridge, MA: Harvard University Press.

St. Pierre, E. A. (2000). The call for intelligibility in postmodern educational research. *Educational Researcher*, 29(5), 25–28.

Wall, S. (2008). A critique of evidence-based practice in nursing: Challenging the assumptions. *Social Theory & Health*, 6, 37–53.

Washburn, J. (2005). *University Inc.: The corporate corruption of higher education*. New York: Basic Books.

Chapter 2 | Four Points Concerning Policy-Oriented Qualitative Research

Frederick Erickson
University of California, Los Angeles

Of the four points that follow, each has a different rhetorical valence in engaging policy audiences. The first point will be stated in a way that is meant to be appealing—consonant with current policy discourse—and the last is stated in a way that is intended to challenge that discourse. The remaining two points are located rhetorically somewhere between the first and the last.

Here is a way to make nice with a policy audience present. When qualitative researchers address policy audiences, they are wise to be explicit and accurate about both the range of variation in phenomena they report and the actual frequencies of occurrence of phenomena. A single narrative vignette or interview quote, however illuminating it might be as a "telling case" (see Merton, 1973, pp. 371–382) does not provide evidence of overall patterns in one's evidence: Was the vignette or quote a typical instance or an atypical one? How many similar ones were observed and how many different ones?

I think it is appropriate to report relative frequency of occurrence and the full range of variation in occurrence of similar or analogous instances to show the reader that one has not cherry-picked evidence in reporting. I know this may sound old-fashioned, but as I teach qualitative research methods to graduate students in education, I teach them, as a matter of self-defense, how to show relative frequency of occurrence as they report their research, because in the field of education I know that they will encounter policy-interested audiences who worry about cherry-picked evidence. And, in my judgment, that is a justifiable worry.

The second point concerns a way to argue for the policy relevance of detailed case study research. In a quite recent volume rather edgily titled *Making Social Science Matter: How Social Inquiry Fails and How It Can Succeed Again,* Bent Flyvbjerg (2001), a Danish urban planner, makes an argument for a kind of social inquiry through case study by which social research stops imitating that of the natural sciences to address directly matters of value, power, and local nuance in policy decision-making. Flyvbjerg says that as long as social inquiry continues to imitate the physical sciences—attempting a social physics or chemistry—it will continue to fail, because social phenomena are far more contingent and labile than are physical phenomena. As Geertz comments in a favorable review of Flyvbjerg's book,

> using the term "science" to cover everything from string theory to psychoanalysis is not a happy idea, because doing so elides the difficult fact that the ways in which we try to understand and deal with the physical world and those in which we try to understand and deal with the social one are not altogether the same. The methods of research, the aims of inquiry, and the standards of judgment all differ, and nothing but confusion, scorn, and accusation—relativism! Platonism! reductionism! verbalism!—results from failing to see this. (Geertz, 2001, p. 53)

Flyvbjerg's argument is an old one in new dress—when I was a graduate student it was indexed by the contrast terms "ideographic" and "nomothetic"—with an intellectual history reaching back to Dilthey's distinction between "Geisteswissenschaft" and "Naturwissenschaft." Mainline social science reached for Naturwissenschaft, yet social science can't identify general laws of social process that enable confident prediction and control. Flyvbjerg argues that that's not actually what policymakers need. They need to understand the particular circumstances at work in a local situation. He uses as an example the planning of auto parking and pedestrian mall arrangements in the Danish city of Aalborg. Given local political interests, particulars of the local built environment and of local history, the parking and pedestrian traffic solution that is best for Aalborg cannot be informed by general knowledge—one cannot average over what was done in Limerick, Bruges, Genoa, Tokyo, and Minneapolis to develop wise policies for Aalborg. What's good for Aalborg involves detailed understanding of Aalborg itself.

Rich local understanding, such as really knowing the particulars of Aalborg, is based on a different kind of knowledge from that of hard science. To show us this, Flyvbjerg turns to Aristotle who, in the *Nichomachean Ethics* (book 6), distinguishes three types of knowledge. The first, "episteme," is what we think of as scientific and mathematical knowledge—general, invariant, cumulative. The second knowledge is "techne"—the knowledge of the craft practitioner—partly today that is manifested in engineering, as well as in handcrafts—what the blacksmith and the gardener knows. The third knowledge is "phronesis," the action-oriented deliberation that an adept policymaker uses to understand the local social ecosystem within which policy decisions need to be made. Aristotle saw this as the highest kind of knowledge—as a virtue—because it led to wise decisions about how to conduct social life.

Translated into Latin as "prudentia," phronesis leads one to prudent decisions—those that actually benefit people as individuals and in society. (Prudence was later seen in the Middle Ages as the chief among the "cardinal virtues"—prudence, temperance, courage, justice. Without prudence none of the other virtues can be realized in action—prudential reflection guides toward actions that are temperate, courageous, and just.) Prudence involves the mature exercise of judgment, and it is thus an intellectual virtue that supports good policy decisions as made by an experienced decision-maker:

> Whereas young people become accomplished in geometry and mathematics, and wise within these limits, prudent young people do not seem to be found. The reason is that prudence is concerned with particulars as well as universals, and particulars become known from experience, but a young person lacks experience, since some length of time is needed to produce it. (Aristotle, 1934, p. 1142)

In his monograph on method, Flyvbjerg goes on to say that the modern equivalent of phronesis is case study, conducted carefully in a local setting over a considerable span of time. It is phronetic understanding that will help policymakers in Aalborg figure out auto parking and pedestrian traffic policies that are fair and workable. (I'm afraid that such case study is still a kind of "realist" ethnography that is no longer fashionable in some circles, but there you are. Yet what Flyvbjerg is recommending is not just a qualitative version of dust-bowl empiricism.) As an illustration of what an analysis based on a phronetic approach looks like, Flyvbjerg (1998) has published a book-length case study of Aalborg and its central district pedestrian mall planning process, titled *Rationality and Power: Democracy in Practice*. He further argues for the policy relevance of case study in an essay on method (2006), titled "Five Misunderstandings about Case Study Research."

The older I get, the more I return to my beginning formation in the humanities and the arts and away from what seems to me to be the overreaching of social science (Erickson 2005). "Science" has become a modern idolatry—we should be much more suspicious of episteme than most of us are. When policymakers ask of research syntheses and meta-analysis "What does the *science* say?" what they actually need is *prudentia*, not *scientia*. They need really good case study—and that doesn't mean that the case study shouldn't be accurate and forthright about those matters of relative frequency of occurrence and range of variation that I mentioned earlier. Prudent decision-making should have such information available and take it into account, as well as taking values and power into account. But most fundamentally for good policy decision-making, case study provides us with a *story* and that helps us to envision policy that is beneficial rather than harmful. As the social philosopher MacIntyre (1984) tells us, "I can only answer the question 'What am I to do?' if I can answer the prior question 'Of what story or stories do I find myself a part?'" (p. 216).

Which leads to my third point. Mainstream social and educational research of the last half of the 20th century was instrumental in focus, attempting to avoid value judgments—emphasizing Weber's "Zweckrational" over "Wertrational." This tendency was accentuated at the end of the century with the emergence of a "New Public Management" (see, for example, the discussion in Barzelay, 2001). The New Public Management is, in Foucauldian terms, a Discourse Formation as well as a set of techniques. Within that discourse, policy choices are framed exclusively in terms of utilitarian ends. Thus, the two questions that dominate current policy deliberations have become "Is this effective?" and "Is this efficient?" In so many current educational policy matters, however, a prior question lurks: "Do we want to do this in the first place?" (i.e., is this a means or an end that is worth pursuing—or, in MacIntyre's terms, is this a story we want ourselves or anyone else to live in?). In my field of professional education, arguments over teaching for basic skills versus for understanding, whether children should be able to use calculators in doing arithmetic, whether racially segregated schools are inherently demeaning and unjust, whether differential spending levels between schools in high- or low-income neighborhoods are wrong or right, whether charter schools are a potential blessing or a curse, whether bilingual instruction should be encouraged or discouraged—and many others—involve issues of value (and of political interest) most fundamentally rather than of instrumental utility. Conventional social scientific inquiry, whether "qualitative" or "quantitative" in method, is ill equipped to deal with the value issues entailed in such policy choices. But prudential social inquiry, a phronetic approach to situated, local understanding, can address value choices as part of a process of deliberation in action. Through prudential social inquiry we can reintroduce ethics into social policy deliberations, reframing the narrowly instrumental rationality of the current discourse.

The fourth and final point is that we need to ask why policy discourse has been so thoroughly overtaken by instrumentally rational hard science framing at this historical moment. It is a superstitious scientism, and in spite of intense critique of blind faith in scientific certainty within the philosophy of science and the sociology of science over the last two academic generations, popular faith in scientism keeps rising up, again and again. Like a zombie it will not die.

I think that the intensification of this superstition in the policy arena has to do with matters of political economy on the world stage. Even before the current economic meltdown, there has been a growing perception among world elites that developed capitalist societies are facing inherent limits on the availability of resources. In the long term for such societies, the economic pie is either never going to expand or it will shrink, and there will be bloody contestations over who gets what amounts from the pieces that remain. The New Public Management Movement can be read as an attempt to find justification for the policy decisions people are making as they try to divide up a pie that becomes smaller and smaller over time. Here lies the surface appeal—the face validity—of efforts to determine accountability for results in the provision of public services and for efforts to introduce scientific evidence-based practice in the conduct of public service delivery. (This is not simply a right-wing impetus—it has been shared in Britain by both Thatcher and Blair/Brown, and in the United States by both Clinton and George W. Bush. It is a general tendency—what Foucault [1979], following Bentham, calls the "panopticon" and what Scott [1998] calls "seeing like a state.")

When we think about the kinds of fields of practice these so-called reforms are claiming to be able to help—such as nursing, teaching, librarianship, medical doctoring—they are all labor intensive. Each is very expensive. In a situation of shrinking resources, it would be great if one could replace physicians with nurses and a computer, using evidence-based advice on what to do with a patient. The same goes for replacing teachers in schools with instructional technology overseen by low-paid classroom assistants who do no teaching but simply keep the kids doing exercises on the computers—a reversion to the 19th century "Lancaster system" of instruction by means of classroom monitors supervising large numbers of students.

Make no mistake—the evidence-based practice movement is a union-busting operation, a de-skilling operation. It is an attempt to substitute general knowledge for the local knowledge entailed in experienced clinical judgment—to substitute *episteme* for *phronesis*. If one values the clinical judgment of skilled practitioners in the human services and believes that there's no substitute for such phronesis, the evidence-based practice claims don't make good sense, however appealing in terms of efficiency and effectiveness they may appear at first glance. Scott (1990, 1998) claims that even though the state wants to see local practices in normalizing, general ways, it can't ever do that completely nor can its mandates for uniformity in the conduct of local practices ever be completely implemented (see also Erickson [2004], concerning the inherently locally opportunistic character—and hence the unrepeatability and unpredictability—of the conduct of everyday life, including that of everyday talk). We need to remember the aphorism attributed to Mark Twain: "History doesn't repeat itself; at best it sometimes rhymes." Qualitative social inquiry gets a lot of mileage out of trying to portray and understand that rhyming, but hard science social inquiry founders on the rhyming of social life. Such social inquiry needs at least synonymy—if not exact repetition—in the words that social life utters.

There's good news and bad news here. The good news about evidence-based practice and pseudo-scientific accountability measurements is that those hard science approaches to the improvement of service in human service fields will never work. Hard science–based policy inquiry can produce lists of "best practices," as evidenced by experimental field trials. But these are not actual local practices—they are general characterizations of practices, considering practices from the point of view of episteme rather than that of phronesis. They are cleaner than life—that is to say, they are sets of square pegs in differing sizes, with all the rough edges rubbed off. Practitioners can try to use such "best practices," but the recurring problem for their use is that in the specific circumstances of their local work practitioners never confront perfectly square holes (see Erickson 1992), so none of the square pegs they are provided with by generalizing scientific inquiry will ever quite fit the particular local circumstance they face. People are starting to figure that out—that the foundations of New Public Management set up a service delivery game that is hopeless to try to realize in actual local enactment. (Ceglowski [1998] presents an argument along similar lines from a case study of service delivery in education.)

The bad news is that it is realistic to assume a future of shrinking resources in late-capitalist societies, and thus an increasingly savage competition over access to resources. In our own society, the competition is not only between people of color and white people or between men and women: It's increasingly becoming an intergenerational struggle, a tug of war between the old and the young. In the face of pervasive shortages, I think we will keep seeing the Discourse of New Public Management emerging again and again from the ashes of its repeated failures to deliver on its own promises because of the recurring needs of elites for political cover as they make zero-sum decisions about resource allocation. Thus, in the continuing discourse of policy analysis, science can substitute for patriotism as the last refuge of scoundrels.

References

Aristotle. (1934). *Nicomachean ethics.* (dual text, trans. H. Rackham). Cambridge, MA: Harvard University Press.

Barzelay, M. (2001). *The new public management.* Berkeley: University of California Press.

Ceglowski, D. (1998). *Inside a Head Start center: Developing policies from practice.* New York: Teachers College Press.

Erickson, F. (1992). Why the clinical trial doesn't work as a metaphor for educational research: A reply to Francis Schrag. *Educational Researcher,* 21, 8–9.

Erickson, F. (2004). *Talk and social theory: Ecologies of speaking and listening in everyday life.* Cambridge: Polity Press.

Erickson, F. (2005). Arts, humanities, and sciences in educational research—and social engineering in federal education policy. *Teachers College Record,* 107(1), 4–9.

Flyvbjerg, B. (1998). *Rationality and power: Democracy in practice* (trans. Steven Sampson). Chicago: University of Chicago Press.

Flyvbjerg, B. (2001). *Making social science matter: How social inquiry fails and how it can succeed again.* Cambridge and New York: Cambridge University Press.

Flyvbjerg, B. (2006). Five misunderstandings about case-study research. *Qualitative Inquiry,* 12(2), 219–245.

Foucault, M. (1979). *Discipline and punish: The birth of the prison.* New York: Random House/Vintage Books.

Geertz, C. (2001). Empowering Aristotle. *Science,* 293, 53.

MacIntyre, A. (1984). *After virtue: A study in moral theory,* 2nd ed. South Bend, IN: University of Notre Dame Press.

Merton, R. (1973). *The sociology of science: Theoretical and empirical investigations.* Chicago: University of Chicago Press.

Scott, J. (1990). *Domination and the arts of resistance: Hidden transcripts.* New Haven CT: Yale University Press.

Scott, J. (1998). *Seeing like a state: How certain schemes to improve the human condition have failed.* New Haven CT: Yale University Press.

Chapter 3

Institutional Review Boards and the Ethics of Emotion

Michele J. McIntosh
York University

Janice M. Morse
University of Utah

In the research arena, institutional review boards (IRBs) have accepted the responsibility to ensure that researchers "do no harm" to participants. Although this mandate is clear in the prevention of physical harm, for social science research that poses no physical risk but the possibility of psychological harm, the issues are less clear. Here, we consider what *harm* may result from interview research—the talking and listening that occurs in qualitative research interviews and is similar to that which occurs in everyday life. Regardless of researchers' statements about the benefits of qualitative inquiry, IRBs consider that research requires oversight and participants need *protection* when participating in qualitative unstructured interviews.

We have selected *unstructured interviews* as the discussion point for this chapter for several reasons: (1) It is the most commonly used method of qualitative data collection; (2) it is a research strategy that allows participants the freedom to tell their stories without the researcher's control of a framework of questions to guide the interviews; and (3) because of the emergent nature of these interviews, the research protocol is unspecified. Participants are free to delve into their innermost emotional lives to the level they choose—and do so using their emotional voice. In this chapter, we examine the participants' response in the context of the ethics of emotion. We discuss if such emotions—or manifestations of distress—are detrimental to the participants, are caused by the researcher and/or the research context, and whether they are harmful. We consider the frameworks within which IRBs consider these issues.

IRBs' Mandate

IRBs are mandated to ensure the protection of participants from harm while at the same time ensuring the production of socially beneficial research. This is achieved by the development of a risk:benefit ratio, considering the risks to participants against the benefits to participants and society. This proportionate review must normally reveal benefit—if not to the individual participant, then to society—and should outweigh the risks to the individual.

Such a weighing of risk to benefit is problematic for social science research, in particular for qualitative inquiry. Although risks and benefits in biomedical research are quantifiable, this is not true for the cost of emotions such as psychological distress. IRBs are further handicapped in risk assessments of emotional distress by an ethics review process governed by guidelines that do not account for emotion. IRB guidelines are dominated by positivistic assumptions that (1) are designed for the evaluation of experimental designs and standardized research; (2) consider emotion, although worthy of investigation per se, as otherwise abjured within research—emotional distress in interviews therefore is regarded as an adverse side effect necessitating post-interview counseling; and (3) believe that the lay public as *subjects* are unable to protect themselves from risk (Kopelman, 2004) and that the IRB alone is authorized to determine how much risk a person should be exposed to.

IRB members are human, empathetic, and well intentioned; the proposed topics of inquiry, particularly those explored in nursing research, are heart-rending. IRB members worry that people who have already suffered will be retraumatized during the interview. When considering the possibility of harm, they use their moral imaginations to place themselves in the shoes of the participants and make decisions "as if" they were the participants themselves. But IRB members are not the participants, nor are they in a relational context with them. Such moral imaginings, therefore, may be inaccurate, unrestrained, and unverifiable.

In this situation, ethical theory provides insufficient guidance. Traditional ethical theory has not yet incorporated a well-developed theory of emotion. Treatment-based counseling theory is inappropriate. Furthermore, there is scant literature on actual participants' experiences and outcomes from qualitative inquiry. Although some qualitative researchers have documented benefits, including those to the participants themselves, these are ignored, and the IRBs focus entirely on the risk of harm. IRBs fear that researchers are unqualified to properly attend to psychiatric issues that may arise during the interview. They are concerned that the interview itself compounds suffering by increasing distress. Their worst fear is that a vulnerable participant will become so despondent that a participant will commit suicide and the university/IRB will be liable.

These issues may account for the fact that qualitative researchers proposing socially sensitive research are twice as likely as others to have their proposals rejected by IRBs, and that the foremost reason given for nonapproval was the protection of human subjects (Ceci, Peters, & Plotkin, 1985; Lincoln & Tierney, 2004).

Unstructured Interviews and Emotional Distress

Unstructured, in-depth, or narrative interviews are shared experiences in which researchers and interviewees come together to create an intimate context in which participants feel comfortable telling their story (Ramos, 1989). The unstructured interview begins with what Spradley (1979) referred to as a grand tour question: "Tell me. ..." Participants are given the freedom to tell their story, beginning wherever they choose, selecting the topics they wish, describing as much detail as they want, and taking as long as they desire. Corbin and Morse (2003) identified the phases of the unstructured interview as: pre-interview, tentative, immersion, and emergence. Participants typically experience emotional distress during the phase of immersion, the point at which "the telling might become distressful to the participant, the story provoking feelings of deep loss and grief, anger, or despair. An interviewee might cry or become too overwhelmed to go on" (p. 343). Indeed, many researchers have noted that becoming emotionally distressed is a characteristic feature of the unstructured interview

(Boothroyd, 2000; Boothroyd & Best, 2003; Carter et al., 2008; Cook & Bosley, 1995; deMarrais & Tisdale, 2002; Dyregrov, 2004; Dyregrov, Dyregro, & Raundalen, 2000; Lowes & Gill, 2006; Rager, 2005). Participants emerge from this phase and enter the emergence phase, which is characterized by less emotional intensity. They are not distressed throughout the entirety of the interview, nor do they leave the interview in a distressed state; often they leave feeling elated and relieved (Corbin & Morse, 2003). Furthermore, participants do not experience emotional distress during other kinds of qualitative interviews, in particular, focus groups or semi-structured interviews, because in these forms the researcher has control of the interview agenda, and this prevents the person from entering a level of intimacy that enables the expression of distress.

Unstructured Interviews Evoke Emotional Distress

Many have attributed participant distress to the unique characteristics of the unstructured interview itself: its structure, length, depth, intimacy, privacy, the degree of trust and rapport established with the participant, the sensitive topic being investigated, and the open-ended nature of its inquiry. All of these may create an emotional space wherein participants relive the experience they are narrating. Many of these features are deliberately established by the researcher to produce rich data (e.g., the establishment of trust) despite knowing that such conditions are likely to evoke distress—this is the researcher's "culpability" (deMarrais & Tisdale, 2002) in a "Machiavellian" aim (Homan, 1992). Without a doubt, unstructured interviews establish conditions that are emotionally evocative. Yet, the question remains: Do unstructured interviews cause emotional distress?

Do Unstructured Interviews Cause Emotional Distress?

The problem with the question of whether interviews cause emotional distress is that implicit in it is the dichotomization, or severance, of emotion from research. Although unstructured interviews may provide contexts for emotional distress to occur, this does not mean that they cause emotional distress. Unstructured interviews invite people to tell stories of events from which they have suffered and are suffering. When participants are invited to tell these stories, they are aware that telling their story will be emotionally distressing, yet, despite this, they accept these invitations. As one participant expressed it, "I was concerned about sharing such an emotional topic experience with a stranger—but in my heart knew that it was the right thing to do" (Cook & Bosley, 1995, p. 166). Emotional distress is not a by-product of interview research, nor even an adverse side-effect or sequela of it. Rather, it is a part of the phenomenon.

Emotion Is Integral to Unstructured Interviews

Qualitative research is intimacy work, and affect, emotion, and the senses are critical components. Indeed, some have asserted that emotion is the essence of qualitative research (Gilbert, 2001). Emotion, including distress, must therefore be ontologically and ethically understood within the context of the data collection; that is, the unstructured interview itself. Recently, Carter et al. (2008) identified three dimensions of her participants' experience of participation in her interview research: purposive/relational, epistemological/ontological, and emotional. Using these dimensions, we will explicate how the original event and emotion are integral to unstructured interview research.

Interviews Are Purposive

The first domain of participants' perspectives of participating in qualitative research was purposive and relational: "Participating made sense if by participating one helped people with whom one had a relationship" (Carter et al., 2008, p. 1273). Many participants report altruistic motives to explain their rationale in participating in interviews. Perhaps most poignantly, persons who were dying stated, "Not everyone gets the chance to know when they are dying, so I say yes let me help" and "It would be a way to give something back now before I die, I would have done something good for the future" (Terry et al., 2006, p. 408). Conversely, participants refuse to contribute to research whose substance or funding is aversive to them (Graham, Lewis, & Nicolaas, 2006).

There are many examples of participants hoping to help the researcher by participating in the study. Carter et al. (2008) quotes "Colin" (one of her participants), as saying, "I hope it helped you a great deal" (p. 1268). However, participants also intended to help others they did not know personally but with whom they shared similar circumstances or belonged to the same community as themselves. For instance, injection drug users wanted to help the drug user community and improve drug-related policies and practices (Barratt, Norman, & Fry, 2007); parents of children with diabetes hoped their participation would "help future parents cope with it" (Lowes & Gill, 2006, p. 590); mothers who returned to the labor market after maternity leave associated the research project with the need to improve the situation for employed mothers and their children (Brannen, 1993); and Bosnian refugees living in Norway "felt a very strong solidarity with all refugees around the world and felt responsible for helping others" (Dyregrov, Dyregro, & Raundalen, 2000, p. 418). Other participants intended to raise public awareness or educate those who were outside of their own community or circumstances to "provide real or true information about drug use" (Barratt, Norman, & Fry, 2007, p. 236) or to tell what it was like to be a woman living with HIV/AIDS (Lather & Smithies, 1997). Dying persons wanted to share their intimate knowledge of pain: "I do feel I'm a bit of an expert in pain, in a way that someone who is not dying might not be" (Terry et al., 2006, p. 408).

In sum, participants are motivated to participate in interview research because they care about others they feel akin to and want to assist or do good for them. Because altruism emerged as a theme particularly in those interviews that addressed a difficult or traumatic situation, Graham, Lewis, and Nicolaas (2006) noted that emotional distress seemed to inspire altruism.

Purposiveness and relationality capture dimensions of research that likewise engage the emotional life of the researcher. Behar (1996), for example, states that it is only worthwhile doing research that "breaks your heart" (p. 161). Emotion provides the impetus to embark on a research topic, but it drives it as well from participant recruitment to conducting the interviews, to transcription, analysis, publication, and living with the results (DeMarrais & Tisdale, 2002; Ellis, 1995; Lather & Smithies, 1997; Rager, 2005).

Interviews Are Relational

Similar to a health care encounter, the interview brings into focus a particular kind of relation that connects strangers together in meaningful and even intimate ways (Bergum & Dossetor, 2005). Carter (in Carter et al., 2008) noted that the relationship, built over time between interviewer and interviewee, clearly had emotional content and importance. Indeed, this emotional connection is an essential component of qualitative interview research. The literature provides some evidence of the importance of this relationship to interview participants: Participants stated that they wanted to be recruited by people they already knew, or they wanted the researcher to be someone with whom they already had an established clinical relationship, and, if there were to be repeat interviews in a study, the majority of participants preferred to have the same researcher conduct all interviews (Terry et al., 2006). For example, in Brannen's (1993) study, 56% of participants would have liked to have been interviewed each time by the same researcher; repeated encounters with the same researcher made the experience more personal, helped them relax, or made it easier to talk. Participants did not want to have to reveal themselves or their circumstances to someone new, so that the research would, in effect, be a product of an already established understanding or rapport.

The basis of this emotional connection is mutual respect. The etymology of the word "interview" is to see the other. Maykut and Morehouse (1994) call on the researcher to understand the participant's point of view; other researchers confirm that qualitative inquiry is not a purely intellectual exercise but rather one for which researchers enter the world of their participants and, at least for a time, see life through their eyes" (Rager, 2005, p. 24). Gilbert (2001) advises researchers to connect with participants cognitively and emotionally.

The literature provides participants' testimonies of such "relational engagement" (Bergum & Dossetor, 2005, p. 103) during interviews. Researchers were informed, knowledgeable, open, interested, and understanding about the participants and their circumstances. In addition, participants appreciated researchers who were empathic, warm, caring, kind, gentle, human, sincere, and nonjudgmental (Cook & Bosley, 1995; Dyregrov, Dyregro, & Raundalen, 2000), who were "not embarrassed by emotion" (Cook & Bosley, 1995, p. 166), who "did not withdraw from our pain" (Dyregrov, 2004, p. 6), who were patient ("gave room for our sadness and crying"), and who inspired confidence and were skillful and professional ("posed the right questions") (Dyregrov, 2004, p. 6). Cook and Bosley write that the "empathic, open-ended style was very hopeful, including the researcher's ability to follow feelings and ideas which emerged through the interview process" (p. 166). Participants appreciate researchers who anticipate the potential for their emotional distress. Similarly, participants appreciated researchers who are flexible during the interview and offer further help and information (Dyregrov, 2004; Dyregrov, Dyregro, & Raundalen, 2000; Lowes & Gill, 2006; Scott et al., 2002; Terry et al., 2006).

Researchers reciprocally experienced care and respect from their informants. Lather recalls the ameliorating effect her informants had on the emotional distress she experienced during her research investigating women with HIV/AIDS: "Two bad cries in such a project testifies to the work the angels did for me, their cooling comfort that let me get on with the book" (Lather & Smithies, 1997, p. 222).

Mutual respect is vulnerable when values clash between the researcher and the participants. Researchers can feel negative emotions such as irritation, annoyance, anger, and confusion. *Discordant emotions*, however, "should be attended to seriously and respectfully rather than condemned, ignored, discounted or suppressed" (Jagger, 1996, p. 183).

Interviews Are Epistemological/Ontological

Through narrative we come into contact with our participants as people engaged in the process of interpreting themselves and seeking meaning in the events that are being suffered. The interviewer and the interviewee are connected, and intimacy is experienced through dialog and intense listening. The interview becomes a particular kind of social relationship wherein both interviewer and participants engage in the co-construction of meaning (Mishler, 1986).

Unstructured interviews are sites of active, reflexive, and reconstitutive practice. This reconstruction of one's extreme experiences and one's self is inescapably emotional (Carter et al., 2008). Hiller and DiLuzio (2004) suggested that people are more likely to take part in research on a topic in which they have some ego involvement, where participation allows for reflection and articulation of their personal experiences, and where they have thoughts or feelings that have few outlets or little legitimacy in current communities of interaction. Dyregrov, Dyregro, & Raundalen (2000) similarly reported that two respondents, before the interview, thought that participation might help them to rethink and analyze their situations. Palliative care patients interviewed by Terry and colleagues (2006) wrote that research participation actively maintained their self-image—"participating in research allowed patients to see themselves and to be seen by others as more than 'a dying person'" (p. 408); one participant in particular stated: "if I'm part of a research I am still real, and if you doctors are doing research I know you think of me as real, too" (p. 408). Other studies corroborate the importance of interest or involvement in the research topic as an important dimension of interview participation (Brannen, 1993; Dyregrov, Dyregro, & Raundalen, 2000). This dimension of research participation, in Carter et al.'s (2008) observation, was the richest and most compelling domain.

Researchers, too, experience the epistemological/ontological dimension of interviews. Lather and Smithies (1997) describe the emergence of Lather's "very personal need to negotiate a relationship to loss" during the course of her research project with women with HIV/AIDS (p. 221). Remarking on Lather's epistemological growth throughout the research project, Amber, one of Lather's informants remarked "You've grown so much and gotten a lot smarter than when I first met you at the AIDS retreat" (Lather & Smithies, 1997, p. vi). Finch (1984), as a result of conducting interviews with women, came to see her researcher-self as potentially dangerous to informants who put their trust in her and her motives.

Interviews Are Emotional

Interview research invites participants to tell life-stories, especially those that have deep and enduring meaning (Chase, 1995). It is theorized that this telling allows the respondent to relive the painful emotions associated with the original experience (Morse, 2002). Life-stories are told through the dialog of emotion as well as words, tears, silences, utterances, and facial expressions.

> We found that in most of our interviews the troubling emotions of anger, frustration, and anxiety were relived by the participants during the process of describing the anger incident. This reliving was expressed by participants in a variety of ways including direct references to "feeling or experiencing the anger again" as well as physical exhibitions in the form of flushed face and neck, shortness of breath, sweaty palms, and facial expressions indicating discomfort, frustration or anger. (deMarrais & Tisdale, 2002, p. 118)

Painful life circumstances are painfully recalled and retold. Life-stories are not, like reports, disconnected from life circumstances but remain embedded in them (Chase, 1995).

Researchers hear, see, feel, and bear witness to the life-stories participants tell. Rager (2005), during her interviews with women who had breast cancer, reports how emotionally drained she was after each interview and how she experienced physical ailments, including pain in her right breast. Similarly, a colleague, in reading her dissertation draft reported that she, too, was emotionally and similarly physically affected. Lather recalls: "Over the course of this project, I broke down badly twice … broken down, crying" (Lather & Smithies, 1997, p. 221). The researcher, also, is an embodied subjectivity: "I remember reaching out to touch Linda's hand as she spoke. I also remember the tears running down my own cheeks as I listened with both my head and my heart to what she was sharing" (Rager, 2005, p. 23).

This emotional distress is but part of an emotional repertoire that is evoked during unstructured interviews. However, according to Carter et al. (2008), although participants experienced interviews as emotional events, they did not regard this as the most significant aspect of their research participation.

Emotional Distress Is Integral to Participants' Experience of Participation in Interviews

Within the context of relational engagement during the interview, participants are invited to tell life-stories of their human suffering. Participants who accept this invitation also assume responsibility for the import of its meaning. Participants tell their story and communicate its import with their emotional voice. The telling of these experiences requires the participant to relive them—this includes the reexperiencing of the emotion originally felt. Emotional distress is integral to emotionally distressing circumstances; emotional distress is likewise integral to the telling of these circumstances in interviews that invite them. But more than this, emotional distress is integral to participants' responses to interview participation; it underpins and interconnects all the dimensions of participants' participation in interviews. Emotional distress motivates purposive participation, creates relational connections, facilitates self-knowledge of participants' and their experiences, and expresses its voice in the emotional space afforded by the interview. It is a gross simplification, therefore, to conceptualize emotional distress as a mere component, by-product, or adverse effect of unstructured interviews. Emotional distress is central to unstructured interview research. If the cardinal sign of worthwhile research is that "it breaks your heart" (Behar, 1996, p. 161), then emotional distress is the heart, the cardinal sign of worthwhile interview research.

Is Emotional Distress Harm?

A paradox is consistently identified in the emerging literature exploring participants' perspectives of their participation in interview research (Carter et al., 2008; Graham, Lewis, & Nicolaas, 2006). Emotional distress, described by participants as hard, painful, sad, nervous, angry, and upsetting (Boothroyd & Best, 2003; Cook & Bosley, 1995; Dyregrov, 2004; Dyregrov, Dyregro, & Raundalen, 2000; Scott, 2002), was not experienced as adverse or harmful. Furthermore, emotional distress coexisted with positive, beneficial experiences of interview participation. Most participants who experienced emotional distress as a response to their participation in interviews evaluate their interview experience as positive and beneficial (Bruzy, Ault, & Segal, 1997; Cook & Bosley, 1995; Corbin & Morse, 2003; Cowles, 1988; Dyregov, 2004; Dyregov, Dyregro, & Raundalen, 2000; Honeycutt, 1995; Kavanaugh & Ayers, 1998; Lee & Renzetti, 1990; Lowes & Gill, 2006; Wong, 1998). For example, participants in Dyregrov, Dyregro, and Raundalen's (2000) study stated: "It hurts to talk, but it also feels good and we need to talk" (p. 415). Other participants concur: "Through the interview I could go through all the details again. That felt good. At the same time, it was painful in many ways" (Dyregrov, 2004, p. 6). How can emotional distress not be considered harmful? Furthermore, how can it coexist with evaluations of interview experiences as positive and beneficial?

This paradox exists only within a conceptualization of emotions as distinctly positive or negative. Contemporary Western scholars have inherited valence and polarity as predominant notions of emotions (Solomon & Stone, 2002). Researchers have suggested a complex relationship between emotional distress and positive benefits of participation (Hutchison, Wilson, & Wilson, 1994).

In the section that follows, we argue that valence and polarity conceptualizations of emotion are too simplistic to account for the complexity of emotion. Emotional distress is not a simple negatively valenced emotion. Emotional distress is a "mixed feeling," not only in the sense of one emotion coupled with another. Within the constellation of emotions that constitute "distress" there are poly-valences. Pain and pleasure are too complex, multidimensional, contextually determined, and "qualitative" than one-dimensional valences can allow (Solomon & Stone, 2002). Emotional distress, therefore, cannot simply be understood in terms of negative emotion or indeed as harm. Ethical approaches that require seeing emotion in these ways are inadequate to make ethical decisions about emotional distress in interview research.

Emotional Valence and Polarity

"The distinction between 'positive' and 'negative' emotions is as ancient as talk about emotions, and it was, under the rubric of virtue and vice, the hallmark of medieval theories of emotion" (Solomon & Stone, 2002, p. 417). Today, the distinction is evident in everyday speech as well as in such sophisticated discussions as professional social science and nursing research publications and ethics review of scientific research. It enters into these discussions through the concept of valence.

> From a global perspective, it seems that past research on emotion converges on only two generalizations. One is that emotion consists of arousal and appraisal. The other, emerging from the scaling literature, is that any dimensional characterization of emotions is likely to include at least the two dimensions of activation and valence. ... (But) the valence dimension (is) the dimension of appraisal. (Ortony, Clore, & Collins, 1988, p. 6)

Thus, valence refers to the appraisal of an emotion as positive or negative, possessing a net positive or net negative charge. Although this positive-negative polarity has its origins in Aristotelian ethics and not in the scientific study of emotion, it has taken on the vernacular of chemistry to serve its purposes—which may include an attempt to scientifically enhance the concept (Solomon & Stone, 2002). Related to the notion of valence is that of emotional polarity or opposites.

Emotions with positive valences are: good, pleasure, happy, conducive to happiness, positive attitude to self, healthy, etc. Negatively valenced emotions are: bad, pain, sad, "upset," conducive to unhappiness, negative attitude to self. Further, pleasure is the emotional opposite of pain. These conceptualizations of emotion, valence, and polarity are evident in discussions of participants' responses to research participation—that is, benefits are positive and harms are negative (Boothroyd & Best, 2003; Cook & Bosley, 1995; Dyregrov, 2004; Dyregrov, Dyregro, & Raundalen, 2000). Emotional distress, as described by participants as pain, sadness, anxiety, anger, and upset, is clearly regarded by IRBs to possess a "negative" valence and thus must be the polar opposite of positively valenced emotions such as those constituting benefit.

Back to the paradox: Clearly there is a problem with such conceptualizations of emotion and participants' actual experiences of them. Indeed, valence and polarity notions of emotion are too simplistic and superficial to account for the complexity of emotion. This is not to dispute "that there is no such thing as valence or no such polarity or contrasts, but rather that there are *many* such polarities and contrasts" (Solomon & Stone, 2002, p. 418).

Context and Consequences of Emotional Distress

The context and circumstances of the emotion are too often confused with the emotion itself. We have already argued that unstructured interviews typically invite participants to tell a life-story of human suffering, and participants become emotionally distressed in the telling of these stories. How can such a clear example of distress be ambiguous?

Suppose the circumstances of the narration involve the tragic diagnosis of a child with a terminal illness. The participant, the child's mother, is clearly grief-stricken. However, is grief, in this context, a negative emotion? Many theorists would argue that it is a negative emotion, a bad emotion, on the grounds that the circumstances provoking it tend to be threatening to one's well-being. But it does not follow that the circumstances that provoke grief might be bad for us, that the emotion of grief itself is bad for us. The emotion of grief might even be perceived as a good emotion, if it propels us toward healing or is cathartic. Aristotle (335BCE/1920), in his Poetics, used the example of fear in the same way—though the circumstances that incite it may be life threatening, the emotion itself enables one to escape such circumstances. Furthermore, Aristotle posited catharsis as an explanation as to why Greek citizens would willingly attend terrifying plays: because it was good for them. The same cathartic incentive may explain why people who experience adverse circumstances agree to be interviewed to talk about them. The circumstances that provoke emotions may be bad, but the emotion itself may not be. Emotional distress, therefore, cannot be conceptualized as "negative" simply in view of the bad circumstances that caused it.

Good and bad emotions can also refer to their various consequences—that they are good or bad for us. Consider the emotion "upset." Much social science, as well as clinical research, fosters the notion that negative emotions make us upset, whereas positive emotions do not (Solomon & Stone, 2002). But upset is also highly ambiguous. Does it refer to the *state* of being agitated or excited (in which case it may be incited by joy or irritation or anxiety)? Or, does upset refer to the *object of emotion*, which is upsetting? In the latter case, Solomon and Stone (2002) note that this upset is a matter of appraisal not arousal. This implies that the "evaluational baggage" of IRBs when considering participants' emotional upset reduces the complexity of emotional distress to one simplistic, superficial feature (Solomon & Stone, 2002, p. 421).

Distinguishing positive-negative emotions by their consequences does not consider subjective relativism. Emotions that make a "person well or happy or ill and unhappy is a very individual matter depending on context and upbringing and history and culture and religion and all sorts of things" (Solomon & Stone, 2002, p. 422). Terry et al. (2006) investigating hospice patients' views on research in palliative care, starkly contrasted how palliative patients regarded harm and benefit of research participation with the views of ethicists. Some ethicists asserted that terminally ill patients with less than six months to live should be disqualified from human subjects research because they are too desperate to be able to distinguish research from treatment (Annas, 1996). In essence, such ethicists believe that terminally ill persons are vulnerable to false hope, that is, the prolongation of life. Terry et al.'s (2006) surprising finding was that "our patients regarded the possibility of an unexpected prolongation of life as an adverse event rather than as a benefit" (p. 412). Thus, the experience of emotional distress is relative to the person experiencing it. Does emotional distress constitute harm? It depends on whom you ask.

Is Emotional Distress Intrinsically "Painful"?

Can emotional distress be conceptualized in terms other than circumstances and consequences? Can emotional distress be intrinsically negative? If emotional distress is *intrinsically* negative, where is this negativity located? Early philosophers, in particular, Spinoza and Hume, located goodness or badness of emotion in the intrinsic sensations (or "impressions") of pleasure and pain. Thus, Frijda (1986) insists that there are just two experiential emotional qualia, pleasure and pain. Others similarly take the pleasure-pain polarity as primary in theorizing basic emotions (Solomon & Stone, 2002).

Solomon and Stone (2002) discuss whether pleasure and pain are true polarities and in what sense can they be compared as well as contrasted:

> The technical notion of "valence" makes it quite clear that plea-sure and pain are quantifiable features of an emotion, very much along the lines of the old "happiness calculus" invented by Jeremy Bentham and the English Utilitarians. Pleasure is positive and pain is negative, both come in degrees or quantities and pleasures and pains can be juxtaposed and compared on a single measuring scale. (p. 423)

Certainly, utilitarianism is a central ethical perspective in IRB guidelines; IRBs regard emotional distress in such one-dimensional terms—their proportionate review of risk compares the pain of participant emotional distress with the pleasure of socially beneficial knowledge. Furthermore,

> Bentham ingeniously laid out a list of dimensions of pleasure and pain such as intensity, duration, certainty, proximity, fecundity, and purity, and insisted that the number of people whose interests are involved be included, but the result was a single value on a single scale with the most pleasure at the top end and pure pain at the bottom. (Solomon & Stone, 2002, p. 423)

Bentham's dimensions of pain are still utilized in IRB pro-portionate review of participants' emotional distress—How pain-ful was the emotional distress? Does it persist after the interview and for how long? How certain is it that participants will expe-rience this in unstructured interviews? Does the timing of the interview to the adverse event make a difference in participants' experience of distress? Thus, pleasure and pain are conceptualized in one-dimensional terms.

Consider the benefits, or *pleasures* of interview participation. Participants report experiencing interviews as beneficial (Carter et al., 2008; Graham, Lewis, & Nicolaas, 2006). The various benefits include: catharsis ("the expression of which provides a sense of relief"); self-acknowledgment ("validation as an individual with integrity and worth"); a sense of purpose ("feeling good about sharing information with researchers that may in turn by shared with other professionals or lay people through publication and presentations"); and facilitating ("movement and change") (Hutchison, Wilson, & Wilson 1994). These benefits, or *pleasures*, are qualitatively different and therefore cannot be quantitatively calculated.

Moreover, these pleasures are not simple positive valences. For example, the benefit (pleasure) of self-understanding is multi-valenced. Participants acknowledge that interviews were thought-provoking and catalyzed insight and self-realization, providing an altered perspective (Carter et al., 2008). The experience of being interviewed enabled participants (new mothers reentering the labor market) to reflect about their return to work after childbirth and reassess their roles as mothers, workers, and partners. As one woman said, it had made her realize which parent spent most time with the child, whereas another noted a number of changes. Reflection enabled participants to articulate issues of worry and concern for them (Brannen, 1993). Nevertheless, such realization is not entirely positive as the worries and concern were highlighted. Solomon and Stone (2002) argue that "pleasure and pain are often far more complex, multi-dimensional, contextually determined, and 'qualitative' than the Bethamite calculus would suggest" (p. 424).

Emotional pain or suffering is interpretive: "We compare pains and measure suffering not just by gauging how much they 'hurt,' but by bringing in all sorts of contextual considerations and cultural expectations" (Solomon & Stone, 2002, p. 425). A review of the literature exploring participants' perspectives of interviews (Graham, Lewis, & Nicolaas, 2006, pp. 9–10) noted: "Feelings of altruism can outweigh anxieties or anticipated pain involved in participation and lead people to participate in research even though they suspect it will be personally distressing." For example, Dyregrov, Dyregro, and Raundalen's (2000) study among refugees in Norway found most participants reported being "anxious, tense and curious" about the interviews before participating, but still rated the potential benefits for others as an important motivation. In Scott et al.'s (2002) study, 47% reported anticipating that research interviews would be painful. However, 94% said they felt eager to participate, and 98% that their participation would be beneficial to others. Thus, emotional pain is measured within the context of altruism.

Despite the dominant view that all positive and negative emotions are reduced to the polarity of pleasure and pain, Solomon and Stone (2002) cogently argue that pleasure and pain do not form a simple polarity and are in no singular sense "opposites." Nor does the rich texture of most emotions allow the assigning of a single "valence" on the basis of pleasures and pains. "It is an essential datum in the study of emotions, this phenomenon of 'mixed feelings,' but this does not just mean one emotion coupled with another. Within the emotions, there can be a number of different 'valences,' even in terms of pleasure and pain" (p. 425).

Participants' responses to interview participation bear out this argument. Emotional distress is hard, pain, sad, nervous, anxious, and angry. Yet none of these emotions are singularly painful valences. Nor are they in any singular sense opposite to pleasure. Indeed, the paradox of participants' responses to interview participation is that emotional distress coexists with benefits. Emotional distress is a richly textured, poly-valent emotion that defies simplistic assignments of negativity and harm.

Are Unstructured Interviews Unethical?

IRBs are concerned about the emotional distress that participants typically experience in unstructured qualitative interviews. This concern for the human protection of participants has caused IRBs to refuse approval for sensitive research (Ceci, Douglas, & Plotkin, 1985). Clearly, in these cases, IRBs regarded emotional distress as harmful and proportionately greater than the benefits to the participants and to society through the knowledge that may have been produced from such research. However, how was this proportionate review of the risk of harm portended by emotional distress conducted?

Utilitarianism is a dominant ethical perspective in ethics guidelines; it underpins the proportionate review of risk. Utilitarianism assesses the morality of actions or policies based on their effects or consequences (Beauchamp & Childress, 2001). IRBs employ utilitarianism to review the risk of harm posed to participants by emotional distress in unstructured interviews. All of the potential good (benefits) outcomes to all concerned are compared with all of the bad (harms) that could ensue to all concerned, in particular, the participants. The morally required or "ethical" action or policy is that which produces the best outcomes. Some utilitarians use the standards of happiness and unhappiness to assess whether consequences are good or bad; others judge consequences in terms of whether they produce pleasure or pain. In any case, utilitarianism works with such standards conceptualized as one-dimensional constructs that can be plotted on a risk-benefit valence scale. Such ethical reasoning that includes the conceptualization of emotional distress as one-dimensional may conclude that unstructured interviews are unethical if they evoke emotional distress. However, as our earlier argument has shown that emotional distress is complex, multidimensional, contextually determined, and qualitative, a utilitarian calculus is too crude to be used for such ethical decisions regarding it. Flawed moral reasoning can lead to unethical decisions.

Traditional ethical theories, perspectives, and principles are insufficient for making ethical decisions regarding emotional distress in interview contexts. These perspectives are too acontextual, objective, absolute, rational, and universal to inform the emotional context of the research interview. Rather, an ethical perspective that is inclusive of emotion and context is required. Emotion is integral to interview research, therefore emotions may, in themselves, be drawn on to ensure participant protection within moral interviews. Furthermore, as emotion is subjective, contextual, and interpretive, this "upheaval of thought" (Nussbaum, 2001, p. 1) must be included in moral reasoning about emotional distress in interview research. Indeed:

> If emotions are suffused with intelligence and discernment, and if they contain in themselves an awareness of value or importance, they cannot, for example, easily be sidelined in accounts of ethical

judgment, as so often they have been in the history of philosophy. Instead of viewing morality as a system of principles to be grasped by the detached intellect, and emotions as motivations that either support or subvert our choice to act according to principle, we will have to consider emotions as part and parcel of the system of ethical reasoning. We cannot plausibly omit them. ...We will have to grapple with the messy material of grief and love, anger and fear and the role these tumultuous experiences play in thought about the good and the just. (pp. 1–2)

Emotion is a crucial component to moral reasoning about participants' distress in unstructured interviews as well as the moral conduct of the interviews themselves.

Despite the painful aspects of the interview, participants appraise the emotional experience of interview participation positively. This is because in large part, we suspect, interviews were emotionally informed. This perspective, *the ethics of emotion,* may both augment IRBs moral reasoning regarding such ethical issues as participants' distress as well as assuage IRBs compassionate concern for the vulnerability of participants in sensitive research.

Toward an Ethics of Emotion

Emotion enhances the moral performance of the interview. Emotions enable the researcher to perceive, judge, and act with moral attitude (Vetlesen, 1994). Acting morally presupposes moral sensitivity—that is, that the morally relevant features of a situation are properly recognized. "In short, moral excellence is based on *perceiving* the salient features of the situation so that moral *judgments* can be sufficiently reliable and so that the *action* itself can display proper respect for the person's dignity" (Nortvedt, 2001, p. 448). Thus, moral sensitivity is the basis for moral judgment and action—how we care for the other. Emotions are an essential component of moral sensitivity and must augment the role of the intellect in moral sensitivity and judgment. The cognitive, affective, and moral dimensions of emotion enable the researcher to comprehend the situation of the participant, to emotionally engage with their emotional distress, and to be morally responsive to the participant, thereby ensuring his or her protection.

Emotions uniquely capture the human import of a situation, which is the true personal significance of human experience (Taylor, 1985). Emotion contributes to moral sensitivity by facilitating the understanding of the significance of an experience to an individual and because it motivates genuine personal human involvement in another's situation. The external manifestations of the participants' emotional distress signify and communicate the importance of the experience to them. Their emotional distress engages the altruistic emotions of the researcher, their compassion, empathy, and concern (Blum, 1980). It is the researcher's emotional engagement that enables him or her to appreciate the other's situation and the degree of significance the pain has to the person who experienced it. Compassion reflects the ordeal and painfulness of human suffering (Norvedt, 2001). This moral understanding could not be achieved without the researcher's emotional engagement with the participant. Analogously, the critical importance of emotional engagement with patients in distress in the clinical setting was previously established by Morse et al. (1992). Recently, moral philosophy has conceptualized ethics in terms of reasoning and justification of actions, thereby missing an important aspect of morality (Blum 1994; Vetlesen, 1994). Although knowledge, thinking, reflection, and cognitive imagination are important, they are not sufficient. To reason about difficult moral cases, and to perceive what is morally at stake in situations of caring for others, emotion is needed to engage one personally (Norvedt, 2001, p. 450).

Human beings are able to respond emotionally to another person's distress because we are relationally and emotionally attached to them. Empathy is defined as an affective response to the human condition of others and a cognitive way of understanding other people's experiences (Hoffman, 2000). Empathy as an affective dimension of emotional sensitivity is sensory, impulse based, and immediate. "This impulse is what works when we feel the hurt of someone else as an aching in our own body" (Norvedt, 2001, p. 456). Researchers of empathy often describe this affective moral impulse as an empathic distress response—the involuntary and forceful experiencing of another's emotion—the distress is often contingent not on our own but someone else's painful experience" (Hoffman, 2000).

Our capacity to be moved by the emotional distress of another is critical to moral agency. "Emotions anchor us to the ethically relevant aspects of a situation so that our rational judgments can be fully informed" (Norvedt, 2001, p. 456). Sometimes, researchers' emotional responses indicate an ethical dilemma (deMarrais & Tisdale, 2000). de Marrais and Tisdale state: "Emotions shown within the interview itself can be a signal to researchers to examine their practices as researchers and attend to the human needs of participants" (p. 120). Empathically informed judgment is exemplified in the decision by Carter et al. (2008) to allow a participant the freedom to continue with the interviews despite the acuity of his suffering heightened by the death of his wife that was so intense it upset the research team: "We *felt* it was important to respect Henry by allowing him to make his own decisions about continuing participation, while repeatedly emphasizing non-obligation and the ability to discontinue at any time" (Carter et al. 2008, p. 1271). In a similar way, emotions facilitate participants' own self-protection. In a study investigating children's experiences of participating in interviews regarding their history of sexual abuse, a young female participant described how emotions helped her to discern danger in a given question. She said that when she felt like she was going to faint, she knew not to answer (Heltne, 2007).

Emotion has an important role in moral action and motivation. "Emotional motivation is significant both because it makes us care for a person's well being and also because emotion helps us care with the proper attitude" (Norvedt, 2001, p. 461). Aristotle (350BCE/1985), in Nichomachean Ethics stated that having virtue is virtue of character. A morally virtuous person acts for the right reason and with the right emotion. The virtuous researcher is well motivated to commit to caring behavior toward the participant. The researcher's emotional attitude shapes the tone, atmosphere, and attitude of interviews, creating the necessary respect and attentiveness that allow the participants' needs to be addressed. Indeed, when asked what researchers had done or said that was most helpful during the interview, the participants indicated: "empathy, warmth, kindness, humanity, knowledge, understanding, and a nonjudgmental and interested attitude" (Dyregrov, Dyregro, & Raundalen, 2000, p. 418).

Coda: Do Participants in Unstructured Interviews Need Protection?

All people who volunteer to participate in scientific research require protection from harm, including participants in interview-based research. Qualitative researchers have been criticized for wielding a moral superiority. Although they assert that the harms participants risk by participation in interview research are no greater than those in everyday life (and are of lesser risk than clinical research), risks to participants exist. For example, betrayal, exploitation, or lack of reciprocity can ensue from the lack of moral respect for research participants (Ellis, 1995).

Ethical oversight of interview research must encompass a wide terrain of ethical perspectives, principles such as informed consent (autonomy) and nonmaleficence remain critical; traditional theories such as deontology also have a role, but these must be augmented by the ethics of emotion. The protection of participants who participate in unstructured interviews is optimized when they and their stories are attended to both cognitively and emotionally—with minds and hearts.

The development of an adequate ethical theory hinges on the development of an adequate theory of emotions including "their sometimes unpredictable and disorderly operation in the daily life of human beings" (Nussbaum, 2001, p. 2). Nussbaum advises turning toward such texts as literature and music to be able to imagine such emotional upheavals of thought in our own lives, to "understand ourselves well enough to talk good sense in ethics" (Nussbaum, 2001, p. 2). Yet the stories of human suffering told in unstructured interviews in qualitative inquiry provide other such texts to inform the role "tumultuous experiences play in thought about the good and the just" (Nussbaum, 2001, p. 2). Moreover, the people who share their stories are also instructive—they remind us that stories have an essential role in a just, human society.

Acknowledgment

The authors thank Dr. Katherine Moore and Dr. Jean Clandinin for their comments on an earlier version of this chapter. This chapter was completed as a part of Michele McIntosh's requirements for a Ph.D. degree at the University of Alberta and was assisted by a CHIR, EQUIPP Pre-Doctoral Fellowship.

References

Annas G. (1996). Old and emerging bioethical issues in research on atoms and genes. Available online at URL:http://subjects.energy.gov/doe-resources/newsletter/winter96-newsltr.pdf

Aristotle. (335BCE/1920). *Aristotle on the art of poetry*. Translator: Ingram Bywater. Oxford, U.K.: Oxford at the Clarendon Press.

Aristotle. (350BCE/1985). *Nicomachean ethics*. Translator: T. Erwin. Indianpolis: Hackett.

Barratt, M. J., Norman, J. S., & Fry, C. L. (2007). Positive and negative aspects of participation in illicit drug research: Implications for recruitment and ethical conduct. *International Journal of Drug Policy*, 18, 235–238.

Beauchamp, T. L. & Childress, J. F. (2001). *Principles of biomedical ethics*, 5th ed. New York: Oxford University Press.

Behar, R. (1996). *The vulnerable observer: Anthropology that breaks your heart*. Boston: Beacon Press.

Bergum, V. & Dossetor, J. (2005). *Relational ethics: The full meaning of respect*. Hagerstown, MD: University Publishing Group.

Blum, L. A. (1980). *Friendship, altruism and morality*. Cambridge: Cambridge University Press.

Blum, L. A. (1994). *Moral perception and particularity*. Cambridge: Cambridge University Press.

Boothroyd, R. A. (2000). The impact of research participation on adults with severe mental illness. *Mental Health Services Research*, 2(4), 213–221.

Boothroyd, R. A. & Best, K. (2003). Emotional reactions to research participation and the relationship to understanding informed consent disclosure. *Social Work Research*, 27(4), 242–251.

Brannen, J. (1993). The effects of research on participants: Findings from a study of mothers and employment. *Sociological Review*, 41(2), 328–346.

Bruzy, S., Ault, A., & Segal, E. A. (1997). Conducting qualitative interviews with women survivors of trauma. *AFFILIA*, 12, 76–83.

Carter, S. M., Jordens, C. F. C., McGrath, C., & Little, M. (2008). Have to make something of all that rubbish, do you? An empiricial investigation of the social process of qualitative research. *Qualitative Health Research*, 18, 1264–1276.

Ceci, S., Douglas, P., & Plotkin, J. (1985). Human subjects review, personal values and the regulation of social science research. *American Psychologist*, 40(9), 994–1002.

Chase, S. E. (1995). Taking narrative seriously. Consequences for method and theory in interview studies. In R. Josselson & A. Lieblich (Eds.), *Interpreting experience. The narrative study of lives*, vol. 3, pp. 1–27, Thousand Oaks, CA: Sage.

Cook, A. S. & Bosley, G. (1995). The experience of participating in bereavement research: Stressful or therapeutic? *Death Studies*, 19, 157–170.

Corbin, J. & Morse, J. M. (2003). The unstructured interactive interview: Issues of reciprocity and risks when dealing with sensitive topics. *Qualitative Inquiry*, 9(3), 335.

Cowles, K. V. (1988). Issues in qualitative research on sensitive topics. *Western Journal of Nursing Research*, 10, 1163–1179.

deMarrais, K. & Tisdale, K. (2002). What happens when researchers inquire into difficult emotions?: Reflections on studying women's anger through qualitative interviews. *Educational Psychologist*, 37(2), 115–123.

Dyregrov, K. (2004). Bereaved parents' experience of research participation. *Social Science and Medicine*, 58, 391–400.

Dyregrov, K, Dyregro, A., & Raundalen, M. (2000). Refugee families' experience of research participation. *Journal of Traumatic Stress*, 131(3), 413–426.

Ellis, C. (1995). Emotional and ethical quagmires in returning to the field. *Journal of Contemporary Ethnography*, 24(1), 68–98.

Finch, J. (1984). "It's great to have someone to talk to": The ethics and politics of interviewing women. In C. Bell & H. Roberts (Eds.), *Social researching: Politics, problems, practice*, 1044–124. London: Routledge.

Frijda, H. H. (1986). *The emotions*. New-York: Cambridge University Press.

Gilbert, K. (2001). Introduction. Why are we interested in emotions? In K. R. Gilbert (Ed.), *The emotional nature of qualitative research*, pp. 3–15. Boca Raton, FL: CRC Press.

Graham J., Lewis, J., & Nicolaas, G. (2006). *Ethical relations: A review of literature on empirical studies of ethical requirements and research participation*. ESRC Research Methods Programme Working Paper No 30. Manchester, UK: National Centre for Social Research (NatCen).

Heltne, U. M. (2007). Qualitative interviews as a method in research with children exposed to family violence: Methodological and ethical dilemmas. Paper presented at the 8th International Interdisciplinary Conference Advances in Qualitative Methods, Banff, Alberta, Canada, September 21–24.

Hiller H. & DiLuzio, L. (2004). The interviewee and the research interview: Analyzing a neglected dimension in research. *Canadian Review of Sociology and Anthropology*, 41(1), 1–26.

Hoffman, M. L. (2000). *Empathy and moral development—Implications for caring and justice.* Cambridge: Cambridge University Press.

Homan, R. (1992). The ethics of open methods. *British Journal of Sociology*, 43(3), 321–332.

Honeycutt, J. M. (1995). The oral history interview and reports of imagined interactions. *Journal of Family Psychotherapy*, 694, 63–69.

Hutchison, H. A., Wilson, M. E., & Wilson, H. S. (1994). Benefits of participating in research interviews. *Image Journal of Nursing Scholarship*, 26, 161–164.

Jagger, A. M. (1996). Love and knowledge: Emotion in feminist epistemology. In A. Garry & M. Pearsall (Eds.), *Women, knowledge, and reality: Explorations in feminist philosophy*, 2nd ed., pp. 166–190. New York: Routledge.

Kavanaugh, K. & Ayres, L. (1998). "Not as bad as it could have been": Assessing and mitigating harm during research on sensitive topics. *Research in Nursing and Health*, 21, 91–97.

Kopelman, L. M. (2004). Minimal risk as an international ethical standard in research. *Journal of Medicine and Philosophy*, 29(3), 351–338.

Lather, P. A. & Smithies, C. (1997). *Troubling the angels: Women living with HIV/AIDS.* Boulder, CO: Westview.

Lee, R. M. & Renzetti, C. R. (1990). The problems of researching sensitive topics. *American Behavioral Scientist*, 33, 510–528.

Lincoln, Y. S. & Tierney, W. G. (2004). Qualitative research and institutional review boards. *Qualitative Inquiry*, 10, 219–234.

Lowes, L. & Gill, P. (2006). Participants' experiences of being interviewed about an emotive topic. *Methodological Issues in Nursing Research*, 55(5), 587–594.

Maykut, P., & Morehouse, R. (1994). The qualitative posture: Indwelling. In P. Maykut & R. Morehouse (Eds.), *Beginning Qualitative research: A philosophic and practical guide*, pp. 23–37. London: Falmer Press.

Mishler, E. (1986). *Research interviewing: Context and narrative.* Cambridge, MA: Harvard University Press.

Morse, J. M. (2002). Emotional re-enactment. (Editorial). *Qualitative Health Research*, 12(2), 147.

Morse, J. M., Bottorff, J., Anderson, G., O'Brien, B., & Solberg, S. (1992). Beyond empathy: Expanding expressions of caring. *Journal of Advanced Nursing*, 17, 809–821.

Nortvedt, P. (2001). Emotions and ethics. In J. L. Storch, P. Rodney, & R. Starzomski (Eds.), *Toward a moral horizon: Nursing ethics for leadership and practice*, pp. 447–463. Toronto, Canada: Prentice Hall.

Nussbaum, M. C. (2001). *Upheavals of thought. The intelligence of emotions.* Cambridge: Cambridge University Press.

Ortony, A., Clore, G. L., & Collins, A. (1988). *The cognitive structure of emotions.* New York: Cambridge University Press.

Rager, K. B. (2005). Self-care and the qualitative researcher: When collecting data can break your heart *Educational Researcher*, 35(1), 23–27.

Ramos, M. C. (1989). Some ethical implications of qualitative research. *Research in Nursing and Health*, 12, 57–63.

Scott, D. A., Valery, P. C., Boyle, F. M., & Bain, C. (2002). Does research into sensitive areas do harm? Experiences of research participation after a child's diagnosis with Ewing's sarcoma. *Medical Journal of Australia*, 177, 507–510.

Solomon, R. C. & Stone, L. D. (2002). On "positive" and "negative" emotions. *Journal for the Theory of Social Behaviour*, 32(4), 417–435.

Spradley, J. P. (1979). *The ethnographic interview.* New York: Holt, Rinehart & Winston.

Taylor, C. (1985). *Philosophical papers*, vol. 2. Cambridge: Cambridge University Press.

Terry W., L. G. Olson, P. Ravenscroft, L. Wilss, & G. Boulton-Lewis. (2006). Hospice patients' views on research in palliative care. *Internal Medicine*, 36, 406–413.

Vetlesen, A. J. (1994). *Perception, empathy, and judgment: An inquiry into the preconditions of moral performance.* University Park: The Pennsylvania State University Press.

Wong, I. M. (1998). The ethics of rapport: Institutional safeguards, resistance and betrayal. *Qualitative Inquiry*, 4, 1.

Chapter 4

Evidence
A Critical Realist Perspective for Qualitative Research

Joseph A. Maxwell
George Mason University

The topic of evidence is so central for research and scholarship that it is extraordinary how little direct attention it has received.

— Chandler, Davidson, & Harootunian, 1994, p. 1

The concept of evidence, largely neglected by researchers in the social sciences for many years, has recently become a hotly contested one, largely because of the rise of movements for "evidence-based" practice and policy (Denzin & Giardina, 2008; Pawson, 2006).[1] Much of the critique of the evidence-based movement by qualitative researchers has been based on a social constructivist or postmodern epistemology that challenges the basic concept of "evidence." This has also been true of the larger debate over evidence in the social sciences, and has "threatened to reduce the role of evidence, facts, and proof to the point of nonexistence" (Chandler, Davidson, & Harootunian, 1994, p. 5).

However, there have also been significant challenges to this movement, and to the push for "science-based" research in general, from a realist perspective (Hammersley, 1992b; Maxwell, 2004a; Pawson, 2006). In this chapter, I argue that critical realism[2] can make important contributions to the critique of evidence-based research, contributions that are particularly relevant to, and supportive of, qualitative research. However, although I think that critical realism is a significant and valuable voice in that critique, I'm not arguing that critical realism is the single, correct philosophical stance for qualitative research. In fact, I'm skeptical that there is such a thing as a "correct" philosophical stance for qualitative research.

My thinking about this approach has been influenced by the work of the sociologist Andrew Abbott (2001, 2004), who has argued for what he calls a "fractal" view of the grand debates over epistemological and methodological issues in the social sciences. (The basic idea of a fractal is self-similarity at different scales or levels.) His view is that if we take any of a large number of debates between polar positions, such as positivism versus interpretivism, analysis versus narrative, realism versus constructivism, and so on, these issues can play out at many different levels, even within communities of scholars that have adopted one or the other of these positions at a broader level. Thus, within the community of sociologists of science, which is generally seen as constructivist in orientation, there are internal debates that play out in terms of realist or constructivist "moves" by particular scholars within that community.

Abbott claims that philosophical paradigms, rather than constituting grand overarching frameworks that inform and control the theories and practices of particular disciplines and subfields, instead function as heuristics, conceptual tools that can be applied in an endless number of specific situations to break out of theoretical blocks and generate new questions and theories. He even suggests that this is the way these grand paradigmatic positions originated: as useful heuristics that later became abstracted and formalized into high-level philosophical systems.

One of the many examples that Abbott provides is Daniel Chambliss's (1989) ethnographic study of competitive swimming. Chambliss argued that there is no such thing as "talent" as an explanation of high performance; it is a social construction that romanticizes and mystifies what he called "the mundanity of excellence." This is a constructivist move in the debate over sports performance. He supported this claim with detailed evidence from observations of, and interviews with, swimmers, showing that high performance is simply the result of dozens of small skills, learned or stumbled on, that are repeatedly practiced and synthesized into a coherent whole. However, an essential part of this argument was a realist move, identifying the actual skills and practices that led to excellence.

Abbott argues that the heuristic uses of such polar positions as realism and constructivism are not aimed at demolishing or debunking the opposition. Instead, their function is to open up the debate, to provoke discussion, and increase understanding, revealing new ways of making sense of the things we study. This perspective has a great deal in common with postmodernism, which rejects "totalizing metanarratives" and emphasizes diversity and irreconcilability (Bernstein, 1992).

From this perspective, philosophical positions look less like the traditional view of paradigms, and more like tools in a toolkit. "Logical consistency" is the wrong standard to apply to a toolkit. You don't care if the tools are all consistent with some axiomatic principle; you care if, among them, they enable you to do the job, to create something that can meet your needs or accomplish your goals. In the same way, consistency is the wrong standard to apply to an individual's or a community's ontological and epistemological views. These views, seen as heuristics, are resources for getting your work done.

The essential characteristic of critical realism (discussed below) is that it combines ontological realism with epistemological constructivism in a productive, if apparently inconsistent, "constellation" (Bernstein, 1992) of positions. Smith and Deemer (2000) argue that this combination is contradictory, and therefore a fatal flaw in critical realism. From Abbott's perspective, this is not a valid criticism, any more than arguing that an automobile having both a battery and a gasoline engine is contradictory. The question is not whether they are logically consistent, but whether they are compatible in their actual functioning. I argue (Maxwell, 2008) that ontological realism and epistemological constructivism are not only compatible, but, like the battery and gasoline engine in a hybrid car, are more effective than a consistent position.

Realism

Schwandt (2007, p. 256) defines realism in a broad sense as "the doctrine that there are real objects that exist independently of our knowledge of their existence," and argues that "most of us probably behave as garden-variety empirical realists—that is, we act as if the objects in the world (things, events, structures, people, meanings, etc.) exist as independent in some way from our experience with them." However, there are many varieties of realism, ranging from naive or direct realism—the view that we directly perceive things as they actually are—to more sophisticated positions that recognize that our concepts and theories necessarily mediate our perceptions of reality.

Many of the latter positions adopt an ontological realism, but an epistemological constructivism, asserting that there is not, even in principle, a "God's eye view" that is independent of any particular perspective or stance. I will refer to these positions as forms of "critical" realism. Lakoff states that such versions of realism assume "that 'the world is the way it is,' while acknowledging that there can be more than one scientifically correct way of understanding reality in terms of conceptual schemes with different objects and categories of objects" (1987, p. 265). Such positions can be seen as postmodern in the sense that they reject the idea that there must be a single correct account or interpretation of a complex reality.

I have argued elsewhere (Maxwell, 2004a, 2004c, 2008) that these positions are both compatible with, and can make a number of valuable contributions to, qualitative research. In particular, they reject the Humean, regularity concept of causation that has dominated both quantitative research and the evidence-based movement and adopt a process-oriented view of causality; they emphasize the importance of context and particular understanding, rather than focusing entirely on general conclusions and laws; and they accept the reality of mental phenomena and the necessity of incorporating these in our understanding and explanation of human action.

In what follows, I present how I see these positions contributing to our understanding of evidence and how they can provide a concept of evidence that is both useful for qualitative researchers and can defend qualitative research from the criticisms of advocates of a narrowly conceived evidence- or science-based approach to social research.

Evidence

Schwandt (2007, p. 98) defines evidence as "information that bears on determining the validity (truth, falsity, accuracy, etc.) of a claim or what an inquirer provides, in part, to warrant a claim." From a different perspective, Chandler, Davidson, and Harootunian, discussing Collingwood's view of evidence in history, likewise argue that "question and evidence are therefore 'correlative' in the sense that facts can only become evidence in response to some particular question" (1994, p. 1).

Schwandt's definition and Collingwood's argument point to the inextricable connections between evidence, claim, and validity. A key property of evidence is that it does not exist in abstraction but only in relation to some claim (theory, hypothesis, interpretation, etc.). There is no such thing as evidence in general; evidence is always evidence *relative to* some particular claim, account, or theory. Evidence is thus in the same position as validity—it can't be assessed in context-independent ways, but only in relation to the particular question and purpose to which it is applied.

In particular, evidence can't be evaluated solely in terms of the methods used to obtain it. Any attempt to establish a context-free hierarchy of kinds of evidence based entirely on the methods used to create that evidence, as proponents of evidence-based approaches typically do, is inevitably flawed. Although this emphasis on the context-dependence of evidence and conclusions is a key feature of critical realist approaches, it is shared by a much broader community of scholars. Phillips states what seems to be a widely held view in the philosophy of science: "In general it must be recognized that there are no procedures that will regularly (or always) yield either sound data or true conclusions" (1987, p. 21).

Shadish, Cook, and Campbell, in what is currently the definitive work on experimental and quasi-experimental research, are quite explicit on this point with respect to validity, and thus for evidence: "Validity is a property of inferences. It is not a property of designs or methods, for the same designs may contribute to more or less valid inferences under different circumstances. ... No method guarantees the validity of an inference" (2002, p. 34).

Brinberg and McGrath make the same point: "Validity is not

a commodity that can be purchased with techniques. ... Rather, validity is like integrity, character, and quality, to be assessed relative to purposes and circumstances" (1985, p. 13)

The philosopher Peter Achinstein, who has probably done the most to systematically critique and reformulate the traditional philosophical view of evidence (2001, 2005), makes the related point that evidence isn't a single thing, but several; there is no essential property that all uses of "evidence" possess (2001, p. 15). This position is strikingly similar to the philosopher Nancy Cartwright's concept of causal pluralism. Cartwright has provided a detailed argument for the view that what causes are and what they do depends on the particular situation in which they are employed. I would similarly argue for evidential pluralism. To borrow Cartwright's phrasing, what evidence is and what it does varies from case to case, and "there is no single interesting characterizing feature of [evidence]; hence no off-the-shelf or one-size-fits-all method for [identifying] it, no 'gold standard' for judging [evidence]" (Cartwright, 2007, p. 2).

In particular, there is a key difference between the uses of evidence in quantitative and qualitative research, or more specifically between what Mohr (1982) called "variance theory" and "process theory." Variance theory deals with variables and the relationship between them, and the main use of evidence is to show that a particular relationship exists between different variables, whether these are constructs measured using a test or survey, or manipulated in an experiment. Process theory, in contrast, is mainly concerned with events and processes, rather than variables, and the main use of evidence (and the primary strength of qualitative research) is to support claims about these events and processes—to get inside the "black box" of variance theory and to argue for what is actually happening in specific cases.

By "what is happening," I (and critical realists in general) include participants' meanings, intentions, beliefs, and perspectives, which are essential parts of these events and processes (Maxwell, 2004a). Evidence for claims about meanings and perspectives, which fall under the general category of "interpretive" claims, require quite different sorts of evidence than claims about behavior, let alone claims about the relationships between variables. Thus, the kinds of claims, and the nature and evaluation of the evidence for these claims, are very different in qualitative research than those in quantitative research, and evidential standards appropriate for quantitative and experimental research can't legitimately be applied to qualitative research.

Achinstein draws a number of other conclusions from this claim-dependence and context-dependence of evidence. First, whether some fact is evidence for a particular claim depends on how the fact is obtained or generated (Achinstein, 2001, p. 8). This does not conflict with the previous point that evidence can't be assessed strictly in terms of the methods used to obtain it. It simply asserts that how the evidence was obtained is often relevant to the support it lends to a particular claim, because the methods used may create certain validity threats that threaten the claim.

Second, the significance of evidence depends on the context of *other* evidence and hypotheses relevant to the claim being supported. A particular piece of data might by itself be evidence for a claim, but not when considered in combination with other evidence. In addition, the degree of support that a particular piece of evidence provides for a particular claim depends on the plausibility of (and evidence for) *alternative* claims regarding the phenomena in question (Achinstein, 2001, pp. 7–10). Achinstein provides several examples from different sciences in which a finding that was once believed to be convincing evidence for a particular claim was no longer thought to be so when new evidence was developed or alternative explanations were proposed. Thus, part of the context that evidence for a particular claim depends on for its assessment is the context of alternative possible theories and explanations for the phenomenon in question.

Achinstein addresses this issue by referring to what he calls the "epistemic situation" in which the use of particular data to support a claim is located (2001, pp. 20–21). This situation consists of what the researcher knew and believed at the time, and what this person was *not* in a position to know or believe. For Achinstein, any justification for saying that a claim is supported by a particular body of evidence is relative to this epistemic situation, rather than being a context-independent truth, and "since justification is relativized to an epistemic situation, so is the concept of evidence based on it."[3] Researchers often agree on the data relative to some claim, but disagree on whether these constitute evidence for the claim. Evidence is therefore an interpretation of the data or observations, and "evidence" is an essentially contested concept.

Third, the previous point entails that whether a fact or observation is evidence for some claim is an empirical question, not a logical one (Achinstein, 2001, p. 9). The evidence can only be assessed in the context of the particular claim that the evidence is asserted to support, the way the evidence was generated, and the epistemic situation in which these claims are made. This context is not given a priori but needs to be empirically discovered. Achinstein argues that one of the main reasons that actual researchers have paid so little attention to philosophical work on evidence is that this work usually presumes that the link between claim and evidence is strictly logical, semantic, or mathematical, something that can be established by calculation rather than empirical investigation.

Finally, Achinstein argues that for a fact to be evidence for some claim, simply because the fact increases the probability that the claim is true isn't enough; there must be some *explanatory connection* between the fact and the claim (2001, p. 145ff.). This is an essential component of realist approaches to explanation in general—that a valid explanation does not simply support the view *that* x causes y, but must address *how* it does so (Manicas, 2006; Salmon, 1998; Sayer, 1992, 2000). This lack of attention to the *process* by which a causal influence takes place is a major flaw in most evidence-based approaches (Maxwell, 2004a, 2008).

A recent study by Leibovici (2001) illustrates this point. Liebovici conducted a double blind, randomized clinical trial of the effectiveness of intercessory prayer on a number of outcomes for hospital patients. To avoid problems of patient consent, reactivity, and patient attrition, the author selected a sample of hospital records of 3,393 adult patients—every patient who had been diagnosed with a bloodstream infection between 1990 and 1996. These records were randomly divided into an intervention group and a control group, and a short prayer was said for the well-being and recovery of the intervention group as a whole. (This intervention took place four to ten years after the patient had left the hospital.)

Examination of the records showed that the patients in the intervention group had had a mean length of stay in the hospital and duration of fever shorter than those in the control group ($p < .01$ and $p < .04$, respectively). Mortality was also lower in the intervention group, but this difference was not statistically significant.

Even if there are doubts that the study was rigorously conducted, the main threat to the credibility of this study's results as evidence for the author's conclusion—that intercessory prayer was effective in reducing the morbidity and mortality of the patients— is that no plausible mechanism can be provided for the causal conclusion. The author addresses this problem head-on: "No mechanism known today can account for the effects of remote, retroactive intercessory prayer said for a group of patients with a bloodstream infection" (Leibovici, 2001, p. 1451). He argues that this case is similar to that of James Lind, who, in 1753, found that lemons and limes cured scurvy without having any knowledge of Vitamin C, let alone an understanding of the mechanism by which this can prevent and cure scurvy.

The difference between these two cases is that for limes and scurvy, even in 1753, the idea that something in limes could cure scurvy was not implausible and could serve as a plausible explanatory connection between the evidence and the claim. For retroactive intercessory prayer, an explanatory connection is difficult to imagine, except in an "epistemic situation" in which the power of God to do anything, even on the basis of a perfunctory prayer said for an entire category of people, is an accepted mechanism.

Achinstein does not directly address the evidence-based approaches that have made evidence a critically important issue for social researchers and evaluators, as opposed to philosophers. However, his reformulations of the concept of evidence challenge many of the premises of these approaches. Evidence is not a context-free entity that can unproblematically be aggregated to generate conclusions about "what works"; what counts as evidence varies from case to case and depends not only on the methods used, but the epistemic situation; and the use of evidence is dependent on the process by which the program or intervention is theorized to affect the outcome, not simply to whether it does so.

The methodologist and evaluation researcher Ray Pawson

(2006) has applied a realist perspective to the evidence-based policy movement, specifically to the central idea of "systematic review" promoted by this movement, particularly by the Cochrane Collaborative (in medicine) and the Campbell Collaborative (in program evaluation). The purpose of such reviews is to produce conclusions about what works based on the "best evidence" culled from available studies.

The failures of this approach that Pawson identifies and systematically criticizes, and the strengths of the realist alternative that he proposes, are too numerous to fully present here, and I will focus on only the most important and intrinsic of these for the use of evidence in research. In particular, I will not address the critique that the very idea that policy should be evidence-based or "research-based" is problematic (Hammersley, 2005; Pawson, 2006).

First, practitioners of the evidence-based approach largely ignore the *process* by which programs or interventions influence the outcomes of interest. Consistent with the Humean, regularity view of causation that they accept, the review focuses on finding evidence on *whether* the intervention influenced the outcome, not *how* it did so—what Shadish, Cook, and Campbell (2002, p. 9) call "causal description" rather than "causal explanation." Instead of trying to understand the mechanisms and processes by which a program has its effects, it attempts to identify causal generalizations, "main effects" across studies and situations.

Second, in seeking these causal generalizations, such reviews systematically neglect the importance of context in understanding why a program may or may not have particular outcomes. For realists, context is intrinsically involved with process in influencing outcomes, and evidence about the effect of the specific context is essential for assessing the likely results of a program or intervention. Causality is thus fundamentally particular rather than general, and an adequate understanding how causes operate requires evidence about the contextual influences operating in the specific case.

Pawson summarizes these two points as follows:

> The nature of causality in social programmes is such that any synthesis of evidence on whether they work will need to investigate

how they work. This requires unearthing information on mechanisms, contexts, and outcomes. The central quest is to understand the conditions of programme efficacy and this will involve the synthesis in investigating for whom, in what circumstances, and in what respects a family of programmes work. (2006, p. 25)

It is ironic that these are issues for which qualitative research can make a significant contribution (Maxwell, 2004a). However, the theory of causation on which the evidence-based movement relies, and the bias toward quantitative and experimental methods that this produces, has largely excluded qualitative evidence from the research syntheses that the movement generates.

In part because of this bias, qualitative researchers have long been either defensive about their use of evidence, or dismissive of the entire concept of evidence. I argue that there is no good reason for either of these reactions. A realist reformulation of the concept of evidence can provide a strong justification for the value of the evidence generated by qualitative research, and qualitative researchers have their own ways of obtaining and using such evidence that are just as legitimate for their purposes as quantitative researchers' are for theirs (Maxwell, 2004c).

Finally, I want to say something about the relationship between ethics and evidence. I would argue that evidence and ethics are separate issues, and that there is sometimes a tradeoff between them. It may be impossible, in any particular study, to maximize both of these. As Hammersley (1992a) has argued about critical theory, it is an illusion to believe that there must be a solution in which all "progressive" goals are compatible and can be optimally achieved.

An example of this tradeoff is Stanley Milgram's experimental studies[4] on obedience to authority (1974), in which he recruited participants to participate in a purported study of reinforcement and learning. This study was clearly unethical in that it subjected participants to potentially psychologically damaging experiences without informing them of the nature of the study or of these risks, but that doesn't discredit the evidence that his study produced to support the view that most people will readily inflict severe pain on others when told to do so by someone seen as an authority. Milgram, in fact, argues that some participants in the study claimed that their lives were transformed by the experience, leading them to be much more concerned about ethical ideals and the need to resist unjust authority.

In conclusion, I am arguing for a dialogical (Greene, 2007), postmodern approach to evidence in qualitative research, one that embraces contrary perspectives such as realism and constructivism and uses these to gain a better understanding of the phenomena we study. This approach can help us make better use of the concept of evidence and help us challenge misguided appropriations of this concept.

Notes

1. An additional work that directly and insightfully addresses many of the issues discussed in this paper, but which was published too recently to be included in the text of the chapter, is Donaldson, Christie, & Mark (2009).

2. The phrase "critical realism" was coined by Roy Bhaskar to refer to his influential version of realism as a philosophy of social science (Archer et al., 1998; Bhaskar, 1978, 1989). However, there are many other systematically developed positions that combine ontological realism with a more constructivist epistemology, by both philosophers (Haack, 2003; Manicas, 2006; Putnam, 1990, 1999) and social scientists (Lakoff, 1987; Lakoff & Johnson, 1999; Pawson, 2006; Pawson & Tilley, 1997; Sayer, 1992, 1999; Shweder, 1991), including qualitative researchers (Hammersley, 1992b; Huberman & Miles, 1985; Maxwell, 1992, 1999, 2004a, 2004b, 2004c, 2008). Although these positions differ on many specific points of philosophy and method, I will refer to all of them, broadly, as "critical realist."

3. Achinstein claims that the dependence of evidence on the epistemic situation still leaves this an objective rather than a subjective definition of "evidence" (2001, p. 21), because the epistemic situation is defined not entirely by what the person believes, but on what the person *is in a position* to know or believe, which can be objectively assessed. However, it is certainly a *context-dependent* definition of what counts as evidence, and includes the person's beliefs as part of that context. In addition, as noted above, Achinstein recognizes that evidence is not a single thing, but a variety of things, one of which he calls "subjective evidence," which *is* based on the subjective beliefs of some person at some time (2001, p. 23). I therefore see Achinstein's position as at least a major step away from objectivism toward a constructivist epistemology. Achinstein is clearly an ontological realist in treating hypotheses and theories as referring to a real world, rather than as simply useful constructions (2001, p. 145 ff., 263–265).

4.   Despite the title, these studies combined quantitative/experimental and qualitative methods. Milgram provided detailed case studies of how particular individuals responded to the experimental situation and interviewed participants following the experimental procedure to understand their perception of the situation and why they responded as they did (Maxwell & Loomis, 2003).

References

Abbott, A. (2001). *Chaos of disciplines*. Chicago: University of Chicago Press.

Abbott, A. (2004). *Methods of discovery: Heuristics for the social sciences*. New York: W. W. Norton.

Achinstein, P. (2001). *The book of evidence*. Oxford: Oxford University Press.

Achinstein, P. (Ed.). (2005). *Scientific evidence: Philosophical theories and applications*. Baltimore: Johns Hopkins University Press

Archer, M., Bhaskar, R., Collier, A. Lawson, T., & Norrie, A. (1998). *Critical realism: Essential readings*. London: Routledge.

Bernstein, R. (1992). *The new constellation: The ethical-political horizons of modernity-postmodernity*. Cambridge MA: MIT Press.

Bhaskar, R. (1978). *A realist theory of science*, 2nd ed. Brighton, UK: Harvester.

Bhaskar, R. (1989). *Reclaiming reality: A critical introduction to contemporary philosophy*. London: Verso.

Brinberg, D. & McGrath, J. E. (1985). *Validity and the research process*. Newbury Park, CA: Sage .

Cartwright, N. (2007). *Hunting causes and using them: Approaches in philosophy and economics*. Cambridge: Cambridge University Press.

Chambliss, D. (1989). The mundanity of excellence: An ethnographic report on stratification and Olympic swimmers. *Sociological Theory*, 7, 70–86.

Chandler, J., Davidson, A., & Harootunian, H. (1994). *Questions of evidence: Proof, practice, and persuasion across the disciplines*. Chicago: University of Chicago Press.

Denzin, N. K. & Giardina, M. D. (2008). *Qualitative inquiry and the politics of evidence*. Walnut Creek, CA: Left Coast Press.

Donaldson, S. I., Christie, C. A., & Mark, M. M. (2009). *What counts as credible evidence in applied research and evaluation practice?* Thousand Oaks, CA: Sage.

Greene, J. (2007. *Mixed methods in social inquiry*. New York: Wiley.

Haack, S. (2003). *Defending science—within reason*. Amherst, NY: Prometheus Press.

Hammersley, M. (1992a). Critical theory as a model for ethnography. In M. Hammersley (Ed.), *What's wrong with ethnography? Methodological explorations*, pp. 96–125. London: Routledge.

Hammersley, M. (1992b). Ethnography and realism. In M. Hammersley (Ed.), *What's wrong with ethnography? Methodological explorations*, pp. 43–56. London: Routledge.

Hammersley, M. (2005). The myth of research-based practice: The critical case of educational inquiry. *International Journal of Social Research Methodology*, 8(4), 317–330.

Huberman, A. M. & Miles, M. B. (1985). Assessing local causality in qualitative research. In D. N. Berg & K. K. Smith (Eds.), *Exploring clinical methods for social research*, pp. 351–382. Beverly Hills, CA: Sage.

Lakoff, G. (1987). *Women, fire, and dangerous things: What categories reveal about the mind.* Chicago: University of Chicago Press.

Lakoff, G. & Johnson, M. (1999). *Philosophy in the flesh: The embodied mind and its challenge to Western thought.* New York: Basic Books.

Leibovici, L. (2001). Effects of remote, retroactive, intercessory prayer on outcomes in patients with bloodstream infection: Randomised controlled trial. *British Medical Journal*, 323, 1450–1451.

Manicas, P. T. (2006). *A realist philosophy of social science: Explanation and understanding.* Cambridge: Cambridge University Press.

Maxwell, J. A. (1992). Understanding and validity in qualitative research. *Harvard Educational Review*, 62, 279–300.

Maxwell, J. A. (1999). A realist/postmodern concept of culture. In E. L. Cerroni-Long (Ed.), *Anthropological theory in North America*, pp. 143–173. Westport, CT: Bergin & Garvey.

Maxwell, J. A. (2004a). Causal explanation, qualitative research, and scientific inquiry in education. *Educational Researcher*, 33(2), 3–11.

Maxwell, J. A. (2004b). Re-emergent scientism, postmodernism, and dialogue across differences. *Qualitative Inquiry*, 10, 35–41.

Maxwell, J. A. (2004c). Using qualitative methods for causal explanation. *Field Methods*, 16, 243–264.

Maxwell, J. A. (2008). The value of a realist understanding of causality for qualitative research. In N. K. Denzin & M. D. Giardina (Eds.), *Qualitative inquiry and the politics of evidence*, pp. 163–181. Walnut Creek, CA: Left Coast Press.

Maxwell, J. A. & Loomis, D. (2003). Mixed methods design: An alternative approach. In A. Tashakkori & C. Teddlie (Eds.), *Handbook of mixed methods in social and behavioral research*, pp. 241–271. Thousand Oaks, CA: Sage.

Milgram, S. (1974). *Obedience to authority: An experimental view.* New York: Harper and Row.

Mohr, L. B. (1982). *Explaining organizational behavior.* San Francisco: Jossey-Bass.

Pawson, R. (2006). *Evidence-based policy: A realist perspective.* London: Sage.

Pawson, R. & Tilley, N. (1997). *Realistic evaluation.* London: Sage.

Phillips, D. C. (1987). Validity in qualitative research: Why the worry about warrant will not wane. *Education and Urban Society*, 20, 9–24.

Putnam, H. (1990). *Realism with a human face*, edited by James Conant. Cambridge: Harvard University Press.

Putnam, H. (1999). *The threefold cord: Mind, body, and world.* New York: Columbia University Press.

Salmon, W. C. (1998). *Causality and explanation.* New York: Oxford University Press.

Sayer, A. (1992). *Method in social science: A realist approach*, 2nd ed. London: Routledge.

Sayer, A. (2000). *Realism and social science.* London: Sage.

Schwandt, T. A. (2007). *Qualitative inquiry: A dictionary of terms*, 3rd ed. Thousand Oaks, CA: Sage.

Shadish, W. R., Cook, T. D., & Campbell, D. T. (2002). *Experimental and quasi-experimental designs for generalized causal inference.* Boston: Houghton Mifflin.

Shweder, R. A. (1991). *Thinking through cultures: Expeditions in cultural psychology.* Cambridge, MA: Harvard University Press.

Smith, J. K. & Deemer, D. K. (2000). The problem with criteria in the age of relativism. In N. K. Denzin & Y. S. Lincoln (Eds.), *The handbook of qualitative research*, 2nd ed., pp. 877–922. Thousand Oaks, CA: Sage.

Section II

Qualitative Inquiry in Post-Disaster America

Chapter 5 ||| Education Research in the Public Interest[1]

Gloria Ladson-Billings
University of Wisconsin-Madison

I watched Katrina from the other side of the Atlantic Ocean. I was attending a conference in London when news from the BBC and CNN International arrived about the strength of the hurricane, the devastation of an area the size of the United Kingdom, and the utter despair of the poor, elderly, and black citizens of the Gulf Coast region. What could we say about the public interest when it appeared that the public institutions most responsible for responding to the most needy segments of the public had almost no interest in them?

The strange contrast between the response to September 11, 2001, and Hurricane Katrina left a sickening feeling in the pit of my stomach. Let me be clear: These are not equivalent events. September 11 was an attack of foreign terrorists that made us all feel confused, horrified, and vulnerable. The nation mourned the death of so many Americans and lifted up the heroism of hundreds of brave first responders. We rallied around a president whose competence (and legitimacy) many of us questioned. New York, the city that never sleeps, became a place that was home to us all. I worried if my family members who live in New York were safe. I heard scores of stories about New Yorkers exhibiting their best selves. There were reports of merchants who handed out sneakers to women who were walking through Manhattan in high-heeled shoes because the transportation system was crippled. There were other reports of children passing out bottles of water to the stunned commuters. Help for victims of 9/11 came in many forms from around the country and throughout the world.

Hurricane Katrina was a natural disaster. It was not contained to a few buildings in New York, Washington, DC, and a field in Pennsylvania. The storm could not be prevented. Indeed, the last few years have seen a number of devastating tropical storms and hurricanes. The state of Florida alone was battered by three or four major storms in the 2004 hurricane season. The shock of Katrina was the way so many U.S. citizens were left to fend for themselves. In an administration that claimed to leave no child behind, large numbers of poor, elderly, and black citizens *were* left behind. Our horror was not over the path of destruction the storm left but rather the gaping hole in the safety net left by twenty-five years of public neglect.

The spectacle that became the Hurricane Katrina crisis forces me to ask: "Which public(s) command our interest and what, if anything, can we say about those publics that we regularly and systematically ignore?" Over forty years ago, Michael Harrington (1962) published the book, *The Other America*, which is credited with launching the "War on Poverty." In it, Harrington described the social and economic isolation that millions of poor urban and rural citizens experience in America. He also described their relative invisible status in the American psyche. During the 2004 presidential campaign, Democratic vice-presidential candidate, John Edwards (D-NC), tried to bring an awareness of the persistence of two Americas to the consciousness of the American electorate:

> Today, under George W. Bush, there are two Americas, not one: One America that does the work, another that reaps the reward. One America that pays the taxes, another America that gets the tax breaks. One America—middle-class America—whose needs Washington has long forgotten, another America—a narrow-interest America—whose every wish is Washington's command. One America that is struggling to get by, another America that can buy anything it wants, even a Congress and a president. (available online at (http://en.wikiquote.org/wiki/John_Edwards, accessed October 6, 2005)

But even Edwards was not referencing the poorest of the poor. His appeal was to the middle class that was slowly but surely feeling the impact of stagnant wages and increasing health care costs. The desperately poor who emerged across our media or were perhaps "washed up" after Katrina represented an entirely new magnitude of poverty to which too many had become insensitive and unaware. Katrina's gift was its in-your-face confrontation of how we are going to define the public and its interests.

Some might question the relevance of Hurricane Katrina to the discourse of education research and the public interest. However, in the aftermath of Katrina—where many cities and small towns are still attempting to pull their lives back together some three years later—we can again witness examples of how the inequities continue to manifest. The hurricane was an equal opportunity destroyer. Million-dollar beachfront homes and casinos were destroyed alongside housing projects, tenements, and "shotgun" houses. But the process of reconstruction reveals very different patterns. Evacuees from the wealthier communities have been able to place their children in private schools or attend public schools outside the urban community of New Orleans. Evacuees from the infamous lower 9th Ward and most of New Orleans proper have been told that their public schools may not reopen for some time.

The public interest aspect of education research is linked to the increasing public *involvement* in education. Since the *Brown v. Board of Education* decisions (1954, 1955), it has been clear that there is a national interest in education. The contour of that interest has shifted with the political winds. There have been times when education barely registered on the national agenda. Ronald Reagan was determined to dismantle the Department of Education. His disdain for what he termed "big government" caused him to urge policies such as school choice vouchers, character education, and an emphasis on back to basics curriculum such as reading, mathematics, and history. However, we must recall that it was during Reagan's administration that the agenda for federal intervention in education was reset. The release of *A Nation at Risk: The Imperative for Educational Reform* (1983) by the National Commission on Excellence in Education set the direction for education reform. This report was followed by a spate of documents and initiatives decrying the terrible state of the nation's educational system.

The response to the alarm that education was failing on all fronts was to raise the bar and depend primarily on standardized assessments to measure academic progress. During the first term of the George W. Bush administration, the Elementary and Secondary Education Act was due for reauthorization. Instead of focusing the reauthorization solely on the compensatory aspects of Title I, the Bush White House made it an omnibus act that impacted all public school. They called their program "No Child Left Behind" (NCLB: Public Law 107-110) and required schools to test students regularly, hire what was termed "highly qualified" teachers, and use "scientifically proven" teaching methods. Unfortunately, these grand plans were not matched with adequate funding from the federal government.

As shortsighted as I think NCLB is, I do think there are aspects of it that do exactly what education needs. For example, NCLB forces schools to disaggregate their data by racial/ethnic group. This is particularly important in suburban and metropolitan districts where so-called good schools were guilty of masking the poor academic performance of students of color by the much greater numbers of their white middle-class students. However, the real genius of NCLB was to include all students—not just Title I students—in the reauthorization. This approach forced many educators off of the sidelines and into the fray. We were no longer talking simply about "other people's children" (Delpit, 1995); we now had to think about our own children. But those points do not outweigh the serious flaws in the legislation or its unfunded mandates.

New Orleans and the Perfect Storm

I reflect back on New Orleans and the aftermath of the hurricane because New Orleans provides a perfect example of what happens when *everything* goes wrong. Before Katrina, the statistics on Orleans Parrish painted a grim picture of life for many of its citizens. According to the U.S. Census Bureau (2000), New Orleans had a population of 484,674 before the hurricane. Sixty-seven percent of that population was African American, with 23.7% of the total population living below the poverty line, and 35% of the African American population living below the poverty line. More than 40,000 New Orleanians had less than a 9th-grade graduation, and 56,804 residents had between 9th- and 12th-grade educations without diplomas. A telling statistic is that 96.1% of the public school population was African American, which means that most of the white families with school-aged children send their children to private schools. Thirteen percent of the public school teachers in the state were uncertified.

Education clearly was not working for those in New Orleans who depended on public schools. It was not working long before the streets were flooded and the roofs were blown away. A well-known Norman Rockwell painting shows a little African American girl walking between federal marshals on her way to school. That depiction represents Ruby Bridges, who, in 1960, was the first African American to integrate New Orleans' schools. Wells (2004) details the history of resistance by white communities bordering New Orleans to allowing African American students to enter their schools. Bridges's story, although compelling, is even more extraordinary in light of the context of school desegregation in New Orleans. Out of 137 African American students who applied to attend formerly all white schools, only four were selected. One of the four was Ruby Bridges. She attended the William Frantz Elementary School; all of the white students then boycotted the school. Only one teacher, a white woman from New York, was willing to teach Ruby. As a consequence of her attending the previously all-white school, Ruby's father was fired from his job and her grandparents were evicted from their tenant farm.

For most of us, the story of Ruby Bridges is a story of courage and heroism—and it is. But the deeper story is the story of how America's fatal flaw—racism—continues to distort and destroy the promise on which the nation claimed to be founded. The same mentality that allowed white citizens to barricade themselves from school desegregation in the 1960s was present among white citizens who armed themselves to prevent desperate black citizens of New Orleans in the midst of the hurricane disaster from seeking refuge from the floodwaters. Which public are we referencing when, in 2005 a public official (a sheriff) points a gun at destitute evacuees and says, "You're not coming in here" and leaves them to wither on a freeway overpass (Glass, 2005)?

This history of New Orleans school desegregation is a part of a larger history of not just educational access denied but rather the history of citizenship denied. Limiting education is just one of the ways to create second-class citizenship. However, it is one of the more effective ways because once a people are *mis*-educated and/or undereducated, society can claim the need to use "merit" as the standard by which decisions for post-secondary decisions (e.g., college admission, job placement) will be made. New Orleans is a municipality where people were *systematically* excluded from social benefits—housing, health, employment, and education: Hurricane Katrina brought to the surface the horror that existed in New Orleans for more than a century.

The horror of Hurricane Katrina is made more frustrating by the history of flooding in the Gulf Coast region. In the great Mississippi flood of 1927, Louisiana officials deliberately flooded African American neighborhoods (allegedly to prevent greater flooding in other parts of the city). Officials dynamited the Poydras levee, which led ultimately to 700,000 people—half of them African Americans—being displaced. More horrific than the flood (which killed about 246 people) were the conditions in the evacuation camps.

Now, almost eighty years later, we see an eerily similar situation. The poor are abandoned and displaced, and we seem to have learned little from the lessons of history. What, if anything, can education research tell us about what we should do to ensure that the rebuilding process in New Orleans does not reproduce the substandard education that had become emblematic of the city?

In many ways, New Orleans has the opportunity to do exactly what Anyon (2005) argues must be done to improve urban schools. The schools must be reformed in tandem with improvements to the entire city. In the case of New Orleans, everything has to be rebuilt and the schools have an opportunity to emerge anew. Unfortunately, some disturbing rumblings have already emerged. The city's power elite, civic leaders, developers, and speculators plan to build a "different" New Orleans—one with fewer poor people and presumably fewer African Americans. Because so many of the city's displaced residents are poor, it is unlikely that they will be able to quickly pick up and return to the city. If they have been fortunate enough to find housing, employment, and decent schooling in another city, we cannot expect them to return to New Orleans. With fewer residents returning to the city, the school population will be smaller. The smaller school population can provide an opportunity for smaller schools (and it is hoped smaller classrooms).

With a smaller school population, New Orleans has an opportunity to be more selective in the hiring of teachers and other school personnel. They even have the opportunity to create a new school district that is not limited to the geographic confines of Orleans Parish. Orfield and Eaton (1996) point out that one of the major problems that school desegregation addresses is the concentration of poverty. A new school district configuration can address that. Delpit (1995), Foster (1997), Hilliard (2000), Irvine (2002), and Siddle-Walker (1996) all address the point that African Americans do know how to educate themselves. Anderson (1988) and Willis (2002) detail the historical pattern of African Americans creating, building, maintaining, and sustaining educational institutions. A new New Orleans school district has the opportunity to build on this legacy of success.

It is important to acknowledge that schools are not the sole site of community and individual development. Rothstein (2004) has consistently argued that in addition to school improvement, policymakers and educators must pursue expanded notions of schooling that include out-of-school experiences, and "social and economic policies that will enable children to attend school more equally ready to learn" (p. 109). The policies that Rothstein references, similar to Anyon (2005), include expanded and affordable health services and housing along with jobs that allow people to make a true living wage. Rubinowitz and Rosenbaum (2000) documented the ability of low-income African Americans to "move to opportunity" by integrating into suburban communities. Comparisons between the people who moved to suburban communities and those who moved within the city show significant differences. Forty percent of the students who attended schools in the suburbs were enrolled in college-track curricula compared to the 24% enrolled in college-tracks in the city. Fifty-four percent of the African American students who moved to the suburbs enrolled in some type of postsecondary education, 27% of whom enrolled in a four-year college. Their city counterparts enrolled in postsecondary programs at the rate of 21%, with only 4% enrolled in a four-year college. On the economic front, 75% of the mothers who moved to the suburbs were working, compared to just 41% of their peers who remained in the city.

But all was not positive in the suburbs. African American students had higher rates of special education placement in the suburbs, with 19% of students placed in special needs categories versus 7% in the city. This special education disproportionality is consistent with Skiba et al.'s (in press) findings on black students in special education placement and discipline referrals.

I recount these figures to point toward the troubling attitudes and behaviors that are likely to emerge even if New Orleans has the opportunity to start over and create a new city that truly provides equal opportunities for all of its residents. Unfortunately, as a critical race theorist I am not optimistic about the likelihood of a just resolution to the reconstruction of New Orleans. If I were forced to predict the outcome of the reconstruction it would resemble the following scenario[2]:

> It is the near-future, and with my eyes closed and ears wide open I can tell I am in New Orleans. The aroma is a mix of savory and sweet—hot and languid. I can smell the down home gumbo, the tangy jambalaya, and a wonder shrimp etouffee simmering on the collective stoves of French Quarter restaurants. My sweet tooth is tickled by the prospect of luscious hot bread pudding and Bananas Foster. Yes, my nose tells me I am in New Orleans. My ears also tell me that I am in the "Big Easy." I hear the strains of Dixieland coming from one street corner and Zydeco coming from another. There is no other town where this music is so prominent and evident in everyday living. However, it is when I open my eyes that I begin to doubt myself. Some aspects of the city are immediately recognizable. I see Jackson Square with the lovely Cathedral of St. Louis on one side and the Mississippi River on the other. The shops of the French Quarter are humming with activity. Tourists are browsing the many souvenir shops. Every now and then I see someone with a t-shirt attesting to their experience of having survived "Katrina."
>
> As I look down Poydras I can see that the horror of the

Superdome and the New Orleans Convention Center have been replaced by a new sports and convention center complex. A gleaming new Hyatt Hotel sits between the two. I decide to grab the trolley on Canal Street and head out toward the zoo. I recognize the grandeur of the Garden District. Organizations like National Historic Preservation have worked hard to make sure the stately mansions were brought back to their timeless beauty. Looking at this community you would never guess that a hurricane and flooding had ever occurred. I step off the trolley at Tulane University where I see a bustling campus, beautifully appointed and clearly a center of academic activity. It looks like the new New Orleans is better than ever.

I return downtown so that I can head toward the places I know best. I want to check out Congo Square in Louis Armstrong Park. I want to see if someone dusted off Marie Laveaux's tomb. I want to see how Xavier, Dillard, and Southern universities came through the disaster. I am buoyed by what I have seen at both Tulane and Loyola. When I get hungry I will probably sneak into Dooky Chase to eat some things that have not been on my diet for years, but Leah Chase is an institution, having cooked at that location since 1946 has earned a special place in my heart. One year while my family and I were in New Orleans for the Sugar Bowl game we had dinner at Dooky Chase. It was late on a Sunday evening and there wasn't much foot traffic. The food was not particularly outstanding but I wanted my teenaged daughter to go to a black New Orleans institution. Some days after we returned home I noticed that my credit card was missing. In attempting to retrace my steps I realized that the last time I used the card was at the restaurant. A quick phone call to New Orleans got me in touch with the maître d', who informed me that he had found the card but did not know how to get in touch with me. In a matter of minutes the card was destroyed and canceled.

Louis Armstrong Park is just where it was. It has been cleaned up and the maker for Congo Square remains. This is the place where former enslaved Africans spent their Sunday afternoons. Their stories of resistance and survival were formulated here. To me, it is sacred ground. I breathe a sigh of relief, but my relief is short-lived. My visits to Dillard, Xavier, and Southern universities are much less satisfying. Both Dillard and Xavier have had to merge with two of the city's predominately white institutions—Xavier with Loyola and Dillard with Tulane. Southern (or

SUNO) has closed and moved its operation to Baton Rouge. The state has decided it can no longer afford to have two branches of the Southern campus.

I decide to pick up my spirits with a shrimp po'boy at Dooky Chase's but when I turn down Orleans Street I barely recognize it. Gone are the ramshackle public housing units and in their place there is nothing. Just as it is in North Philadelphia, Detroit, South Central Los Angeles, East Oakland, East St. Louis, and countless other U.S. cities, there has been no attempt to rebuild in this area. The infamous 9th Ward that was home to a large number of the city's poor and African American community lays fallow. It is caught between the greedy land developers from the east coast and the holier-than-thou environmentalists from the west coast. The two groups are mired in litigation while squeezed in the middle are the poorest of the poor who would like to return but have nowhere to live.

Without a 9th Ward, Orleans parish schools were a very different place. Instead of 60,000 students it now had less than half that number with about 28,000 students. When the first residents returned to repopulate the city, those with school-aged children were offered vouchers to take to private schools because the public system was not yet fully online. By the time the city was up and running, the damage that this diversion of students from the public system had taken its toll. The failure to bring all segments of the community back into the city means that there was a smaller tax base upon which to build a school system.

The booming downtown area was deceptive. Yes, there were gleaming new hotels and department stores. In fact, several corporate headquarters had relocated to the newly reconstructed New Orleans. These companies were able to make sweet deals with the city fathers. They were promised tax credits and a variety of workplace waivers that allowed them to hire people for their low level jobs (e.g. janitors, cafeteria workers, clerks) without providing full benefits. Housing was at a premium in the new city. Condos and town homes dominated the downtown area. The stately mansions remained in the hands of the city's 'old money' families. The poor were locked out. A few of the poor were able to find some housing across the river in the Algiers section of the city but there is not much in the rebuilt city that can accommodate people of modest means.

For many months New Orleans was known as the "childless

city" (MSNBC, 2005). Those poor families with children did not return because they did not want to risk moving their children out of the somewhat stable school environments they had found in other communities. Others worried that the level of contamination caused by the sewage, standing water, and lack of sanitation created a toxic environment that they could not risk with their children and still others recognized that the limited social services—day care, after school, community centers—meant that there was not enough community infrastructure in which their children could flourish.

New Orleans had become a city of odd demographics. It reminded me of the District of Columbia. It was a place where almost no families sent their children to public schools. Private schools were springing up all over the place. In a nod to its French heritage the city became home to several lyceums attended by the wealthiest residents. The public schools, although smaller, were not much better than before the disaster. Few "highly qualified" teachers returned to the system. Most of the newer teachers had found jobs in other communities. Large numbers of veteran teachers retired. This smaller school system had its share of "competent" teachers but a better assessment was that most of the system's teachers were mediocre.

The pattern of racism seemed clear to me but I was assured that race had nothing to do with how the city was reconstructed. I was shown how a variety of old line (read: Creole) families were an integral part of the rebuilding. Indeed, the mayor was black. No, racism had no place in New Orleans. The city was just adamant about not allowing an unsavory element to repopulate the new city. I had been in this place before. Every time someone said the words "urban renewal," I witnessed the dissolution of poor African American communities, the loss of community control, the influx of high-end homes, and the disappearance of strong public schools.

The new New Orleans is an adult city—a kind of Las Vegas south. The needs of low- to moderate-income families are not taken into consideration. There is a need for some low-income people to do service work in the hotels and growing number of casinos that jumpstarted the economy after the hurricane. Many of these workers are migrant and undocumented. They rarely demand social services for fear of being harassed by government officials regarding their immigrant status. Many of these workers work two (and sometimes three) jobs.

The strange thing about this new New Orleans is that so many people are so positive about the reconstruction. The newspapers are filled with good news stories about new hotels, restaurants, and businesses opening. The Bureau of Tourism is thriving, and conventions and meetings are at an all-time high. As a part of the redevelopment, the city provides huge discounts for organizations to book their conferences and conventions in New Orleans. The voices of the suffering poor are muted and their advocates are regularly dismissed. The only thing they can hope for is another devastating hurricane. Then the nation will be forced to gaze on them once again.

Coda

Some might argue that the chronicle I detailed is far-fetched and has no basis in reality. However, the story has a basis in the historical reality of generations of New Orleans families. In both the flood of 1927 and Hurricane Betsy, the African American community was the most vulnerable. Rumors of deliberate levee breaches and slow responses (or responses primarily motivated by the possibility of political gain) have kept African Americans suspicious and distrustful of their governments at all levels—local, state, and federal.

The one thing that many planners and reconstruction gurus have not understood is the incredible pull of family in the African American community in New Orleans. Many of the residents of the 9th Ward have not lived anywhere other than New Orleans. With family members deceased and dispersed because of Hurricane Katrina, many African Americans have lost their moorings. Their extended families provided the safety net that kept them from starvation and homelessness. The complex and vital social networks of mothers, grandmothers, aunts, uncles, and cousins are what kept people connected to and functioning in the city, no matter how marginal those existences were.

What, then, can education research offer to a place of such utter devastation and despair? My initial response is nothing. But as I think about our work, I am convinced that the hurricane also gave us an opportunity to recapture our humanity. Our work is not merely about data points and effect sizes. It is also about what difference our work can make in the lives of real people. Hurricane Katrina brings shame on us all. We have no excuse for our ignorance about poverty. We cannot keep writing about schools as some idyllic, romantic places where a few students are failing. The work we have to do must be done in the public interest. We cannot hide behind notions of neutrality or objectivity when people are suffering so desperately. The questions we pursue, the projects we choose, the agenda we champion have to be about more than career advancement. If education research is going to matter, we have to make it matter in the lives of real people around real issues. It is just too bad that we had to have a disaster to make this clear to us.

Notes

1. This chapter draws from and reworks arguments in the introduction to my recent book *Education Research in the Public Interest: Social Justice, Education, and Policy*, coedited with William F. Tate (Teachers College Press, 2006).

2. Critical race theory relies heavily on storytelling and counter-storytelling. Here I am using Derrick Bell's (1987) notion of the chronicle to set this scenario.

References

Anderson, J. D. (1988). *The education of Blacks in the South, 1860–1935.* Chapel Hill: University of North Carolina Press.

Anyon, J. (2005). *Radical possibilities: Public policy, urban education and a new social movement.* New York: Routledge.

Bell, D. (1987). *And we are not saved: The elusive quest for justice.* New York: Basic Books.

Delpit, L. (1995). *Other people's children: Cultural conflict in the classroom.* New York: The Free Press.

Foster, M. (1997). *Black teachers on teaching.* New York: The New Press.

Glass, I. (Ed.). (2005). After the flood. This American Life, Public Radio Broadcast. Available online at http://www.thislife.org/pdf/296.pdf (accessed October 15, 2005).

Harrington, M. (1962). *The other America: Poverty in the United States*. New York: Macmillan.

Hilliard, A. G. (2000). Excellence in education versus high stakes testing. *Journal of Teacher Education*, 51, 293–304.

Irvine, J. J. (2002). *In search of wholeness: African American teachers and their culturally specific classroom practices*. New York: Palgrave/St. Martin's Press.

MSNBC. (2005). New Orleans faces months without children. Available online at http://msnbc.msn.com/id/9480718/ (accessed October 16, 2005).

National Commission on Excellence in Education. (1983). *A nation at risk: The imperative for education reform. A report to the nation and the Secretary of Education, University States Department of Education*. Washington, DC: Government Printing Office.

Oliver Brown et al. v. Board of Education of Topeka et al. (a.k.a *Brown v. Board of Education*). (1954). 347 U. S. 483. Appeal from the United States District Court for the District of Kansas. No. 1. Argued December 9, 1952. Reargued December 8, 1953. Decided May 17, 1954.

Oliver Brown et al. v. Board of Education of Topeka et al. (a.k.a *Brown v. Board of Education II*, or *Brown II*) (1955). 349 U.S. 294. Appeal from the United States District Court for the District of Kansas. Reargued on the question of relief April 11–14., 1955. Opinion and judgments announced May 31, 1955.

Orfield, G. & Eaton, S. (1996). *Dismantling desegregation: The quiet repeal of Brown v. Board of Education*. New York: The New Press.

Rothstein, R. (2004). A wider lens on the black-white achievement gap. *Phi Delta Kappan*, 86, 105–110.

Rubinowitz, L. S. & Rosenbaum, J. E. (2000). *Crossing the class and color lines: From public housing to white suburbia*. Chicago: University of Chicago Press.

Siddle-Walker, V. (1996). *Their highest potential: An African American community in the segregated South*. Chapel Hill: University of North Carolina Press.

Skiba, R. J., Michael, R. S., Nardo, A. C., & Peterson, R. (in press). The color of discipline: Sources of racial and gender disproportionality in school punishment. *Urban Review*.

U.S. Census Bureau. (2000). *Census 2000*. Washington, DC: Government Printing Office.

Wells, A. (2004). Good neighbors? Distance, resistance, and desegregation in metropolitan New Orleans. *Urban Education*, 39, 408–427.

Willis, A. I. (2002). Literacy at Calhoun Colored School, 1892–1943. *Reading Research Quarterly*, 37(1), 8–44.

Chapter 6 ||| Performing Pedagogies of Hope in Post-Katrina America[1]

Michael D. Giardina
University of Illinois

Laura H. Vaughan
Independent Scholar

I hope we realize that the people of New Orleans weren't just abandoned during the hurricane. They were abandoned long ago—to murder and mayhem in the streets, to substandard schools, to dilapidated housing, to inadequate health care, to a pervasive sense of hopelessness.

—Barack Obama, 2005

The tragedy of both gulf crises must do more than provoke despair or cynicism, it must spark a politics in which the images of those floating bodies in New Orleans and the endless parade of death in Iraq serve as a reminder of what it means when justice, as the lifeblood of democracy, becomes cold and indifferent in the face of death.

—Henry Giroux, 2006a

It was the images that struck you first: the lifeless body of a fellow citizen cast off to the side of a street, a starving dog gnawing at a bloody limb. A mother gripping her infant daughter at the New Orleans Convention Center, begging—pleading—for someone, anyone, to whisk them away from their uncertain future. An elderly man in a wheelchair, clinging to his last shards of breath. A news reporter breaking down into frustrated tears on national television. People—fellow human beings—rummaging in garbage cans or blown-out storefronts for food and water because FEMA had yet to realize that New Orleans was, in fact, a city located in the United States.[2] The collapse of civil society: live and in unliving color.

The mood was somber. Reflective. Harsh. Sad. Kim Segal, a segment producer at CNN caught in New Orleans (henceforth the colloquial NOLA), recalled the scene unfolding through her journalistic eyes: "It was chaos. There was nobody there, nobody in charge. And there was nobody giving even water. The children, you should see them—they're all just in tears. There are sick people. We saw … people who are dying in front of you" (CNN.com, 2005).

A photojournalist from NBC agrees, declaring that a third-world country he once covered was better off than conditions downtown. CNN's Sanjay Gupta, a medical doctor by trade (and potential nominee for Surgeon General in the Obama administration), relays the shocking brute force of horror in one of NOLA's hospitals: "When patients die in the hospital, there is no place to put them, so they're in the stairwells. It is one of the most unbelievable situations I've seen as a doctor, certainly as a journalist as well. There is no electricity. There is no water. There's over 200 patients still here remaining" (CNN.com, 2005).

And hardened journalists such as Anderson Cooper and Sheppard Smith break down numerous times during live shots, the former snapping at U.S. Senator Mary Landrieu (D-LA) during an interview,[3] the latter barking at his on-air colleagues for not "getting" what he was physically witnessing as they sat back in the comfort of their broadcast studio.

Yet in the midst of this hellish event came the voices and actions of dedicated people who were motivated to help, to become engaged with the event, to be "present to the scene," as Lauren Berlant has said. For example:

- Three Duke University students drove to New Orleans from Durham, North Carolina, forged a set of media credentials, gained access into the cordoned-off city, and rescued several people. (*Duke Magazine*, 2005)
- Davy Jones Locker, a volunteer-run store serving Navy and civilian personnel and their family members at Stennis Space Center in Mississippi, distributed basic sundries such as soap, dishes, and cat food free of charge.

- Kuwait donated US $500 million for Katrina relief; the Red Cross raised more than US $750 million in aid.
- Web sites such as http://www.katrinaconnections.com, http://katrina.im-ok.org, http://hurricanekatrinasurvivors.com, and http://katrinasafe.com quickly sprang up, connecting thousands of lost and displaced families. Internet blogs such as DailyKos played a similar role in disseminating crucial information (as well as critically informed commentary).
- A medical team from Anne Arundel County, Maryland, traveled to and operated a makeshift hospital in Jefferson Parish, Louisiana; treated more than 1,000 patients; returned a hurricane-battered four-story hospital to satisfactory operating conditions; and restored faith in the public trust.
- The National Football League hosted a historic Monday Night Football doubleheader featuring the New Orleans Saints in a part-game/part-telethon that raised over US $25 million (see King, 2005).
- The popular-public sphere started to take notice.

A few days after Katrina came ashore, I received the following e-mail from an old friend of mine:

> I just wanted to take a minute and ask you all for your thoughts and prayers this weekend. My roommate, boyfriend [now husband], and I will be heading down to Baton Rouge this weekend to assist in volunteer work for the hurricane survivors. We really don't know what we'll find there, but we're definitely moved to go down and help out in any way that we can. So think of us this weekend.

Although I was obviously proud of her commitment to get her hands dirty as part of the on-the-ground relief efforts (especially while I was sitting back in the comfort of my office writing about the *mediated* images of post-Katrina NOLA cascading across my television screen), a side of me worried about her essentially doing "risky" (Stewart et al., this volume) or "dangerous" (Madison, this volume) ethnography, literally hours after the storm had hit: How many media reports had there been about "toxic soup" and other health concerns in Louisiana, I thought to myself?

But it's her story, not mine. She should re-present it.

"How can I help you?"

It was a simple question, asked and answered many times over on many other days in so many other places. But not here. Not today. I approached the elderly woman as she began to sift through the men's clothing laid out on makeshift tables. From a distance, she looked like a dozen other elderly women I had met yet, as I got closer, I could see the strain in her eyes. Her stooped posture and reluctant smile spoke of a weariness and despair. Yet smile lines were evident around her eyes, hinting at a kind spirit within, revealing a calm inner presence and integrity.

"I need to find some pants fo' my gran'son. He takes a 30, but he's real tall. They made that boy tall and skinny," she said, tiredly shaking her head from side to side.

I knew that we had nothing in that size, but I pulled out two pairs that would come close.

The woman looked up at me with a tired sigh and said, "Those will have to do. He has nuthin' now."

With a slight smile masking her disappointment, she thanked me for my assistance and began to walk away. I felt a saddened pressure in my chest, the weight of her disappointment pressing down on my shoulders. My heart thumped, skipping an old Jazz beat:

I *wanted* to tell her that I was sorry.

I *wanted* to tell her that I could make things better for her.

I *wanted* to tell her that everything was going to be okay.

(But did *I* even believe that?)

Around me milled other volunteers and about a dozen "shoppers"—a crude euphemism if ever there was one. The sounds of a guitar, dulcimer, and banjo playing Brumley's "I'll Fly Away" rose above the makeshift partition separating the "dining area" from the "clothing distribution center." Yet the cacophony of voices echoing throughout the gym of the large Baptist church became muted, melting away into the background like the images cast in an Astrid Kirchherr photograph of John Lennon—I could only see the face of the old woman as she began to turn away. Her weathered countenance was like so many faces represented in media accounts in the aftermath of Katrina.

"Do you need anything for yourself?" I called after her.

She turned, faced me, and shook her head softly.

"Are you here from New Orleans?" I asked.

The woman nodded a distant, tired nod. "My fam'ly an' I are up here stayin' with a cousin."

The tears swelled in her eyes as Jenny Wren[4] recounted a story that was shared by so many others in this city whose population exploded nearly overnight with evacuees rescued as the creeping floodwaters devoured their city, their lives:

"We came up here whenna floods got bad. Seventeen of uss'er stayin' wit' her now."

"I hope she has a big house," I said, revealing my oblivious naiveté at the individual hells unleashed by Katrina.

"We all sleepin' 'onna floor. She only got two bedrooms an' a bathroom, but at least we not in shelters like a lotta folks." Jenny's jaw tightened noticeably, pulling back her stooped shoulders as a new determination flowed into her melodic voice. "I din't have much before the storm. I had a house, and lived there wit' ma son and gran'son. My house is gone now. I got nothin' left."

"What are you going to do now?"

She simply sighed and shrugged. "We'll get by. We always do."

"Rebuilding" New Orleans

In the days following Katrina, calls rang out from all corners of the country to "rebuild New Orleans." Congress authorized an initial $50 billion in emergency funds.[5] The American Red Cross pledged untold funds and dispersed thousands of volunteers to the region. Even President Bush stated that New Orleans would be rebuilt "better than before." (Was that a Halliburton logo I saw?)[6]

Better than before. I suppose that is all a matter of perspective: Even from the outset, it was clear that if the powers-that-be were to have their way, it certainly wasn't going to look much like *old* New Orleans. Rep. Richard Baker (R-LA) admitted as much when he told the *Wall Street Journal,* "We finally cleaned up public housing in New Orleans. We couldn't do it, but God did" (as quoted in Babington, 2005). Of course, by "cleaned up public housing," Rep. Baker meant that he was thankful that the hurricane displaced those (largely poor, largely black) residents who were living in impoverished dwellings, in effect making the now-abandoned or destroyed land prime for real estate (re)development. In fact, Alphonso R. Jackson, then-secretary of Housing and Urban Development, predicted that New Orleans would be "whiter" after its pre-Katrina population of more than 500,000 African Americans had largely been dispersed across the country, many to Houston, Texas, and other neighboring urban areas (see DuBose, 2005).[7]

And in its place, did anyone expect the rebuilt city to be anything more than an expansion of the Time Square Lite facade that already existed—a place where jazz music, Cajun/Creole food, and French historical inflections were reduced to banal touristic caricatures that saw "neighborhood radicalism and protest as entertainment, myth, human-interest story, or a peculiar spectacle to be gazed at by a curious middle-class" (Mele, 2000, p. 308)? Of course not! If anything, the new branding dynamic that was sure to take hold in NOLA would be "embedded in highly marketable, sanitized styles and signs of subversion, anti-authoritarianism, and experimentation that designate it as an 'alternative' space" (Cole, 2001, p. 117). As Friedman, Andrews, and Silk (2004) contend with respect to privatized urban "redevelopment" projects, one of the primary results of such "consumption-based, visitor-oriented redevelopment could be in creating little more than a veneer of change and vitality within the city" in which beneath the shiny new façade of an improved national image, "the underlying realities of urban life frequently remain unaltered" (p. 130).[8]

In the immediate aftermath of the devastation, the direction needed was clear. Said Mark Krasnof, a cofounder of the Civic Center Shelter on the Louisiana-Texas border, which helped house many who were lucky to escape Katrina's wrath:

> The very soul of Louisiana is now at stake. ... If our "leaders" have their way this whole goddamn region will become either a toxic graveyard or a big museum where jazz, zydeco and Cajun music will still be played for tourists but the cultures that gave them life are defunct or dispersed. (quoted in Davis & Fontenot, 2005)

Fighting against what many perceived as the inevitable, Glen Ford and Peter Gamble (2005) of *The Black Commentator* pleaded that

> priority must be given to the right to preserve and continue the rich and diverse cultural traditions of the city, and the social experiences of Black people that produced the culture.

The second line, Mardi Gras Indians, brass bands, creative music, dance foods, language and other expressions are the "soul of the city." The rebuilding process must preserve these traditions. THE CITY MUST NOT BE CULTURALLY, ECONOMICALLY OR SOCIALLY GENTRIFIED INTO A "SOULLESS" COLLECTION OF CONDOS AND tract home NEIGHBORHOODS FOR THE RICH.[9]

It is important to remember, also, as Gloria Ladson-Billings (2002) reminded us in her recent address to the American Educational Researchers Association meetings in New Orleans, that the cultural history of NOLA had *already* been whitewashed many times over, renarrated through capitalism's ghoulish eyes: "They sold slaves in this city. They made a tourist stop out of the place where they sold slaves!"

And yet, despite the continued pillaging of the city and its surrounding parishes, the spirit of NOLA continued to live on undaunted in the hearts and minds of its many multigenerational residents, as one diarist from New Orleans stated quite poetically on DailyKos.com:

> New Orleans isn't what most people think it is. It's not just the French Quarter. It's your neighborhood po'boy shop. It's City Park on a Sunday afternoon. It's sitting on a blanket with your sweetie on the Lakefront at night under a canopy of stars and in front of a carpet of black water. It's going to the funeral of an old acquaintance from Schoen's to Lake Lawn Cemetery. It's the box of beads in your attic from all the Mardi Gras parades you ever went to. New Orleans is our family, friends, foes and fellow city dwellers. She cries out to have her children back with their hustle and bustle and vibrancy. (*DailyKos*, 2005)

In the days following Hurricane Katrina, it was a deep-rooted Christian faith that prompted me to act and frustration that charted my course; I just couldn't sit comfortably by doing *nothing*; I'd seen too much. Spurred on by this inner drive, two friends and I decided to cancel vacation plans and set out for Baton Rouge, Louisiana, to pitch in. On a limited budget, and with only a small window of time, we were able to take time off from our respective jobs, and we contacted a number of local churches in the Annapolis, Maryland, area to organize donations.

Not surprisingly, we were greeted with a bevy of hesitations in the face of uncertainty:

"There's no gas … you'll get stranded there."

"What about that toxic sludge? Won't you get sick?"

"You won't have enough time to really do anything."

"Aren't they still shooting at people and looting?"

Others who we knew were stunned that three late-20-somethings would actually be motivated to set aside their day-to-day agendas and stitch themselves into the moment. Still others offered canned food, toys, and clothing to bring with us. But what I found to be the most striking donation was a large monetary one given to us with the caveat of strict instructions:

> I want this to go to someone who needs it, someone who doesn't have food or prescriptions or anything else. I want it to really make a difference on a personal level, to connect with them. I want them to know that there are people out there who care for them and who are praying for them. A donation to a big impersonal organization wouldn't be the same. I want it to mean more than that.

This would be nearly effortless, I thought before we left. Just look at the human suffering on television! This money would make a small difference to anyone in this time of uncertainty. But as we drove past shelters, social service centers, and churches, the need before us was overwhelming. Everywhere we turned there were people who had lost everything: lines of our fellow citizens stretching for blocks around distribution centers, trees snapped in two that had landed haphazardly on houses and vehicles, and wearied relief workers trying to manage the chaos. Everywhere we turned there were people who had lost everything; everywhere we turned there were people to whom a large monetary donation might surely go far in restoring their faith in the world around them and in giving them hope for the potential of a rebuilt future. Or, not any less significantly, at least helping them to buy a hot meal, a bus ticket, or a place to sleep for the night.

But who was I to decide who among the now-homeless, the now-parentless, or the now-childless was to benefit from the charity of others?

"Erasing" New Orleans

Let's cut to the chase. Race and class were the primary factors in the rising death toll following Katrina. As Democratic National Committee Chairman and former Vermont Governor Howard Dean stated shortly thereafter in his 2005 address to the National Baptist Convention of America, "We must ... come to terms with the ugly truth that skin color, age, and economics played a deadly role in who survived and who did not" (quoted in Kalette, 2005).[10] More so than that, perhaps, Mark Anthony Neal (2005) is correct in his observation that although rap star Kanye West's nationally televised statement that "George W. Bush doesn't care about black people" was largely accurate, it is a sentiment that we must complicate: "The initially tepid and lazy response to Katrina in New Orleans wasn't *just* a product of racist neglect, it was also the product of the devaluation of whole communities because they didn't posses political capital." His strong words are echoed by former U.S. senator and ambassador to New Zealand Carol Moseley-Braun (D-IL), who spoke out about the general neglect of poor and underprivileged citizens in New Orleans: "I think it's a sin of omission more than anything. They don't see poor people. They don't even think about them, they don't plan for them. How do you tell people to evacuate and then turn your back on those who don't have money for cab fare or who don't have cars?" (quoted in Cole, 2005, p. 368)

Summing up the general sentiment of the day, Rev. George Clements, a Catholic priest who founded the One Church, One Family effort to care for storm survivors, stated:

> [Bush said] "The storm didn't discriminate and neither will [the recovery effort]." Well ... then why were 95 percent of the poor people [displaced by the storm] black? ... People ask, "When did all of this business about Hurricane Katrina and the fact that there were so many black victims start?" And I tell everybody it started in 1619 when those first slaves got to Jamestown. (quoted on The Cliff Kelly Show, WVON-AM 1450, Chicago)

Consider for a moment the Superdome during Katrina as a transient site for the mediation of blackness in the United States: For a few fleeting days during and after the storm, the

Superdome—home to the New Orleans Saints professional football team, as well as many Super Bowls and other major sporting events—found itself officiating between two seemingly warring camps about "urban" blackness: the story of productive black bodies disciplined through sport to entertain and profit privileged fans and owners, and that of undisciplined black bodies that threaten the social good and burden the U.S. economy (Cole & Giardina, forthcoming). That is to say, although stories of heartfelt suffering, struggle, tragedy, and rescue rang out from all corners of the Gulf Coast region, this narrative was countered by a narrative of upheaval signaled by the apparent breakdown of law and order in the Superdome that rendered visible a long familiar trope in the United States: the always-already pathologized bodies of black men were used to signal "incomprehensible crimes" (Cole & Giardina, 2005, p. 4).

Stories about rape and gang violence in and around the Superdome abounded (although largely exaggerated and/or unfounded)—to listen to cable news reports, a *Mad Max*–meets–*New Jack City* shroud had become draped over a dark, twisted, evil city languishing in chaos. Other reports about "roving [black] gangs" and [black] "snipers" were given cultural purchase across the spectrum of broadcast and print media. For example, on his highly viewed neoconservative propaganda vehicle on Fox News Channel, *The O'Reilly Factor*, host Bill O'Reilly (2005) blatantly inferred that the majority of NOLA's Katrina victims—particularly those caught in the Superdome—were uneducated, poor drug addicts who lived a "gangsta" lifestyle akin to that of the *Grand Theft Auto* video game world:

> Every American kid should be required to watch videotape of the poor in New Orleans and see how they suffered, because they couldn't get out of town. And then, every teacher should tell the students, "If you refuse to learn, if you refuse to work hard, if you become addicted, if you live a gangsta-life, you will be poor and powerless just like many of those in New Orleans."[11]

Yet the story "on the ground," as it were, never quite seemed to match up with what was being reported or televised. As *Washington Post* columnist Eugene Robinson (2005) was quick to point out, the prevailing mediated pedagogy dominating the

Katrina landscape just wasn't true in an empirical reality:

> I got there five days after the deluge, when the story, as the whole world understood it, was one of *Mad Max* depravity and violence. Hoodlums were raping and pillaging, I just "knew"—even shooting at rescue helicopters trying to take hospital patients to safety. So it was a surprise when I rolled into the center of the city, with all my foreign-correspondent antennae bristling, and found the place as quiet as a tomb. The next day I drove into the French Quarter and was struck by how pristine St. Louis Cathedral looked, almost like the castle at Disney World. I got out of the car and walked around the whole area, and I wrote in my notebook that except for the absence of tourists, it could have been just an ordinary Sunday morning in the Big Easy. Then I got back into the car, and on the radio a caller was breathlessly reporting that, as she spoke, a group of policemen were "pinned down" by snipers at the cathedral. I was right there; nobody was sniping at anybody. But the reigning narrative was *Mad Max*, not Magic Kingdom. Thanks to radio, television and the Internet, everyone "knew" things that just weren't true. (p. A23)[12]

However, as Ezra Klein (2005) cogently explicates, it isn't enough to simply point out that incendiary news coverage was just spotty work done by lazy or inept reporters. He states,

> Those horror stories, now proved [mostly] untrue, were not simply mistaken, they were racist. From the widely reported but never confirmed rapes in the Superdome all the way to the false accounts of sniped rescue workers and roving gangs of looting blacks, Katrina exposed a latent cultural racism that many Americans assumed had vanished. These were tropes more suited to the Deep South of the 1800s than the cable networks of the 21st century.

In working through and unmasking this latent, systemic cultural racism, we must reject outright such outlandish claims that the people of New Orleans brought this tragedy on themselves, or that those who did not have the means to vacate lacked "values." Alongside O'Reilly in the domain of public demagoguery, Senator Rick Santorum (R-PA) heartlessly suggested *punishing* those who are unable to leave a disaster-stricken area, when he stated, "I mean, you have people who don't heed those warnings and then put people at risk as a result of not heeding those warnings. So there may be a need to look at tougher penalties, candidly, on those who decide to ride it out and understand there are consequences to not leaving" (quoted in Hamill, 2005).

Likewise, we must also be mindful of the disturbing corollary to Rep. Baker's aforementioned theo-conservative "blame-the-victim" statement that, in effect, "God cleaned up public housing in NOLA": A nationwide poll of 1,003 Americans conducted several weeks after Katrina hit found that 23% of Americans believe that "hurricanes are a deliberate act of God" (see also Miller, 2006).[13] This absurd implication—that Katrina was a deliberate, punitive act by God unleashed against the citizens of NOLA—was propagated en masse by those on the far right, such as Michael Marcavage (2005), director of Repent America (a Philadelphia-based ministry), who stated in a press release: "Although the loss of lives [*sic*] is deeply saddening, this act of God destroyed a wicked city. From 'Girls Gone Wild' to 'Southern Decadence,' New Orleans was a city that had its doors wide open to the public celebration of sin" (Marcavage, 2005).

Rev. Bill Shanks, pastor of the New Covenant Fellowship of New Orleans, touched a similar chord:

> New Orleans now is abortion free. New Orleans now is Mardi Gras free. New Orleans now is free of Southern Decadence and the sodomites, the witchcraft workers, false religion—it's free of all of those things now. .... God simply, I believe, in His mercy purged all of that stuff out of there—and now we're going to start over again. (quoted in Brown & Martin, 2005)

And, not to be outdone, Pat Robertson claimed on his September 12 broadcast of *The 700 Club* cable program that Katrina was punishment for the "legalization of abortion."[14]

This attitude simply cannot continue to go unchallenged in the public discourse without dire consequences for the popular-public sphere. As Cole and Giardina (2005) have argued, the blame-the-victim narrative so prevalent in the immediate aftermath is symptomatic of yet another form of protecting the white public from so-called damaging media images—it is the story that will salvage white American innocence and allow for a cathartic adventure experience in place of activism to change the historical and political circumstances that led to such a crisis in the first place. (p. 9). This narrative is unacceptable. We can do better than this.

Jenny left the clothing section to find a place with her family among the rows of wooden picnic-style tables to rest and enjoy a hot meal of chili and cornbread prepared by a disaster relief group from Oklahoma. She had a quiet grace about herself—a spirit of resilience in the face of despair. Her story had struck a chord in my innermost being: Jenny was unassuming and unselfish; she wanted only pants for her grandson, even though she herself had nothing left. I just stood there for a few minutes, caught in a rush of emotions, thoughts swirling in my soul. I rushed out of the clothing area, heart a-flutter, scanning the tables for the elderly woman in a lime green short-sleeve shirt who had shared a bit of her life story with me, a twenty-something physical therapist forty-plus years her junior.

I found her in the middle of the gym with her son and grandson. "Can I have just one minute of your time?" I asked her.

A look of distant puzzlement crossed over the weariness that was so apparent in our first meeting, but she followed me over to the side of the gym anyway.

"Look ... umm ... the reason I came here ... I'm not sure if ... you see ... uh ..." I stuttered, sounding more like an awkward middle-schooler than the strong-willed, independent-minded grownup the latest faux-feminist Nike commercial tells me I should be.

"What I mean is ..." I sighed, finally finding my composure lost amid the sea of grief. "A friend of mine wanted to help someone out on a more personal level than just donating some money to a big charity. She wanted it to go to a person. So she gave me some money... and ... well ... I know that you've been through so much, and this will only help for a little while ... but would you be offended if I offered it to you?"

She stood there, silent.

(I stood there, nervous.)

Gradually, a smile crept ever so slowly across her face to her eyes. The commotion around us continued, but in that moment, Jenny, an elderly woman from New Orleans, and I, a young, professional woman from Maryland who knew very little of what it meant to be in need ... connected. Our gazes locked, and the outside world evaporated in on the moment.

"Thank you," she whispered, barely audibly.

I handed her the thick fold of $20 bills. She accepted it with outstretched hands, her eyes welling up with tears. She reached up and hugged me. Held me.

"Thank you. Thank you. Thank you. Thank you," she repeated over and over again. As we slowly broke our embrace, she looked at me and whispered something once again: "God bless you." Tears began to spill from my eyes, overwhelming me. The doubts I had had about having even a small—yet potential personal—effect on someone seemed to melt away, warmed by the smiling eyes of a woman I didn't even know.

I couldn't possibly hope to replace all that Jenny had lost; it would have been an exercise in shallow self-aggrandizement to think so. I'd like to think that I was able to offer her hope and compassion, a belief that we're not all cold-hearted yuppies turning our backs on the open wound of poverty, racism, classism, and crony capitalism that Katrina ripped open live on television for the whole world to see. I'd like to think that maybe—somehow—my contribution (and that of my friend who initiated the process)—my attempt at being present to the scene—might possibly have helped Jenny start to rebuild some small portion of her family's life. Maybe it illustrated that God could act through a stranger. Maybe it just helped get her through the day. I'll never really know. But as Julie Delpy said to Ethan Hawke in *Before Sunrise*, the answer must be in the attempt, right?

What I do know is this, however: In that moment of unexpected connection, we were no longer just a seventy-something African American woman from New Orleans and a twenty-something white woman from Annapolis; we were witnesses to hope.

Eventually, the days since my encounter with Jenny waned, and I returned to my comfortable existence where there were no ravaged houses, uprooted trees, or emergency shelters. I was no longer immediately surrounded by the sheer amount of public despair and need (though it was clearly still there, shielded by comfortable everyday lives at the local Starbucks). However, the impact of those brief few minutes shared with another human being remains burned to my core, as I was able to stand as witness to the unflinching spirit of hope and human dignity in the face of tragedy, revealed in the eyes of someone I didn't know but who could just as easily have been my own grandmother ... or yours.

"If Not Us, Then Who?"

As the days following Katrina turned into weeks and the weeks into months, two more powerful hurricanes slammed into the southern coast of the United States. This time, the discourse was in place, the hero-narratives well planned. Law and order was back up and running (allegedly), organized (allegedly). News reports focused on federal help that actually managed to arrive.[15] Racial issues, of course, were soon ignored once again in the mainstream media. (The running "joke" becoming, "Well, two weeks for a national conversation on race seems about right.") Mainstream discussions about poverty and class silently receded into the mist as attention was once again focused on such pressing infotainment issues as the Tom Cruise–Katie Holmes marriage, supermodel Kate Moss's arrest on drug charges, or Terrell Owens's suspension from the Philadelphia Eagles football team.[16]

Yet for the people living in Louisiana, theirs was and is a very different reality. One that, although epically tragic, somehow still offers hope—a vision of the future, perhaps—of the joining together of hands in the negotiation of race, class, and gender issues at the local level. As Mike Davis and Anthony Fontenot (2005) revealed at the time:

> The folks of Ville Platte, a poor Cajun and black Creole community [in Louisiana] with a median income less than half that of the rest of the nation, have opened their doors over the past three weeks to more than 5,000 of the displaced people they call "company" (the words "refugee" and "evacuee" are considered too impersonal, even impolite). Local fishermen and hunters, moreover, were among the first volunteers to take boats into New Orleans to rescue desperate residents from their flooded homes. Ville Platte's homemade rescue and relief effort—organized around the popular slogan "If not us, then who?"—stands in striking contrast to the incompetence of higher levels of government as well as to the hostility of other, wealthier towns, including some white suburbs of New Orleans, toward influxes of evacuees, especially poor people of color. Indeed, Evangeline Parish as a whole has become a surprising island of interracial solidarity and self-organization in a state better known for incorrigible racism and corruption. What makes Ville Platte and some of its neighboring communities so

exceptional? ... There is a shared, painful recognition that the land is rapidly sinking and dying, as much from the onslaught of corporate globalization as from climate wrath. (p. 6)

Against a multifaceted onslaught ranging from corporate globalization and inept political machinery to global warming and the undercurrents of economic despair, this literal realization of a performative popular-public sphere (see Giardina, 2005) in which the promise of common citizens once again participating with hands joined forward in their common future—coming together in common cause to "forge a new American Century from the bottom up" (Trippi, 2004, p. 125)—gave us (some) reason to be hopeful.[17]

A year on, New Orleans remained an empty shell of its past glory. As Spike Lee's (Lee & Nevins, 2006) powerful documentary *When the Levees Broke* so dramatically detailed, decomposed bodies were still being pulled from the wreckage; garbage and debris remained strewn in the streets; the local economy was faltering. To mark the one-year anniversary, President Bush spun empty platitudes about how the hurricane launched "a moment of great sadness" and how "although a year has gone by, it's really the beginning of the renewal and rebuilding" (MSNBC, 2006).

Yet it was poet Andre Codrescu (2006)—not Bush—who offered perhaps the most spot-on commentary of the yearlong fiasco when he states

Katrina was just a storm, but what followed was so hideous that one year later, we can only shake our heads and vomit. ... In the space of one year, our commander in chief has evolved from a flyover disaster to a profligate dispenser of cash ... [in which] the only thing wrong with the vast billions that are supposedly heading our way is that they may actually be handed out in the form of checks instead of being thrown down from helicopters so the groveling masses can wrestle for them like a proper Mardi Gras crowd [because] hurling cash into the streets would, in fact, be a much more equitable way of dispensing treasure than handing it over to people like Congressman Jefferson or a mayor who has been invisible to us since his re-election. (p. 1)

Contra Bush, and in the spirit of Codrescu's stinging narrative, the words of Howard Dean's (2006a) address marking the Katrina anniversary set the stage to help us begin to imagine an alternative to the sorrows of the Bush imperium, of the divisiveness knocking on our door[18]:

> Katrina was a terrible tragedy, not just for New Orleans and Mississippi, not just for the people who died or still have not been able to move home. Katrina was a tragedy for America. ... [W]hat we experienced a year ago was not just the personal loss and tragedy to all of our lives, because so many of us knew people or had family in New Orleans or Mississippi. ... [S]eeing, unmasked, the incompetence, and failures, and indifference, of the president and the Republican majority, we need a new direction for America where no one is left behind!
>
> The American people are extraordinary people. What we saw was great acts of generosity, and courage and heroism, of people coming together and opening their hearts, reaching out to help one another. That reminds us that the American people will transcend the incompetence of our leaders. We need a new direction where we are as competent and fair and qualified and caring as the American people showed themselves to be a year ago. We can do better. We will have a new direction of hope and opportunity in America, based on the idea that we are all in this together. Not just those in the Democratic Party, not just those in urban America. We will reach out to those who disagree with us, we will reach out to Evangelical Christians, to rural Americans, we are all in this together. It is time to end the divisiveness.

Afterword: Toward a Politics of Hope?

The response to Katrina was effectively the end to the President's presidency in the sense that people all of a sudden saw the small man behind the curtain.

—Howard Dean, 2006b[19]

Let's take stock. It is now three years and a few months since Katrina came ashore. A few weeks ago, Barack Obama was sworn in as the 44th president of the United States. Wars in Iraq and

Afghanistan still wage on. The economy is in a deep recession the likes of which haven't been witnessed for decades, resulting in the politically charged passage of a nearly $1 trillion stimulus package. The banking sector is in disarray, as is the crumbling U.S. auto industry. Political scandals abound, ensnaring members of both parties (e.g., Blagojevich in Illinois, Richardson in New Mexico, Coleman in Minnesota, etc.). Yet it is Katrina that Matthew Dowd, Bush's pollster and chief strategist for the 2004 presidential campaign, returned to most notably in a retrospective interview given to the *Village Voice* about the eight-year reign and the moment when the wheels came flying off:

> Katrina to me was the tipping point. ... The president broke his bond with the public. Once that bond was broken, he no longer had the capacity to talk to the American public. State of the Union addresses? It didn't matter. Legislative initiatives? It didn't matter. Public relations? It didn't matter. Travel? It didn't matter.

———

We face an uncertain future. This much is true. But there is hope. In an Obama administration, yes, to a degree. But more so in the sheer number of people—especially young people—who became involved (some might say enthralled) with the campaign for change waged by Obama on his way to assuming the presidency. In corners near and far, social activism is on the rise, especially as related to politics, of becoming active participants once again in public debate. The feelings are noticeable, palpable. It's our job as scholars and educators to foster those feelings, before it's too late.

Notes

1. This chapter extends and revises slightly Michael D. Giardina and Laura A. Hess (now Vaughan), 2007.

2. *The New York Times,* among other media outlets, reprinted former FEMA Director Michael Brown's shocking e-mails from the time New Orleans was first under siege. These e-mails contained, among other statements, Brown telling one staffer the following: "If you'll look at my lovely FEMA

attire you'll really vomit. I am a fashion god [*sic*]. ... Anything specific I need to do or tweak? Do you know of anyone who dog-sits? ... Can I quit now? Can I come home? ... I'm trapped now, please rescue me." The disregard for human life by Brown et al. was further typified by his bizarre statement on September 1, 2005: "Considering the dire circumstances that we have in New Orleans, virtually a city that has been destroyed, things are going relatively well."

3. After introducing Sen. Landrieu (D-LA), Cooper immediately asked her, "Does the federal government bear responsibility for what is happening now? Should they apologize for what is happening now?" Landrieu responded, "[T]here will be plenty of time to discuss those issues," and she proceeded to begin thanking various government officials for their disaster relief support. Cooper then interrupted her and passionately stated the following:

> Senator, I'm sorry ... for the last four days, I have been seeing dead bodies here in the streets of Mississippi and to listen to politicians thanking each other and complimenting each other—I have to tell you, there are people here who are very upset and angry, and when they hear politicians thanking one another, it just, you know, it cuts them the wrong way right now, because there was a body on the streets of this town yesterday being eaten by rats because this woman has been laying in the street for 48 hours, and there is not enough facilities to get her up. Do you understand that anger? ... There are people that want answers, and people want someone to stand up and say: "We should have done more."

4. The name was changed; also, it is our homage to Paul McCartney (who likewise borrowed the name for his 2005 song of the same name from Charles Dickens's novel *Our Mutual Friend*). Those familiar with the Dickens novel will appreciate the inclusion of the name here.

5. Relatedly, when Bush proposed $62 billion in emergency reconstruction aid for New Orleans alone, a question remained as to where the funds were going to come from. Would there be across-the-board tax increases? Cuts in defense spending? Perhaps getting out of Iraq a bit earlier (and merely transferring Halliburton's accounts to the Gulf Coast)? True to form, the president was vague in answering such a question. However, the Cato Institute, a right-wing think tank heavily favored by the Bush administration, would have none of that talk about tax increases or cutting funds from other areas of defense spending (such as the $5.3 billion per month spent in Iraq). Instead, policy analysts such as Chris Edwards and Stephen Slivinski proposed:

> cutting NASA in half, slashing energy research and subsidies just as Congress [was] gearing up to increase them in the face of soaring gasoline prices, cutting the U.S. Army Corps of Engineers' budget by

$4.6 billion after its levees failed to protect New Orleans, and eliminating $4.2 billion in homeland security grants while lawmakers are debating the nation's lack of preparedness. (Weisman & VandeHei, 2005, p. A01)

6. Yes it was. On September 1, 2005, Grieve of *The Houston Chronicle* reported that the U.S. Navy had hired Houston-based Halliburton to restore electric power, repair roofs, and remove debris at three naval facilities in Mississippi damaged by Hurricane Katrina.

7. And still, twelve weeks after Katrina hit, "no one [had] an answer to where people [who want to return to NOLA] should go. An estimated 80,000 homes had no insurance, and for now, the biggest grant a family can get from the federal government is $26,200" (CBS.com, 2005).

8. As "tourist bubbles" or "islands of affluence," these rewritten, whitewashed landscapes actively work to "project a reassuringly dislocated experience and perception of safety, fun, and vitality for downtown areas" (Eisinger, 2000, p. 318). Sarah Vowell (2003) got it right when she said, "There are few creepier moments in cultural tourism than when a site tries to rewrite its past" (p. 36).

9. For more, see Ford and Gamble's (2005) "New Orleans Citizen's Bill of Rights."

10. According to the 2000 census, the per capita annual income for Whites in New Orleans, $31,971, was $10,000 higher than the national average. The per capita income for African Americans, $11,332, was $10,000 less than the national average. This $20,000 gap between white and black residents of New Orleans compared to a gap of less than $10,000 nationwide.

11. This sharp divide of public opinion toward "black" and "white" survivors was vividly captured in the main of America's popular-public sphere when *Agence-France Presse* and the *Associated Press* news agencies became embroiled in a case of image captioning that set off a mini firestorm of debate. The first photo, from *Agence-France Press*, highlighted a picture of two white individuals (a man and a woman) wading through water carrying bags of food with the description: "Two residents wade through chest-deep water after finding bread and soda from a local grocery store after Hurricane Katrina came through the area in New Orleans, Louisiana" (WikiNews Service, 2005). The second photo, from the *Associated Press*, highlighted a picture of an African American man carrying similar items with the description "A young man walks through chest-deep flood water after looting a grocery store in New Orleans on Tuesday, Aug. 30, 2005."

12. At least they weren't true in the sense of what was being reported. More than three years later, for example, a report by *The Nation's* A. C. Thompson (2008) revealed how white vigilante groups "patrolled" the streets (especially in Algiers Point) in the days after Katrina and hit and shot at least eleven black men "like it was pheasant season in South Dakota."

13. It is important to point out that the division between income/education levels and responses is quite stark: 31% of respondents with a high school diploma or less reported believing that hurricanes are a deliberate act of God (compared with 61% who said no), whereas only 11% of those with a college degree or higher reported believing hurricanes are a deliberate act of God (79% said no). (The keyword here is *deliberate*.)

14. With this context in mind, we side with Rev. Dr. Maurice O. Wallace (2005) in being "grievously troubled by the popularity of a commercial Christianity that romanticizes ... faith for the sake of capital campaigns, political favor and box office receipts." See also DailyKos.com (2006), which touches on similar themes related to right-wing political organization, theocratic nationalism, and the commercialization of religion in the United States.

15. That such a development as the federal government doing something adequately was hailed as a resounding success is perhaps the clearest indication of the disaster of the Bush years.

16. Despite the ineffectual mainstream media, which has since all but forgotten about Katrina other than in package-reports about the failures of the Bush administration, critical scholars have had much to say on the matter. See, for example, Henry Giroux's (2006b) *Stormy Weather: Katrina and the Politics of Disposability*; David Brunsma's (2007) *The Sociology of Katrina: Perspectives on a Modern Catastrophe*; Chester Hartman and Gregory D. Squires's (2007) *There Is No Such Thing as a Natural Disaster: Race, Class, and Hurricane Katrina*; Michael Eric Dyson's (2006) *Come Hell or High Water: Hurricane Katrina and the Color of Disaster*; and the South End Press Collective's (2007) *What Lies Beneath: Katrina, Race, and the State of the Nation*. See also Naomi Klein's (2007) *The Shock Doctrine: The Rise of Disaster Capitalism*, for more on the impact of neoliberalism on the privatization of post-Katrina New Orleans.

17. How we go about enacting such politics of transformation is at the core of Denzin and Giardina's (2006) book of essays *Contesting Empire/ Globalizing Dissent: Cultural Studies after 9/11*. They argue that we need "critical, humane discourses that create sacred and spiritual spaces for person and their moral communities—spaces where people can express and give meaning" (p. 4) to the world around them. In so doing, they outline a four-pronged strategy for a repositioned cultural studies project organized around the moral clarity and political intervention (i.e., a focus on the personal and the biographical, the launching of critical discourse at the level of the media and the ideological, the fostering of a critical international conversation that helps us develop a contextual theory of radical politics and social democracy, and the enacting of critical interpretive methodologies that can help us make sense of life in an age of the hyperreal, the simulacra, TV wars, staged media events, and the like). Such a project embraces a public intellectualism on the order of Noam Chomsky's 1967

article "The Responsibility of Intellectuals," in which he argues that we (i.e., you, dear reader) have a moral and professional obligation to speak the truth, expose lies, and see events in their historical perspective.

18. In this vein, it is fair to say that Howard Dean anticipated Barack Obama's general election strategy and is perhaps philosophically the one person outside of Obama's inner-circle most responsible for shaping the public tenor of the Democrats grassroots, bottom-up message (Berman, 2008). As Joe Trippi argued, since 1960, "only two [candidates] have been bottom-up. One was Dean. The other was Obama." That the Washington establishment has seemingly ostracized Dean is testament to his critical voice for change.

19. Once again, Dean's comment was right on the money. It took until December 2008 for former Bush administration officials to admit the same. Added Dan Bartlett, former White House communications director and later counselor to the president: "Politically, it was the final nail in the coffin."

References

Babington, C. (2005). Some GOP legislators hit jarring notes in addressing Katrina. *Washington Post.* Available online at http://www.washington-post.com/wp-dyn/content/article/2005/09/09/AR2005090901930.html (accessed September 11, 2005).

Berman, A. (2008). The Dean legacy. *The Nation.* Available online at http://www.thenation.com/doc/20080317/berman (accessed March 1, 2008).

Brown, J., & Martin, A. (2005). New Orleans' residents: God's mercy evident in Katrina's wake. AgapePress.com. Available online at http://headlines.agapepress.org/ archive/9/22005b.asp (accessed September 17, 2005).

Brunsma, D. (2007). *The sociology of Katrina: Perspectives on a modern catastrophe.* Lanham, MD: Roman & Littlefield.

CBS.com. (2005). New Orleans is sinking. Available online at http://www.cbsnews.com/stories/2005/11/18/60minutes/main1056304_page2.shtml (accessed November 22, 2005).

Chomsky, N. (1967). The responsibility of intellectuals. *The New York Review of Books* (Special Supplement), 8(3). Available online at http://www.nybooks.com/articles/12172 (accessed December 1, 2008).

CNN.com. (2005). A big disconnect in New Orleans. Available online at http://www.cnn.com/2005/US/09/02/katrina.response/ (accessed September 3, 2005).

Codrescu, A. (2006). Mourning for a flooded crescent city. NPR Radio. Available online at http://www.poynter.org/column. asp?id=52&aid=109898 (accessed September 7, 2006).

Cole, C. L. (2001). Nike goes Broadway. *Journal of Sport & Social Issues*, 25(2), 115–117.

Cole, C. L. (2005). Katrina's wake-up call. *Journal of Sport & Social Issues*, 29(4), 367–368.

Cole, C. L., & Giardina, M. D. (2005). Revelation at the Super Dome: The "other" America. Paper presented at the annual conference of the North American Society for the Sociology of Sport, October 26–29, Winston-Salem, North Carolina.

Cole, C. L., & Giardina, M. D. (forthcoming). Revelation at the Super Dome: Race, class, and neoliberalism in America. In D. L. Andrews & M. L. Silk (Eds.), *Sport and neoliberalism*. Philadelphia: Temple University Press.

DailyKos.com. (2005). The wound of Katrina slowly festers. Available online at http://www.dailykos.com/story/2005/11/21/152843/01 (accessed November 22. 2005).

DailyKos.com. (2006). Six Flags over Jesus. Blog entry by redmcclain. Available online at http://www.dailykos.com/story/2006/5/29/193711/698 (accessed May 29, 2006).

Davis, M., & Fontenot, A. (2005). Hurricane gumbo. *The Nation*. Available online at http://www.thenation.com/doc/20051107/davis/6 (accessed October 26, 2005).

Dean, H. (2006a). Speech to the Democratic National Committee, August 18, Chicago, Illinois.

Dean, H. (2006b). Interview with Wolf Blitzer. Cable News Network, August 23.

Denzin, N. K., & Giardina, M. D. (Eds.). (2006). *Contesting empire, globalizing dissent: Cultural studies after 9/11*. Boulder, CO: Paradigm.

DuBose, B. (2005). HUD chief foresees a "whiter" Big Easy. *The Washington Times*. Available online at http://www.commondreams.org/headlines05/0930-07.htm (accessed October 5, 2005).

Duke Magazine (2005). In Katrina's aftermath, Duke responds. Available online at http://www.dukemagazine.duke.edu/dukemag/issues/111205/depgaz2.html (accessed June 13, 2006).

Dyson, M. R. (2006). *Come hell or high water: Hurricane Katrina and the color of disaster*. New York: Basic Civitas Books.

Eisinger, P. (2000). The politics of bread and circuses: Building the city of the visitor class. *Urban Affairs Review*, 35, 316–333.

Ford, G., & Gamble, P. (2005). The battle for New Orleans: Only a real movement can win this war. *The Black Commentator*. Available online at http://www.blackcommentator.com/156/156_cover_battle_for_no.html (accessed November 4, 2005).

Friedman, M., Andrews, D. L., & Silk, M. L. (2004). Sport and the façade of redevelopment in the postindustrial city. *Sociology of Sport Journal*, 21(2), 119–139.

Giardina, M. D. (2005). *Sporting pedagogies: Performing culture & identity in the global arena*. New York: Peter Lang.

Giardina, M. D. & Hess, L. A. (2007). If not us, then who? Performing pedagogies of hope in post-Katrina America. *Cultural Studies/Critical Methodologies*, 7(2), 169–187.

Giroux, H. (2006a). Katrina and the politics of disposability. In These Times, available online at http://www.inthesetimes.com/article/2822/ (accessed January 4, 2009).

Giroux, H. (2006b). *Stormy weather: Katrina and the politics of disposability*. Boulder, CO: Paradigm.

Grieve, T. (2005). Halliburton gets its share, where has Cheney been? Salon. com. Available online at from http://www.salon.com/politics/war_room/2005/09/03/halliburton/index.html (accessed September 10, 2005).

Hamill, S. D. (2005). Santorum retreats on evacuation penalty remarks. *The Post-Gazette* (Pittsburgh). Available online at http://www.postgazette.com/pg/05250/566844.stm (accessed September 10, 2005).

Hartman, C. & Squires, G. D. (2007). *There is no such thing as a natural disaster: Race, class, and Hurricane Katrina*. London: Routledge.

Kalette, D. (2005). Dean: Race played a role in Katrina deaths. *The Associated Press*. Available online at http://www.breitbart.com/news/2005/09/07/D8CFNMPG0.html (accessed September 10, 2005).

Kelly, C. (2005). *The Cliff Kelly Show*. WVON-AM 1450. Chicago, September 14.

King, S. J. (2005). Sport culture, the "War on Terror," and the emergence of jockocracy. Paper presented at the annual conference for the North American Society for the Sociology of Sport, October 26–29, Winston-Salem, North Carolina.

Klein, E. (2005). The media of 100 years ago, today. *The American Prospect Online*. Available online at http://www.prospect.org/archives/archives/2005/10/index.html (accessed November 4, 2005).

Klein, N. (2007). *The shock doctrine: The rise of disaster capitalism*. New York: Picador.

Ladson-Billings, G. (2002). Egon Guba distinguished lecture. Presented at the annual meeting of the American Educational Research Association, April 25–27, New Orleans.

Lee, S. (Director) & Nevins, S. (Executive Producer). (2006). *When the levees broke: A requiem in four acts.* United States: 40 Acres & a Mule Filmworks (in association with Home Box Office).

Marcavage, M. (2005). Hurricane Katrina destroys New Orleans days before "Southern Decadence." *Repent America.* Available online at http://www. repentamerica.com/pr_hurricanekatrina.html (accessed September 15, 2005).

Mele, C. (2000). *Selling the lower east side: Culture, real estate, and resistance in New York City.* New York: New York University Press.

Miller, T. (2006). The American people cannot be trusted. In N. K. Denzin & M. D. Giardina (Eds.), *Contesting empire, globalizing dissent: Cultural studies after 9/11,* pp. 121–135. Boulder, CO: Paradigm.

MSNBC. (2006). Bush sees rebirth from "sadness" of Katrina: As bells toll on anniversary, President says New Orleans "still a mess." Available online at http://www.msnbc.msn.com/id/14567350/ (accessed September 3, 2006).

Neal, M. A. (2005). Race-ing Katrina. *NewBlackMan.* Available online at from http://newblackman.blogspot.com/2005/09/race-ing-katrina.html (accessed September 17, 2005).

Obama, B. (2005). Speech on the floor of the United States Senate. Washington, DC, September 13.

O'Reilly, B. (2005). *The O'Reilly Factor.* Available online at http://www.pfaw. org/pfaw/general/default.aspx?oid=19453 (accessed November 4, 2005).

Robinson, E. (2005). Instant revisionism. *Washington Post,* October 7, p. A23.

South End Press Collective. (2007). *What lies beneath: Katrina, race, and the state of the nation.* Boston: South End Press.

Thompson, A. C. (2008). Katrina's hidden race war. The Nation. Available online at http://www.thenation.com/doc/20090105/thompson (accessed December 21, 2008).

Trippi, J. (2004). *The revolution will not be televised: Democracy, the Internet, and the overthrow of everything.* New York: Regan Books.

Vowell, S. (2003). *The partly cloudy patriot.* New York: Simon & Schuster.

Wallace, M. O. (2005). "Our tsunami": Race, religion and mourning in Louisiana, Mississippi, and Alabama. *NewBlackMan.* Available online at http://newblackman.blogspot.com/2005/09/our-tsunami-race-religion-andmourning.html (accessed September 10, 2005).

Weisman, J., & VandeHei, J. (2005). Bush to request more aid funding: Analysts warn of spending's impact. *The Washington Post.* Available online at http://www.washingtonpost.com/wp-dyn/content/article/2005/09/14/AR2005091402654_pf.html (accessed September 17, 2005).

WikiNews Service. (2005). Controversy over New Orleans photo captions. Available online at http://en.wikinews.org/wiki/Controversy_over_New_Orleans_photos_captions (accessed September 5, 2005).

Chapter 7

Power-Shifting at the Speed of Light
Critical Qualitative Research Post-Disaster

Gaile S. Cannella
Tulane University

Michelle S. Perez
Arizona State University

Everyone is familiar with the critical reactions to hurricanes Katrina and Rita in 2005, whether related to the slow response of the U.S. government to life/death circumstances; the racism, classism, and sexism that have been evident in recovery plans; or recent colonialist discourses that characterize a diverse city like New Orleans as a den of violence (Denzin, 2007; Giardina & Hess, 2007; Kellner, 2007; Troutt, 2007). "Saviors" have traveled to disaster locations around the United States to sell manufactured housing, corporatize public schools in the name of recovery and achievement, or study the "psychological effects" of disaster experiences. Further, as various stakeholders and others interact within a context that fosters the fusion of physical/emotional survival with corporatization/profiteering, the dire circumstance can result in the shifting of power that is irregular, constant, and unpredictable.

Post-Katrina New Orleans is a case that illustrates these unpredictable and continued power shifts (a circumstance that accelerates even Foucault's notion of the complexity of power that produces and is produced). Yet, actions following hurricanes Katrina and Rita are probably not unique; devastating disastrous events and circumstances around the globe are increasingly serving as locations in which power shifts at the speed of light, in which privilege and counter-democratic discourses and agendas are so swiftly imposed that our research perspectives and methodologies fail to notice until it is too late.

Qualitative researchers can be faced with data collection that is erroneous, illusive, and misleading as all forms of "knowing" are challenged. Although critical work brings to light new and/or reinscribed forms of oppression and social injustices under such circumstances, the revelations are often too late to counter newly created structures, discourses, and privileged ways of interpreting and approaching problems. Catastrophic, disastrous circumstances can/may lead to problem identification and solving in which critique is prohibited because of the immediacy required for survival. This chapter focuses on the need for critical qualitative research methodologies that respond to pressing immediate circumstances (that may even be direct and physical) while, at the same time, unmasking and making "public" stealth power maneuvers when those with privilege would use survival and urgency to accelerate and advance their own agendas.

Post-Disaster New Orleans: Examples of Power Shifting

As individuals who have now lived in New Orleans for almost two years beginning in 2007, we want to first provide examples of the multiple instances of urgency and stealth power maneuvers that we have experienced in daily life. We must admit that these experiences are both personal and professional, as we have attempted to determine how we work as researchers and scholars in a location that has literally been referred to as a "great experiment." Although qualitative and critical work has been the focus of our professional practices for many years, when whole communities—individuals, families, children, schools, neighborhoods, churches, even businesses—are referred to as an experiment, we question the moral agendas behind the discourse (as well as the appropriateness of gathering data ourselves for publication).

Even our qualitative data collection and analysis methods that would recognize the social and collaborative construction of naturalistic and ethnographic work with community members cannot represent the complexity of lives that have been turned upside-down and are continually disrupted; we have questioned the American-Eurocentric error (Jaimes, 1992) that assumes we can know what's in the "minds" of "others" even without the dire circumstance of disaster. Yet, we know there are people who are not being heard, who need help, and are being ignored—how should we function as researchers during such urgent circumstances? As critical scholars and pedagogues, we have learned to be suspicious of power and privilege (both hierarchically and infused) and to recognize that urgent circumstances may facilitate great advantage for those with resources and institutional power, while disproportionately harming, labeling, and discrediting groups and individuals who were already victims of societal injustices (even before the disaster occurred). However, critical research has most often taken time and involved historical analysis. Time and history are important components, but under conditions of urgency and shifting power, we must ask: When dire circumstances require immediate action for survival, can research be generated that makes "public" the multitude of hidden, and shifting power agendas before people and the institutions that serve them are, in the name of immediate assistance, permanently harmed and even eliminated?

Although Hurricane Katrina is, in national public discourses, referred to as a major disaster for the Gulf Coast (of the United States), dominant discourses rarely mention that the New Orleans disaster was not the storm, but flooding that poured water though man-made levees as well as lack of food and shelter for residents who were displaced and labeled as unprepared, looters, violent, and lazy. Although the flooding occurred on August 30 and supply trucks distributed food and water to stranded residents on September 2, as early as September 10, Republican congressman Richard Baker made the following comment: "We finally cleaned up public housing in New Orleans. We couldn't do it, but God did it" (quoted in Long, 2007, p. 795).[1] On September 13, 2005 (just two weeks after the storm, while residents continued to be displaced and disenfranchised), the Heritage Foundation (an U.S. conservative think-tank) hosted a meeting to create a list of ideas for responding to Hurricane Katrina to be used by President George W. Bush. The agenda included: suspension of Davis-Bacon federal living wage laws in times of disaster, waiving regulations in the region related to economic competition, and labeling the Katrina-affected area as a free-enterprise zone. Nonlocal funeral conglomerates were hired to retrieve bodies; local morticians were forbidden from handling them. Within weeks, Kellogg Brown & Root (now KBR, Inc.), then a subsidiary of Halliburton, received a $60 million reconstruction grant; private military contractor Blackwater USA (later known as Blackwater Worldwide, and rebranded later still as "Xe" on February 13, 2009) was hired to protect outside FEMA employees from "looters" in New Orleans; and all local unionized teachers were fired. Immigrants were hired as construction workers, yet paid little or nothing because they were awakened in the night and told to leave because they would be arrested. The Katrina/Rita Gulf Coast disaster area (and especially New Orleans) was created, using power maneuvers in the name of survival and urgency, as an Iraq-like green zone (Klein, 2007). One can imagine thousands of similar actions (not listed here) taken in the name of disaster survival and recovery between 2005 and 2007.

We now fast forward to fall 2007, because we each moved to New Orleans to begin the 2007–2008 academic year as part of our work. Without using interviews, focus groups, or well-designed document analyses, we have experienced the ways that disaster, and the use of disaster by particular groups, continue to impact the community. We are in education, so we'll use education examples. However, simply as part of daily life, we experience power shifting at the speed of light—and constructed in hidden and clandestine locations—in all areas that impact human beings, from the eradication of affordable housing, to the redeployment of tax payer money for corporate education agendas, to the absence of transportation and services that contribute to the public good.

By simply reading the newspaper, completing elementary school volunteer work, attending community meetings, and listening to conversations, we have experienced the following related to education:

- parents turned away when they took their children to the local neighborhood school on the first day;

- volunteer work in schools that involved gathering research data (rather than assisting children with learning) for scholars outside the area that asked questions to groups of children like "What did you lose in the storm?";

- closing of a school in November legitimated by using the rhetoric of environmental conditions that sent children to three different locations;
- more children expelled from a particular school in one academic year than graduated;
- public education discourses, committees, and boards controlled by local business leaders and private school interests;
- public conversations that advantage the creation of decentralized public schools;
- federal action that funds recovery grants tied to "choice" and "charter" schools while refusing to fund more traditional public orientations toward schooling;
- increased numbers of teachers without experience and requiring less pay from programs like Teach for America;
- eighty schools labeled as "public" run by twenty-nine different operators some of whom are corporate;
- silence regarding the city and state history that has supported private, religious schools;
- community leaders from a particular neighborhood visiting New York to request creation of a charter school by Edison (and a seeming lack of awareness regarding the general business and school operation failure of Edison; see Saltman, 2007); and
- surprise in the media that charter schools are having trouble providing special education services.

We could go on and on regarding education rhetoric and actions that are legitimated using the discourse that past New Orleans schools were failures, while ignoring the institutional racism, sexism, and power orientations that have generated past circumstances and supported a failure label. Further, this discourse uses the urgency of disaster, whether related to physical facilities or quality defined as high stakes tests, to convince the public that private, corporate choice is the only way to "save" children. Anyone who disagrees is labeled closed-minded, not current, uncaring, and/or unable to focus on the best interests of those in need.

Research methods that assume consistency and stability, whether related to human constructions or the location of power (however circulating or dispersed), are likely to overlook or even disregard power that is continually shifting and masked within locations that claim to rescue victims and make survivors the first priority. Even critical qualitative research methods that assume that social justice, power, and oppression should always be considered and that acknowledge power circulation can fail to comprehend accelerated power shifts that disperse resources and generate the acceptance of new forms of domination as public practice. The use of disaster as a form of social engineering creates a contemporary condition in which rethinking and reconceptualizing possibilities for critical research, and ways of disseminating that work, have never been more important.

Rethinking Critical Qualitative Research: Critical Pedagogies, Anti-Colonialist Social Sciences, and Recognizing Contemporary Agendas

Scholars from a range of perspectives and fields have pointed to the need for critical conceptualizations of research purposes and practices. Yet, this work has not usually challenged domination in everyday life. The context of disaster (whether natural or planned), and the possibilities for exploitation and radical social engineering generated by that context, results in a contemporary circumstance in which researchers must accelerate their own critical methodologies and rethink the purposes of those practices. This rethinking requires a "multilogical critical" research perspective and can employ methodological critical bricolage that becomes a multiperspectival process (Denzin & Lincoln, 2000; Kincheloe, 2001, 2005, 2008a, p. 4; Kincheloe & Berry, 2004). Further, anti-colonial understandings that would privilege egalitarian activist perspectives and support collective reciprocal relations (Cannella & Manuelito, 2008; Lincoln & Cannella, 2007) can facilitate this critical bricolage, which incorporates diversality with the recognition of the broader ideological, cultural, and political context (Kincheloe, 2008a, 2008b). This rethought research conceptualization would be especially useful for revealing circumstances that construct and promote cycles of disaster as well as conditions of exploitation, invisibility, and erasure from within disaster.

Critical Bricolage: Emergent and Immediate

Critical bricoleurs (Denzin & Lincoln, 2000) employ "theoretical dexterity" (Kincheloe, 2008a, p. 5), engaging with the multiple—like feminisms, poststructuralism, queer theory, and anti-colonial orientations as well as multiple methods like the variety of forms of textual analyses, ethnographic data collection, semiotics, "even dramatic and theatrical forms of observing and making meaning" (p. 4), and emergent methods like situational mapping and contextually generated researcher methods (Kincheloe, 2008a). In addition to multiple knowledges and methodologies, critical bricolage requires an intellectual agility and flexibility that facilitates revision of research conceptualizations and purposes as data is collected and analyzed. This dexterity can also respond to and critique the accuracy of conditions of urgency as they are "used" as forms of legitimation for immediate actions by those in power.

Kincheloe (2008a) describes critical bricolage as moving beyond interdisciplinarity into new conceptual domains. Deep understanding of theories and conceptual lenses from a range of life, geographic, and even power locations is considered necessary for the rigorous practice of critical bricolage. As researchers, critical bricoleurs use knowledges from the multiple, from those who have been disenfranchised and/or oppressed, from diverse experiential locations, to generate multidisciplinary insight along with a critical mode of self-awareness. Indigenous ways of knowing and knowledges that have been silenced by dominant Western ideologies are considered transformative. The critical bricoleur uses diverse worldviews to enhance the imagination and awareness regarding diverse circumstances and sociopolitical agendas and to learn to recognize power struggles and new forms of human suffering that either go unnoticed or are purposely ignored. Research purposes can be/are rethought from such multidisciplinary, "multilogical" (Kincheloe, 2008a, p. 5) locations. An example of this rethinking is the way that feminists of color and poststructuralists have used multidirectionality and the feminine organic archetype to generate research that does not separate the mind and body.[2]

Critical bricolage can be neither rigorous nor critical without knowledges necessary to recognize contemporary and contextual ideologies, cultural practices, and dominant political agendas that surround the situation to be researched. Describing the dismissal of context and process knowledge as "an insidious and effective way of hiding the influence of dominant power and maintaining the status quo," Kincheloe (2008a, p. 8) stresses that critical work requires cultural, political, and local knowledge to avoid reductionism and positivist "episto-power" orientations that exclude and limit public knowledge.

Most importantly, intellectual dexterity and multilogicality can result in a researcher or team of researchers who is/are profoundly environmentally aware. This agility facilitates the moment-to-moment conscientization necessary for the recognition of lightening power shifts and the revision of actions related to new power shifts that would narrow possibilities for social justice. In essence, the critical bricoleur can become a hybrid body that is researcher, cultural worker, investigative journalist, and activist/communicator for the public good.

Recognizing the Context and Politics of Knowledge: Contemporary Ideologies and Cultural Agendas

Faced with circumstances of disaster, needed contextual knowledge is required from a range of sources—ideologically, culturally, and locally. These knowledges include the ideologies that dominate contemporary forms of logic and may therefore impact the disaster locations and actions taken within that location (e.g., neoliberal free-market capitalism, 21st-century Christianity, U.S. patriarchy). Cultural knowledge may include information constructed by a range of groups (e.g., local histories and ways of interacting, academic knowledge concerning disaster). To illustrate the types of knowledge required for rigorous critical bricolage related to post-Katrina New Orleans, we overview two of those contextual knowledges below—the contemporary U.S. privileging of market ideologies (and perspectives that relate those ideologies to disaster) and diverse scholarly interpretations of disaster.

Contemporary Acceptance of Market Ideologies and Local Applications to Post-Katrina New Orleans

Identified as classical economics, free market democracy, and Reaganomics in the United States, and neoliberalism, free trade, or globalization around the world, Milton Friedman's free market manifesto (1962) has been imposed whenever possible by leaders around the world from the Chilean dictator Pinochet in the 1970s to Ronald Reagan (United States) and Margaret Thatcher (United Kingdom) in the 1980s to George W. Bush in the 21st century (Klein, 2007). The ideology has come to so dominate the globe, and especially perspectives in the United States, that to question it is often treated as heresy. Even in contemporary conditions (the latter half of 2008) in which values in stock markets indices are falling and major businesses have failed, the notion of fundamentalist free market capitalism as necessary for democracy remains largely unquestioned. This dominant political ideology certainly influenced New Orleans before, during, and after Hurricane Katrina.

As a professor at the University of Chicago, Friedman framed his work as the practice of freedom, which meant freeing the market from the state. He literally describes devoting his life to a battle of ideas against those who believe that the market should be softened by government (Friedman & Friedman, 1998) to protect the less fortunate. Using the languages of math and science, his vision has always supported the interests of corporations, and especially multinationals, putting forward three demands—government deregulation, privatization, and major cuts in spending for the common good. Klein (2007) describes Friedman's use of what he called "shock treatment" (Friedman & Friedman, 1998, p. 592) to take advantage of crisis or disaster to impose sweeping economic reforms (that would privatize, deregulate, and cut programs) without restraint by taking advantage of temporary collective trauma to obtain consensus. The "war on terror" is an example of the use of the Friedman perspective to construct a "disaster capitalism complex" by the Bush administration (Klein, 2007, pp. 14–15), fully supported by right-wing think tanks like the Heritage Foundation, the American Enterprise Institute, and the Cato Institute that had long been associated with Friedman and his fundamentalist capitalism.

Immediately following Hurricane Katrina in the fall of 2005, Friedman moved to apply this shock treatment to the New Orleans schools. As with other social programs designed for the common good, Friedman (2005) believed that a public school system represents socialism and wrote in the *Wall Street Journal*: "It is an opportunity to radically reform the education system." His push for vouchers, so that students could attend private schools, was seized on by the Bush administration that had in recent years promoted charter schools (that could be run by a range of administrative entities including corporations) as a method for privatizing the public that is less challenged (than vouchers) by the public. Within eighteen months, most schools were privately run (if open at all), the New Orleans teachers' union contract was shredded and almost 5,000 members fired, and some children were (and are) denied entrance. Fundamentalist, free market capitalism appears to be the response to post-disaster schooling in New Orleans.

Academic Perspectives on Disaster

Research on catastrophic events was first initiated in the United States during World War II (Janis, 1951) and gained momentum in the beginning stages of the cold war because of concern of about public response to a possible nuclear war (Tierney, 2007). Event inquiry led researchers to use the study of natural disasters as a context for studying human behavior during and after traumatic circumstances (Quarantelli, 1987). In 1963, the Disaster Research Center was established at Ohio State University. During the 1960s and 1970s, mostly qualitative research methods were used to study collective and organizational behavior during and after disaster and during moments of civil unrest like riots.

The natural hazards perspective was also influential in early disaster research. Led by geographer Gilbert White, the Natural Hazards Center (NHC) was founded in 1967 at the University of

Colorado and funded by the National Science Foundation. The NHC concentrated on the cycle of hazards as a whole by studying human and societal adjustments like land-use planning, avoiding extreme events by imposing codes and regulations on building, providing insurance, and preparing for extremes (White, 1974). Most of this work is positivist in nature and assumes the unexpectedness and unpredictability of disaster.

However, a range of scholars point to disasters as reflections of societal values and characteristics. Gender is increasingly considered a variable in disaster studies, either related to gender roles and responses to disaster or linked to studies on families in disaster circumstances (Drabek, 1986; Wenger & James 1994). As research on gender and disaster has become more common, intersectional research has focused on the ways that race, class, and gender interact to shape disaster circumstances (Enarson & Morrow, 1998; Flothergill, 2004). Gender also has been studied more recently as a factor in susceptibility to a higher risk of death, lack of respect for authoritative decision-making, and the ability to be able to prepare and respond during disaster (Ariyabandu, 2006; Enarson, 2005; Enarson & Fordam, 2001; Flothergill, 2003; Morrow & Phillips, 1999). Moving beyond woman-as-victim grand narratives, research has also been done on the way in which gender allows for specialized knowledge and social networking skills that are utilized for disaster preparedness and relief efforts (Enarson, 2000; Neal & Phillips, 1990).

Further, industrialization and urbanization are examples of societal practices that are believed to result in particular forms of disaster; attempts to control the environment, economics, and Western practices of domination are used to explain disastrous events (Davis, 1998; Hewitt, 1998; Pellig, 2003). Sociopolitical ecology describes environmental disasters as the result of modernity. "Regimes of production and accumulation" are described as causing environmental disasters as well as making particular populations and communities more vulnerable to extremes (Foster, 2005; Gould, Pellow, & Schnaiberg, 2004; Tierney, 2007, p. 518). Machine politics and the use of vulnerable spaces for economic gains are described as the mechanisms that construct future disasters. Additionally, Blanchot (1995) illustrates that disaster can establish conditions for a perceived unity that is actually false; although uncertainty may ultimately result, regimes of power legitimated in the name of unity that would address the crisis are inscribed. Further, disaster "ruins everything, all the while leaving everything intact" (p. 1), a condition that facilitates entrepreneurialism and the construction of devalued markets for future economic development. These forms of scholarship—that bring to light possible ways that societal values play a role in the construction of disaster—are obviously lenses through which critical bricolage can be informed.

Critical Diversality: Multiple Lenses

A variety of theories and perspectives concerning power can be used to unveil multiple logics, insight, and open-endedness (Kincheloe, 2008a). As examples: A poststructuralist focus on the construction of regimes of the normal (as posed by Foucault, 1978) can shed light on the use of discourses of disaster to inscribe/credit particular forms of behavior and discredit others. Or feminist conceptualizations of the unmarked category—the male, Caucasian, heterosexual, capitalist economic practices, the unquestioned category of privilege—can be used to unveal ideologies that are accepted as universals. Interpretations of power by indigenous peoples or others who have been traditionally disenfranchised provide possibilities for generating expanded and multiple constructions of issues and in this case power. The following is an example using a woman-of-color perspective as applied to disaster in contemporary neoliberal United States.

Black Feminist Thought

A feminist perspective generated by Patricia Hill Collins (2000) from a life experience that recognizes the intersection of oppressions, known as black feminist thought, is an example of a lens from which critical bricolage can engage with diversality. Acknowledging that power is circulating and that everyone (dependent on context) is both oppressor and oppressed, Collins refers to strategically organized systems of intersecting oppressions that are labeled matrices of domination. These matrices are then conceptualized as consisting of structural, disciplinary, hegemonic, and interpersonal domains. These power domains can be used directly to question, explore, and analyze disaster.

Societal institutions like schools, social services, and the law are *structured* in ways that privilege the knowledges, resources, and ways of functioning of those in power. These structures maintain both the status quo for institutions and power for those who construct and interpret them. For example, related to research and disaster, the notion of structural domains of power could lead to questions like: To maintain a capitalist society, is a cycle of planned disaster necessary for the devaluing/revaluing of property? How is the notion of disaster preparedness an inequitable construct? How do our dominant interpretations of disaster privilege individualism? Determinism? Linearity?

Matrices of domination are also viewed as grounded within disciplinary practices or *disciplinary* power domains. This form of power is imposed using social and institutional regulatory practices and is perhaps the most visible and direct, while probably being the most accepted during conditions of disaster. Because urgency and life/death conditions can so easily be exploited, control can literally be maintained through an accepted militarization. Further, demobilization and destabilization serve as disciplinary power. Questions like the following are necessary: Is an imposed displacement necessary? How does required movement mask inequities? Are there methods that would promote survival that are not being heard? Implemented? How are dominant ways of functioning contributing to destabilization?

Hegemony is the replacement of multiple subjugated knowledges by the specialized knowledge and ways of being of those in power (Collins, 2000). *Hegemonic power* is made possible through the intersecting of structures and forms of disciplinary power that silence diverse voices related to disaster experiences and discredit multiple ways of interpreting those experiences. When only particular disaster discourses are used, specific knowledge is publicly accepted as universal and correct information. Recognition of societal hegemony necessitates posing such questions as: How is using language like the "unprepared" or "those who refuse to move/be helped/listen" a moral discourse? How is the dichotomy of victim and savior perpetuated? When dominant societal discourses (like the acceptance of capitalism) are combined with disaster circumstances, who is privileged? Who is harmed, disenfranchised, or labeled as inferior?

Finally, the *interpersonal domain* of power directly reflects the ways that individuals and groups accept and construct themselves, either consciously or unconsciously from within dominant structures, forms of discipline, and hegemonic knowledge. Further, the complexities of oppressions, intersecting power, and resistance are literally demonstrated by, and imposed on, the bodies of individuals. In disaster circumstances in which neoliberal market philosophies are privileged, necessary inquiry may include issues like: How am I constructing my identity regarding the catastrophic circumstances? What discourses have I accepted? How is power generated for the well-meaning philanthropist? Corporation? Disaster worker? What history—whose voices, what actions— does this power exclude? Generate? Even the researcher must consider the interpersonal domain and ask questions like: Am I using this work to foster my own "marketability?" How? How do I embody an entrepreneurial researcher self? Who can this way of functioning privilege and harm?

Collective Reciprocal Relations

Critical qualitative research can most likely benefit profoundly from the construction of a critical research team that includes both researchers and community activists in collective reciprocal relations, workers like *promatoras* in the El Paso, Texas, area or community activist in the New Orleans area. Collectivist perspectives like calls for women to identify with women (Jaimes, 2003; Walker, 1999), for indigenous living with the land, or for reciprocal interactions between the bioregion and human cultures (Jaimes Guerrero, 2004) can be used as models for collectivist diversity and the unthought. This diversity is needed to support a research condition that would generate "new ways of seeing" social science and the collaborative construction of informed rigorous inquiry (Kincheloe, 2008b, p. 12).

Coda: Egalitarian Activism

Finally, some researchers have always considered their scholarly work to be activism. We also know that many of us have faced academic and public power brokers who attempt to silence, ignore, or discredit our work as unscientific, idealistic, unrealistic or lacking rigor. For various reasons, a range of critical work has not impacted the public imaginary, much less the conditions of oppression that are experienced by many. Because crisis and disaster are literally life threatening, are often reproduced, and generate conditions through which even greater social injustices can be inscribed, research activism becomes even more important. This activism requires new, even previously unthought, and immediate forms of dissemination and critical behaviors. As an integral component of an action research process and the continued struggle to maintain and increase egalitarian social justice, critical qualitative inquiry in crisis circumstances must include questions (and actions) like the following:

- How are our skills as researchers most beneficial to groups struggling to resist oppression and exploitation under difficult survival conditions?

- How can we use our skills as researchers to help communities stay informed when power is rapidly shifting and changing under crisis circumstances?

- How does disaster demobilize resistance? Are there collaborative methods that can be generated that mobilize and empower?

- Are there research practices that allow information to be disseminated quickly enough so that counter actions can be directly taken to avoid exploitation?

- How do we avoid perpetuating acts that dehumanize and objectify people and communities that we hope to support?

- Are we quickly uncovering and changing perspectives, practices, and conditions that are causing immediate risks (whether physical, educational, or otherwise)?

Notes

1. Most of the public housing units were not actually damaged, but residents were kept out through military force as well as conditions in which power, supplies, and resources like transportation were not available to make return possible.

2. To illustrate, see Mohanram (1999), women's bodies as coded to represent nation; Anzaldúa, (1987, 1990), border bodies and *mestiza* consciousness; and Spivak (1996, 1999), bodies and the reconstitution of the colonized.

References

Anzaldúa, G. (1987). *Borderlands/La frontera*. San Francisco: Aunt Lute Books.

Anzaldúa, G. (Ed.). (1990). *Making face, making soul*. San Francisco: Aunt Lute Books.

Ariyabandu, M. M. (2006). Gender issues in recovery from the December 2004 Indian Ocean tsunami: The case of Sri Lanka. *Earthquake Spectra*, 22, 759–775.

Blanchot, M. (1995). *The writing of disaster* (trans. A. Smock). Lincoln: The University of Nebraska Press.

Cannella, G. S. & Manuelito, K. D. (2008). Feminisms from unthought locations: Indigenous worldviews, marginalized feminisms, and revisioning an anticolonial social science. In N. K. Denzin, Y. S. Lincoln, & L. Tuhiwai Smith (Eds.), *Handbook of critical indigenous methodologies*, pp. 45–59. Thousand Oaks, CA: Sage.

Collins, P. H. (2000). *Black feminist thought: Knowledge, consciousness, and the politics of empowerment*, 2nd ed. New York: Routledge.

Davis, M. (1998). *Ecology of fear: Los Angeles and the imagination of disaster*. New York: Metropolitan Books.

Denzin, N. K. (2007). Katrina and the collapse of civil society in New Orleans. *Cultural Studies↔Critical Methodologies*, 7(2), 145–153.

Denzin, N. K., & Lincoln, Y. S. (2000). *Handbook of qualitative research*, 2nd ed. Thousand Oaks, CA: Sage.

Drabek, T. E. (1986). *Human system responses to disaster*. New York: Springer-Verlag.

Enarson, E. (2000). We will make meaning out of this: Women's cultural responses to the Red River Valley flood. *International Journal of Mass Emergencies and Disasters*, 18, 39–62.

Enarson, E. (2005). Women and girls last? Averting the second post-Katrina disaster. *Understanding Katrina: Perspectives from the social sciences*.

Available online at http://understandingkatrina.ssrc.org/Enarson/ (accessed August 5, 2008).

Enarson, E., & Fordham, M. (2001). From women's needs to women's rights in disasters. *Entironmental Hazards*, 3, 133–136.

Enarson, E., & Morrow, B. H. (Eds.). (1998). *The gendered terrain of disaster: Through women's eyes*. Westport, CT: Praeger.

Foster, J. B. (2005). The treadmill of accumulation: Schnaiberg's environment and Marxian political economy. *Organizational Environments*, 18, 7–18.

Fothergill, A. (2003). The stigma of charity: Gender, class, and disaster assistance. *Sociological Quarterly*, 44, 659–680.

Fothergill, A. (2004). *Heads above water: Gender, class, and family in the Grand Forks flood*. Albany: State University of New York Press.

Foucault, M. (1978). *The history of sexuality* (trans. R. Hurley). New York: Penguin Books.

Friedman, M. (1962). *Capitalism and freedom*. Chicago: University of Chicago Press.

Friedman, M. (2005). The promise of vouchers. *Wall Street Journal*, December 5, p. A20.

Friedman, M., & Friedman, R. D. (1998). *Two lucky people: Memoirs*. Chicago: University of Chicago Press.

Giardina, M. D. & Hess, L. A. (2007). If not us, then who? Performing pedagogies of hope in post-Katrina America. *Cultural Studies↔Critical Methodologies*, 7(2), 169–187.

Gould, K. A., Pellow, D. N., & Schnaiberg, A. (2004). Interrogating the treadmill of production: Everything you wanted to know about the treadmill but were afraid to ask. *Organizational Environments*, 17, 296–316.

Hewitt, K. (1998). *Interpretations of calamity: From the viewpoint of human ecology*. Boston: Allen & Unwin.

Jaimes, M. A. (1992). La raza and indigenism: Alternatives to autogenocide in North America. *Global Justice*, 3(2–3), 4–19.

Jaimes, M. A. (2003). "Patriarchal colonialism" and "indigenism": Implications for mative feminist spirituality and native womanism. *Hypatia-A Journal of Feminist Philosophy*. Available online at http://rdsweb1.rdsinc.com.ezproxy1.libasu.edu/texis/rds/suite2/+sceJjD6emxwwwwwFqz6 (accessed February 4, 2006).

Jaimes Guerero, M. A. (2004). Biocolonialism and isolates of historic interest. In M. Riley (Ed.). *Indigenous intellectual property rights: Legal obstacles and innovative solutions*, pp. 251–277. Walnut Creek, CA: AltaMira Press.

Janis, I. L. (1951). *Air war and emotional stress: Psychological studies of bombing and civil defense*. Santa Monica, CA: RAND.

Kellner, D. (2007). The Katrina hurricane spectacle and crisis of the Bush presidency. *Cultural Studies↔Critical Methodologies*, 7(2), 222–234.

Kincheloe, J. L. (2001). Describing the bricolage: Conceptualizing a new rigor in qualitative research. *Qualitative Inquiry*, 7(6), 679–692.

Kincheloe, J. L. (2005). On to the next level: Continuing the conceptualization of the bricolage. *Qualitative Inquiry*, 11(3), 323–350.

Kincheloe, J. L (2008a). *Critical pedagogy*, 2nd ed. New York: Peter Lang.

Kincheloe, J. L. (2008b). Critical pedagogy and the knowledge wars of the twenty-first century. International Journal of Critical Pedagogy. Available online at http://freire.education.mcgill.ca/ojs/public/journals/Galleys/IJCP011.pdf (accessed August 12, 2008).

Kincheloe, J. L., & Berry, K. (2004). *Rigor and complexity in educational research: Conceptualizing the bricolage*. London: Open University Press.

Klein, N. (2007). *The shock doctrine: The rise of disaster capitalism*. New York: Metropolitan Books.

Lincoln, Y. S., & Cannella, G. S. (2007). Ethics and the broader rethinking/reconceptualization of research as construct. In N. K. Denzin & M. D. Giardina (Eds.), *Ethical futures in qualitative research: Decolonizing the politics of knowledge*, pp. 67–84. Walnut Creek, CA: Left Coast Press.

Long, A. P. (2007). Poverty is the new prostitution: Race, poverty, and public housing in post-Katrina New Orleans. *The Journal of American History*, 94(3), 795–803.

Mohanram, R. (1999). *Black body: Women, colonialism, and space*. Minneapolis: University of Minnesota Press.

Morrow, B. H., & Phillips, B. D. (Eds.). (1999). Special issue: Women and disasters. *International Journal of Mass Emergencies and Disasters*, 17(1).

Neal, D. M., & Phillips, B. D. (1990). Female-dominated local social movement organizations in disaster threat situations. In G. West & R. Blumberg (Eds.), *Women and social protest*, pp. 243–255. New York: Oxford University Press.

Pellig, M. (Ed.). (2003). *Natural disasters and development in a globalizing world*. London: Routledge.

Quarantelli, E. L. (1987). Disaster studies: An analysis of the social historical factors affecting the development of research in the area. *International Journal of Mass Emergencies and Disasters*, 5(1), 285–310.

Saltman, K. J. (2007). *Capitalizing on disaster: Taking and breaking public schools*. Boulder, CO: Paradigm.

Spivak, G. C. (1996). Poststructuralism, marginality, postcoloniality, and value. In P. Mongia (Ed.), *Contemporary postcolonial theory: A reader*, pp. 198–223. London: Arnold.

Spivak, G. C. (1999). A *critique of postcolonial reason: Toward a history of the vanishing present*. Cambridge, MA: Harvard University Press.

Tierney, K. J. (2007). From the margins to the mainstream? Disaster research at the crossroads. *The Annual Review of Sociology*, 33, 503–525.

Troutt, D. D. (Ed.). (2007). *After the storm: Black intellectuals explore the meaning of hurricane Katrina*. New York: The New Press.

Walker, A. (1999). *In search of our mothers' gardens: Womanist prose*. San Diego, CA: Harvest.

Wenger, D. E. & James, T. F. (1994). The convergence of volunteers in a consensus crisis: The case of the 1985 Mexico City earthquake. In R. R. Dynes & K. J. Tierney (Eds.), *Disasters, collective behavior, and social organization*, pp. 229–243. Newark, NJ: University of Delaware Press.

White, G. F. (1974). *Natural hazards: Local, national, global*. New York: Oxford University Press.

Section III

Human Rights and Radical Performance

Chapter 8 ||| Dangerous Ethnography

D. Soyini Madison
Northwestern University

The Merriam-Webster pocket electronic dictionary describes "dangerous" as an adverb, defining it first as: (1) hazardous, perilous (a dangerous slope); and second as: (2) able or likely to inflict injury (a dangerous man)

—Madison

I. Three Vignettes

1. It was 1988, my first year teaching at the University of North Carolina (UNC) at Chapel Hill. My advisor, Dwight Conquergood, had flown in from Northwestern University in Evanston, Illinois, to give final approval of what I hoped would be the last draft of my dissertation. The dissertation needed to be completed within a few weeks for me to be awarded the Ph.D. that year and to be promoted from lecturer to assistant professor at UNC (this was the agreement UNC mandated on my hire). While Dwight was managing all-nighters proofing dissertation chapters at my kitchen table and I was running back and forth between my study and the kitchen giving him chapter after revised chapter, hot off the computer, one night we took a break from the intensity of dissertation deadline madness and starting talking about the nature of fieldwork and the notion of a "dangerous ethnography."

Earlier that morning, Dwight went to campus with me to talk to a group of people who were interested in his fieldwork with

Chicago street gangs. At the end of his presentation, the familiar question rose again: "Professor Conquergood, you are involved in very dangerous work with some very dangerous characters—are you safe?" Dwight, affectionately referred to in those days as the "Indiana Jones" of performance studies, was asked versions of this question time after time. At my kitchen table that night, he slowly shook his head and quietly said, "With these communities and entire families in peril, everyone is more worried about the lone white man."

2. Ten years later, in 1998, as an associate professor I was on my way to Ghana, West Africa, to conduct fieldwork with local human rights activists. Before I left for Ghana, the investigative television news magazine *60 Minutes* aired a feature on a traditional cultural practice in a particular region of Ghana where the reporter depicted innocent women and girls being forced and condemned to village shrines where they were placed in bondage as reparation for a crime committed by a family member, usually a male. After the *60 Minutes* program, when I mentioned to certain individuals that I was going to Ghana to research human rights in the rural areas, the response was "Be careful, Soyini, it is dangerous there. They steal women and put them in shrines." An entire country had been reduced to a unique location with no critical questions regarding the *60 Minutes* representation or concern for the women and girls reported.

3. Now, in 2008, as a full professor, I remember a transatlantic phone call from my student Hannah Blevins several years ago. I was in Ghana continuing my fieldwork on human rights and local activism and Hannah was in southern Appalachia in the last stages of her fieldwork to complete her dissertation on the cultural economy of the coal mining community and black lung disease. Hannah called from Tennessee to tell me she was going down into one of the mines that had recently been closed. Her purpose was to see for herself where so many miners had worked and died. I was silent, but my immediate thought was, "No, you cannot, it is too dangerous." Sensing my fear through the phone, Hannah said it would be safe. She said experienced miners would guide her and protect her through the passageways of the mine. We talked for a bit. Hannah *did* go deep into the mine and completed

a brilliant dissertation. But while she was thousands of feet below ground in a closed mine—to go where the miners had gone, to enter the risky knowledge of the body—I was on the other side of the Atlantic thinking of her and in fear of the danger.

II. Flipping the Script on Danger: Danger in Reverse

What if we stop for a moment and rethink the "dangerous"? What if we were to consider putting the dangerous in reverse? Instead of conventionally positioning the dangerous inside the field, what might happen if we think of *ourselves* as being dangerous? What if danger is no longer somewhere "out there" in the field? What if we carry danger with us, embody it, and carry it with us *into* the field? Consider the option that we, ourselves, could be dangerous. Consider what it might mean to be an *agent* of danger, what it might mean to become dangerous ethnographers doing dangerous ethnography. "Flip the script" and reposition the dangerous from individuals or communities that are and can be dangerous to some of us (i.e., a street gang member, a shrine in the Third World, a restricted coal mine) to now include the structures of power that generate and sustain what is systematically dangerous to *all* of us: systematic poverty, the machinery of imperialism, structures of homophobia, and phallocentric power. What if we were dangerous to the force of these dangers? What if we were dangerous to the systematic abuse of power? What if we were to be perpetrators of danger to that which is dangerous to our universal well-being?

The street gang member, a village shrine, and a restricted coal mine are dangers at the surface; structures of urban poverty, phallocentrism, imperialism, and homophobia are dangers at the root. An ethnography that labors to injure the foundation and the root cause of what is dangerous and that is not diverted by its symptoms or surfaces of danger might contemplate a new appropriation of danger. We can speak truth to power and we can also be dangerous to its perpetuation and continued abuse. Don't get me wrong: We must and should pay attention to the dangers at the tip and the surface, because they are no small matters. A troubled gang member, a shrine of slaves, and a restricted coal mine legitimately invoke fear and are dangerous at a number of levels. *Both* root and surface are forceful, significant, and scary. A dangerous ethnography seeks to enter surfaces, but, moreover, enters what is often hidden in plain sight—the convolutions and complications below the surface, the systems that generate and keep surfaces in place.

We will keep listening with our hearts and minds to the poignant ethnographic accounts of Darfur because the human horror is too great for us not to hear or care. A dangerous ethnography will carry those stories forth while not ignoring how oil money funds government weapons, how the militias are aligned with national and transnational exploitation, and how ignorance is warming the globe and drying up the land to spark one of the most vicious ethnic conflicts in recent history. Every story about the horror of Darfur is not only a story of human suffering that must be heard, it is also about oil and the warming of our planet. Another example of dangerous ethnography might include entering various urban dance communities to examine how everyday city life is identified, sustained, contested, and remade through the labor, imagination, and global connections of community dance dancers. A dangerous ethnography is reflected in the work of Judith Hamera, who unearthed the urban political infrastructures of dance to critique and complicate notions of difference, cosmopolitanism, the distributions of urban space, and the politics of globality and urban migration. Another example is the intimate ethnography of Della Pollock and her retelling of birth stories, documenting them as reperformances of how men and women recast the ritual of giving birth. Within the poetics of birth narratives, Pollock lends a penetrating analysis of U.S. medical discourse, reproductive technologies, and the tensive intersections of maternity, sexuality, and reproduction as well as how pain is constituted and represented.

My plea is for us not only to speak truth to power but also to put power in peril, in jeopardy, to endanger it. This all comes quite frankly from being weary of being angry. I have made up my mind in my golden years that I shall aim to be a danger to dangerous power, from the tip to the root, from the surface to the foundation.

III. The Body as Bearing Witness

I will argue that a *dangerous ethnography* does not begin with interventions on political economies or structures of the state or the nation, on global capitalism or corporate greed, or even on ideologies of neoliberalism or fundamentalism—these are the targets of a dangerous ethnography (with some complication) but they are not the starting point, not the inspiration. My inspiration for a dangerous ethnography begins with performance—that is, the body in performance.

In performance studies, we do a lot of talking about the body. For performance ethnographers, this means we must embrace the body not only as the feeling/sensing home of our being—the harbor of our breath—but the vulnerability of how our body must move through the space and time of another—transporting our very being and breath—for the purpose of knowledge, for the purpose of realization and discovery. Body knowledge, knowledge through the body, is evidence of the present. It is the truth that I exist with you—with myself—right here, right now. Further, it is evidence that I am not anywhere, I am not nowhere, I am not over yonder, I am not absent. I am not dead. I am alive here and now and I am vulnerable to this feeling/sensing present moment. My body breathes here unmediated and unprotected. The Other can reach across me and touch my wounds, can feel the beating of my heart, can hear my nervous breathing, can strike me down and make my blood flow.

This is intersubjective vulnerability in existential and ontological order, because bodies rub against one another flesh to flesh in a marked present and where we live on and between the extremes of life and death. Another can love me and another can kill me; I can love and kill in the corporeal present tense of another. I cannot live or die in my body's absence—I can only die and live in the present moment, in the presence of my body, and where my body is present. The immortality of the soul withstanding, we end when our bodies end and we begin when our bodies begin—body presence with another is fraught with intersubjective risks.

So what is my point? The point is that where my body is I am vulnerable to the radical extremes of life and death; the point is that where my body is I am vulnerable to the disgust and desire of all my senses; and finally, the point is that because my body is vulnerable to life and death in this particular ethnographic moment as well as the penetrating depths of its sensual meanings, I am living evidence that this moment, in this time and space, does exist and I am a surviving witness to its living realities of life and death and the infinite in-between. This is why, for better and for worse, we say: "Are you safe?" "Is it dangerous?" "I am afraid for you."

So how is the body specifically implicated in a dangerous ethnography? The body must testify, it must speak—it must provide a report—it must bear witness to the surfaces and the foundations, the symptoms and the causes.

"What should I do with what I have witnessed?" I have strong responses to what I witnessed during my fieldwork. These responses demanded that I be responsible for providing an opportunity for others to also gain the *ability* to respond in some form.[1] I bear witness and in bearing witness I do not have the singular response-ability for what I witness but the responsibility of invoking a response-ability in others to what was seen, heard, learned, felt, and done in the field and through performance. As Kelly Oliver states, "We have an obligation not only to respond but also to respond in a way that opens up rather than closes off the possibility to respond by others" (2001, pp. 18–19). Steven Durland says, "A person who bears witness to an injustice takes responsibility for that awareness. That person may then choose to do something or stand by, but he may not turn away in ignorance" (1987, p. 65).

Response, response-ability, and responsibility became aligned with advocacy and ethics. To be an advocate is to feel a responsibility to exhort and appeal on behalf of another or for another's cause with the hope that still more others will gain the ability to respond to your advocacy agenda. Being an advocate has a different intent than speaking in the manner of a ventriloquist, in the sense of muting Other voices to only amplify one's own. Being an advocate is to actively *assist* in the struggles of others, or (and) it is learning the tactics, symbols, and everyday forms of resistance of which the subaltern *enact* but "do not speak" (Spivak, 1988) so that they may provide platforms for which their struggles can be known and heard.[2] As advocates, we aim for a cycle of responses that will set loose a stream of response-abilities that will lead to something more, something of larger philosophical and material effects.

In addition, the position of advocate and the labor of advocacy are riddled with the pleasure and burden of representation that is always already so much about ethics. Advocates represent who and what they are advocating for: their names, narratives, histories, and their logics of persuasion as well as imagining what more is needed in the service of advocacy. All this requires labor that is entrenched in power relations and representations that are inextricable to ethics. Representation happens at different points along power's spectrum—we are all "vehicles and targets" of power's contagion and omnipresence.[3] As advocates, surrounded by the far and wide entanglements of power's disguises and infinite forms, we aim to invoke a response to its consequences—a response-ability—to its operations. In doing the work of advocacy, whether we consider ethics or not, it is always already present within the horizons of representation and the machinations of power. Because ethics requires responsibility (and the ability to respond), it is inherently antithetical to apathy.

If apathy cannot rest beside the ethical responsibility to respond and if ethics also includes providing opportunities for others to gain access to the ability to respond, then performance can form a vibrant and efficacious partnership with ethics. Ethics and advocacy now pave the way as we move from the field to the stage. Stage performance becomes a dynamic space where response-ability, advocacy, and ethnics are heightened and ultimately culminate.

The fieldwork data *travel* to the public stage with the hope that the performance will invoke a response (ability) among a group or spectators. It is said that theater and performance *show ourselves to ourselves* in ways that help us recognize our behavior and life worlds as well as the behavior and life worlds of others, for better or worse, as well as our/Others unconscious needs and desires. Victor Turner said, "When we act in everyday life we do not merely re-act to indicative stimuli, we act in frames wrested from the genres of cultural performance" (1982, p. 122). He also said:

> It might be possible to regard the ensemble of performative and narrative genres, active and acting modalities of expressive culture

as a hall of mirrors, or better magic mirrors. ... In this hall of mirrors the reflections are multiple, some magnifying, some diminishing, some distorting the faces peering into them, but in such a way as to provoke not merely thought, but also powerful feelings and the will to modify everyday matters in the minds of the gazers, for not one likes to see himself as ugly, ungainly, or dwarfish. Mirror distortions of reflection provoke reflexivity. (p. 105)

These performances not only reflect who we are, they shape and direct who we are and what we can become. The major work of performance ethnography is to make performances that do the labor of advocacy and do it ethically to inspire realms of reflection and responsibility. Bertolt Brecht reminds us that performance must also proceed beyond that of a mirror reflection to become the hammer that breaks the mirror, distorts the reflection, to build a new reality. Brecht's charge to "build a new reality" leads us closer to a methodology of *dangerous ethnography* and beckons the need for utopian performatives.

IV. Utopian Performatives

Performance scholar Jill Dolan reminds us that utopian performatives aim for "a different future, one full of hope and reanimated by a new, more radical humanism." She goes on to state that a Utopian Performative is capable of lifting us "above the present, into a hopeful feeling of what the world might be like" and that it is always already "a 'doing' in linguistic philosopher J. L. Austin's sense of the term, something that in its enunciation *acts*—that is, performs an action as tangible and effective as saying 'I do' in a wedding ceremony" (Dolan, 2005, pp. 5–6; emphasis in the original). Therefore we may understand Utopian Performance, in their "doings" as making palpable an affective vision of how the world might be better.

What is significant here is that Dolan is rearticulating the move from the ideal fantasy of Utopia in the Marxist sense by asserting that the utopian is "historical," it is "*this*-worldly" and involves human agency (Bamer, 1992, p. 6). That is, as Bamer states, we need to replace the idea of a Utopia as something fixed, a form to be fleshed out, with the idea of "the Utopian" as an *approach toward*, a movement beyond set limits into the realm of the not-yet-set. At the same time, I want to counter the notion of the utopian as unreal with the proposition that the utopian is powerfully real in the sense that hope and desire (and even fantasy) are real, never "merely" fantasy. It is a force that moves and shapes history. (Bamer, quoted in Dolan, 2005, pp. 5–6; emphasis added)

This notion of a utopian performative is articulated as a characteristic of the theater and stage performance but it is also appropriated by performance ethnographers and, I would argue, is the very motivation and inspiration leading us toward a dangerous ethnography. Adapting the philosophy of a utopian performative means that danger is not simply a threat to life but a praxis toward a better life and future that moves us from "as is" to "what if." I will now outline how a utopian performative, within critical performance ethnography, "flips the script" on danger through the ontology of performance.

First, performance invites us to understand the body as its own evidence. Our research is radically animating the intersubjective (corporeal) vulnerability of a particular present. We are not only participant-observers with Others, but flesh-to-flesh co-performative witnesses in the risky business of a contagious desire, passion, and urgency that affects us all, propelling back and forth between us/among us through our feeling/sensing vulnerable bodies. The utopian performative of a dangerous ethnography does not simply observe but bears the responsibility of witnessing, and it does not simply participate but embodies performance with a deeply felt sensing empathy.

Second, performance invites us to understand that "bearing witness" is a form of truth. The truth of not what precisely happened here but what profoundly and phenomenologically happened here to me, to us—to an/Other. It is a different measure than quantifying accuracy, because it constitutes the multiple makings of subjectivity and the emotional processes of witnessing, not for witnessing sake but for politics and praxis. Bearing witness to the culminating affects/effects of social live and symbol-making in action and the living narrative(s) that swirl within and against the creation and consequence of life and symbol are different encounters and challenges than the culminating answers, numbers, and checked boxes held as evidence, as more true.

Third, performance invites us to understand that the performative is always and already about a doing—a doing that transforms a reality. Again, "the performative is something that in its enunciation *acts*," makes action and makes action possible in its "affective dimensions" (Dolan, 2005, p. 5).

V. Coda

The current historical moment requires morally informed performance and arts-based disciplines that will help people recover meaning in the face of senseless, brutal violence, violence that produces voiceless screams of terror and insanity.

—N. K. Denzin, 2003

My hope is that we strive to be a danger to "the face of senseless, brutal violence" in the creation of its demise and that the "violence that produces voiceless screams of terror and insanity" (Denzin, 2003, p. 7), endangered by utopian performatives and our labors of love for the future, comes to an unalterable end, but, like a troubled memory and a regrettable history, inspires the words "ever again."

Notes

1. This concept draws from Kelly Oliver (2001).

2. This is a reference to Gayatri Chakravorty Spivak's classic essay, "Can the Subaltern Speak?" (1988). I am appropriating Spivak here to assert the temporalities of speaking within indigenous locations where the subaltern speaking subject escapes and/or transgresses the bounds of allowed speech constituted by Western epistemologies and venues.

3. I am drawing here from Michel Foucault's articulation of power as set forth primarily in *Discipline and Punish* (1991).

References

Bamer, A. (1992). *Partial visions: Feminism and utopianism in the 1970s.* London: Routledge.

Denzin, N. K. (2003). *Performance ethnography: Critical pedagogy and the politics of culture.* Thousand Oaks, CA: Sage.

Dolan, J. (2005). *Utopia in performance: Finding hope at the theater.* Ann Arbor: University of Michigan Press.

Durland, S. (1987). Witnessing: The guerrilla theater of Greenpeace. In J. Cohen-Cruz (Ed.), *Radical street performance*, p. 65. New York: Routledge.

Foucault, M. (1991). *Discipline and punish: The birth of the prison* (trans. A. Sheridan). London: Penguin

Oliver, K. (2001). *Witnessing: Beyond recognition.* Minneapolis: University of Minnesota Press

Spivak, G. C. (1988). Can the subaltern speak? In C. Nelson & L. Grossberg (Eds.), *Marxism and the interpretation of culture*, pp. 271–313. Champaign: University of Illinois Press

Turner, V. (1982). *From ritual to theatre: The human seriousness of play.* New York: PAJ Publications.

Chapter 9 ||| Risky Research

Investigating the "Perils" of Ethnography

Karen A. Stewart
Arizona State University

Aaron Hess
Arizona State University

Sarah J. Tracy
Arizona State University

H. L. Goodall, Jr.
Arizona State University

Our chapter is a collection of stories about risks we've faced as practicing ethnographers. We wanted to tell our risky stories because, conceptually, "risk" has a distinct relationship with qualitative methods, and ethnography in particular. All ethnography is inherently risky, at least to some degree. The contingent nature of fieldwork—our primary method of inquiry—places us in dynamic, unusual, or otherwise unfamiliar social settings where we are expected to interact with new people and new ideas and, ultimately, make sense of our surroundings. This process, at best, is ambiguous and situates ethnography as a less-than-predictable form of investigation. Experience, and a healthy dose of common sense, tells us this is risky work.

Historically, risk has been conceptualized as the mental and physical challenges the ethnographer faces in the field. Robert J. Flaherty's (1922) documentary film *Nanook of the North* and similar early ethnographies helped establish this precedent. And this concept of risk is perpetuated by the continuing practice of presenting ethnographic research as a kind of adventure story where the "researcher/hero" marches off into some great "unknown" and, through his or her physical talents, mental abilities, and amazing social skills manages to navigate the situation bravely. The researcher/hero then returns with an amazing story only an adventurer could tell.[1]

Given the ease in which ethnographic research is linked to adventure stories, it is not surprising many people in both academia and the general public at large continue to conceptualize the relationship between research and risk in this manner. As practicing ethnographers, however, we are aware there are less obvious and less glamorous risks associated with the process of ethnography. We are also aware that qualitative scholars need more opportunities to identify and discuss the types, interactions, nuances, and implications of these risks. We need to understand more fully why these kinds of risks exist and why they can be as serious and derailing to our research as actual physical harm.

Our goal here is not to discount the literal risks of ethnographic fieldwork, but to extend the concept of risk to include a wider range of considerations. With ethnography often presented as a methodological challenge to postpositivism, and as a method self-aware of its colonial legacy, the concept of risk can and should be expanded to include the ethical, institutional, paradigmatic, methodological, epistemological, and reception challenges ethnographers face throughout their entire research process. At any given point, any one of these issues can inhibit the progress of ethnographic research and potentially harm the researcher or the research subjects involved in the project.

In this expanded context, we perceive risk as a relational dynamic, operating on multiple levels, and manifesting as interrelated research considerations. We also see risk as exponential. A risky decision made early in the process can later lead to riskier consequences. This is especially true when ethnographers submit their research for publication only to find their entire study called into question over issues of scientific validity, institutional review board (IRB) approval, methodological rigor, ethical reflexivity, and/or the stylized presentation of data.

By sharing our risky stories, we want to draw attention to and investigate the complexity of risk. We also want to draw attention to its fluctuating nature. By working together to produce our narratives, we have come to realize risk is as much about researcher perception as it is about real-world considerations. Each of us is at a different point in our academic career. One is a fourth-year doctoral student, one a newly minted Ph.D. Another is a recently tenured associate professor, and the fourth is a veteran ethnographer. Risk looks and feels differently to each of us. Our perception of risk has taken on different degrees of relevancy and urgency depending on our experience and status. We also see different risks depending on our personal, professional, and research goals.

The subjectivity of risk should not, however, be discounted. We believe it serves as an effective reminder that ethnographic research is never a singular, uniform experience—a necessary reminder for fundamentally challenging the practice of reducing risk to a single, historically limited concept. It also reminds us that no one, at any stage of his or her research or career, is immune from the implications of risk. Risk is integrated in the overall production of qualitative research. Given this continual presence, risk warrants deeper consideration.

We offer the following narratives as launching points for this discussion.

Are You Serious?

Striving toward Theoretical and Disciplinary Legitimacy

Sarah J. Tracy

I vividly remember my beloved doctoral advisor suggesting that I change the title of my first sole-authored article from "Smile, You're at Sea," to "Becoming a Character for Commerce." The second title provided a cloak of authenticity around my commercial cruise ship research site—a context that my advisor correctly assumed might be judged as questionable for a young woman who wanted to be taken seriously as an organizational communication scholar. Indeed, the decision of research site has crucial consequences for ethnographers, affecting our data, the theories that we might examine, and our researcher well-being.

Perceived Seriousness and Transferability of Research

Risk often begins with the choice of research site. Throughout my career, I have found myself attracted to settings quite different from the Fortune 500 companies, large nonprofits, or social service organizations that are common among organizational communication and emotional labor research.

My first field research experience was hanging out with 911 call-takers during the hot summer of 1995 (Tracy & Tracy, 1998). Throughout the late evening hours, I sat with call-takers at CityWest Emergency Communications Center, listening into calls, chatting, and socializing with them at breaks and off-hour cocktail gatherings. At the time, emotional labor was a new concept to communication scholars, and my hope was that my nontraditional site of study might help problematize and extend the scholarship.

Soon after my 911 experience, I set my sights on another research venue that seemed poised for extending emotion labor research—a commercial cruise ship. I figured the venue would be perfect for understanding the construction of employee identity in relation to panoptic and virtually inescapable discourses of control within a total institution setting (Tracy, 2000). The main challenge was entrée. Very little research is available about cruise ship organizations, largely because cruise lines are quite secretive about their operating practices. Furthermore, it is difficult to negotiate field research within an organization that only periodically touches on the same geographic ground and one in which lodging is an extremely scarce and valuable commodity.

I solved the entrée issue by becoming an employee for eight months. It was not until I got off the ship and began to try to write up my research that I faced judgments that such a research site may not be considered serious or important. I remember hearing comments like: "If you are interested in organizations, you should want to be able to generalize from your own research to other organizations. Yet, here you go insisting on doing research in organizational settings like 911 and cruise ships."

My most recent in-depth ethnographic fieldwork has been with correctional officers at a prison and jail (Tracy, 2005). Very little scholarship qualitatively examines the well-being and dilemmas of the "watchers" and "keepers" of prisoners. The research that does exist is mostly self-reported survey data and focuses on employees' individual aspects of burnout. I wanted to understand how organizational structural norms and practices affected the ways correctional officers performed the emotion work of showing respect and nurturing inmates, maintaining stoicism, and managing danger, fear, and disgust.

In each of these venues, I connected research findings with extant research on emotion, stress, and burnout done in more traditional work settings. In doing research in these settings, I faced the risk that people might not take my scholarship seriously. However, the reward has been extending emotion labor theory in ways that would have been more difficult or impossible if I would have done research in a "safer" more known and common venue. Because I studied emotion labor among employee populations whose jobs were in total and closed institutions (cruise ship and prison) and employees who had to "service" lower status others (911 and prison), I was able to name a practice termed "double-faced emotion management" (Tracy & Tracy, 1998, p. 407) and argue that the difficulty of emotion labor has as much to do with enacting low-status emotional identities as it does with faking it (Tracy, 2005).

Risks Associated with Organizational Entrée and IRB Approval

Getting access has been one of the most difficult parts of doing organizational field research. I entered the cruise ship venue as a "junior assistant cruise director" without clear-cut plans for research. Once I had been on board for a month or so, I approached the cruise director who granted participant observation research permission and proceeded to have all interviewees sign informed consent forms. I thought all was fine, but when my first article was about to go to press in *Management Communications Quarterly*, I received a note from the editor asking that I add a footnote indicating IRB approval. There was one catch: I did not have it. I had not been employed by the university at the time, and as a twenty-five year old with two years of graduate school behind me, I had no clue that such approval was necessary.

With no IRB approval, the publisher was concerned that the article (which did not paint a pretty picture of behind-the-scenes cruise ship life) might result in a lawsuit. As a result, I edited out a potentially damning section of the piece and assured the publisher that I had obtained signed consent forms from participants and gone through a number of steps to ensure confidentiality. Tragedy averted. They published the piece, and I made a promise to myself to never proceed again without the proper types of permissions in place. Unfortunately, I quickly learned that IRB approval is not always enough.

Getting access to do research behind the locked doors of prisons and jails required lots of cold-calling, networking, and proposal-giving. I finally received organizational access after going through the program's volunteer training, passing multiple background checks and billing myself as a "volunteer researcher" studying the emotional highs and lows of correctional officers. I received a letter of research permission from the prison's volunteer coordinator and was approved to do human subjects research through my university's IRB. I gave a whoop of joy, glad to have permission in hand.

Eight months into my data collection and analysis, I came home to a sinister voicemail message, the gist of which was this: "Hello, I'm calling for Ms. Sarah Tracy. This is the director of research for the Department of Corrections. I have recently learned that you have been conducting unauthorized research in our women's prison. This research has not been authorized or approved by our office. Please call us immediately."

Through several panic-filled phone calls with the director of research, I learned that I had gone through the wrong routes to receive research permission. Furthermore, my participant observation research was extremely unconventional, and the department usually only allowed researchers to do one-time surveys. And, when they did allow researchers into the organization, they usually required significant experience and specific research goals. Needless to say, my open-ended ethnographic research did not "fit" any of these criteria. However, at this point, data collection was virtually complete and I was able to assure the director of research that no harm had been done. Fortunately, I was able to get retroactive permission for the research and carry on with my analyses.

Several months later, I met the director and shared my research findings. He was especially interested with a framework

I developed about correctional officer burnout and structural level contradictions—a framework that was only emergent through the process of the ethnography. I asked the director if he would have provided me access to do the research if, at the beginning, I just indicated that I wanted to examine the emotional highs and lows of correctional officers. His response came without a beat: "No way."

So, ironically, if I had actually gone through the formal correct channels for receiving research permission I never would have received access and none of the research would have been possible. Sometimes, following the rules may be the biggest risk of all.

The Risk that Sensational Data Can Distract from Theoretical Contributions

Consider the following two excerpts from my 911 research. The excerpts as written below were included in an original version of the article.

> One of the most revolting calls that came in during my participant observation was when I was sitting with Christy. The female caller said that her sister's baby ate some hamburger and now it's "stuck in her rear and won't come out." The call-takers also reminisced about a case where a woman had to go to the emergency room to literally get disconnected from her German shepherd because his penis was stuck inside of her.

These excerpts clearly illustrate that call-takers need to do significant work in managing their disgust and disdain in the service of efficiently providing police assistance. However, in early internal reviews of the article, I was told by several peers and an instructor that the excerpts were so graphic that it was difficult for the reader to think about anything but visions of hamburger stuck in a baby's rear end and a woman sexually attached to her German shepherd. (Tracy & Tracy, 1998).

In response to these critiques, I chose to keep the hamburger-baby example but delete the discussion of bestiality. I felt as though this was the best compromise. Although the baby-hamburger story still risked overshadowing my theoretical contributions, it was a risk I was willing to take to provide clear evidence of emotional work required by 911 call-takers to accomplish neutrality—a type of emotional labor that, until then, had not been investigated or very well understood.

Reflecting on These Risks

A common (if clichéd) question about risk is: Was it worth it? I am not convinced this is the best question to ask. Instead, I wonder whether risk is even an option. My experience suggests risk is part and parcel of ethnographic methods. Creativity emerges when we let go of our grip on certainty. Further, when we question and challenge the status quo, we not only learn about ourselves, but extend theory and understanding.

The Perils of (What) "I Don't Know"

Risk and Reward in Ethnographic Advocacy

Aaron Hess

Weekend after weekend, new recruits are found in the rave scene. On my first night working with DanceSafe, as I stood in the desert outside of Tucson, Arizona, a pair of bright-eyed ravers came to the table. One, adorned in the usual beads, visor, and flashy colors, had a new friend who he had "birthed" into rave culture. Introducing a new person into the scene came with the title of rave "parents." This particular pairing came up to get some candy and check out the table. The paternal raver, according to DanceSafe members, was a usual in the scene.

"Here," he said as he handed an ecstasy information card to his newly indoctrinated recruit, "read this."

She looked at the card and flipped it over to the all-important, drug education side.

He continued, "See, this tells you what is going to happen to you and all the side effects and stuff." Looking up at the group of us behind the table, he added, "She *just took* her first hit of ecstasy."

She excitedly smiled at us, proud of her decision, and continued to read the information.

Dismayed at the order of decision-making, I asked the DanceSafe members what they can do in this instance. How do you help them if they've already ingested the pills?

Lisa, the chapter co-president, replied, "You do what you can. Tell them to pay attention to their bodies and come back if they need help."

That same night, another young woman came to the table seeking assistance. She told us that she had taken two hits of ecstasy and two pills of Vicodin, and asked simply, "What's going to happen to me?"

I've got a lot to learn.

————

In my work with the harm-reduction organization DanceSafe, I travel to local raves—all night dance parties featuring music, glowing lights, and drug-induced youth. The drug of choice is 3,4-methylenedioxymethamphetamine (MDMA, more commonly known by its street name, ecstasy), a drug known for its stimulant, empathy-producing, and hallucinogenic properties. Users of the drug often experience profound interactions with others, even complete strangers, as if they have known them for entire lives. DanceSafe is dedicated to educating youth about drugs and drug use from a harm-reduction perspective, which offers neither criticism nor judgment of users. Instead, the organization provides information about safer use practices, such as testing kits to determine ecstasy pill contents. As a member of the group, I frequently interact with drug users while they are on drugs in an effort to learn and perform DanceSafe's advocacy.

Such advocacy is complicated by the nature of substance use and abuse. Young drug users would come to DanceSafe seeking information or advice about how to do drugs more safely. But there are a lot of drugs out there, with a lot of side effects. And young drug users are experimental, often combining different substances to produce the perfect high. DanceSafe volunteers, as local experts in the scene, are supposed to be the repository of drug literature, experiences, and more importantly, *answers.* Armed with binders full of information, glossy educational cards for young drug users to take home, and personal experiences, DanceSafe members conduct a questionable health advocacy for youth. Youth come with questions Mom and Dad would refuse to answer and youth dare not ask in school; questions about combining acid and ecstasy or how to kick a heroin habit.

And I'm supposed to have the answers.

When I joined the group in 2006, I was shocked at the amount of drug use in the rave scene and the impossible task that DanceSafe volunteers had undertaken. On the one hand, ravers were remarkably dismissive of DanceSafe's purpose. Looking over our wares, they would collect the information cards, loudly proclaiming, "I've had that one and that one and that one." Toward the end of any given night, DanceSafe members would scour the warehouse or desert to collect discarded drug information to recycle it back onto the table. On the other hand, DanceSafe members are faced with moments when their advocacy did exactly what it was supposed to do. Ravers approach the table with pertinent questions, earnestly seeking more information to make a decision about what to do *that night*. "What happens if I mix antidepressants with ecstasy?" "Have you tried this pill?" "Does LSD make your brain bleed?" "Do you know where I can find free drug treatment? I don't have insurance."

Every answer was loaded.

"I—I don't know."

Especially that one.

As a researcher, I came to my first rave with a notebook and pens, foolishly believing that I was prepared. At the time, I didn't realize that I was expected to know which neurotransmitters are released when MDMA hits the brain or about contraindications between methamphetamine and selective serotonin reuptake inhibitors. When ravers approached the table, they asked about who we were and what we were doing. At first, I didn't know how to respond and just wanted to observe. But from the other side of the table, I *was* DanceSafe. Wearing my name badge, I looked as much a part of the team as any other member. But when questions surface about mixing three different drugs, I am called on to answer. To *know*.

What if I get it wrong?

I quickly learned that much of my ethnography was learning to be a proper advocate for DanceSafe. It was learning about the different effects of drugs, learning about how ecstasy testing kits work, learning how to dispel the many urban legends about drugs. It wasn't that joining DanceSafe was risky for me; it was that my joining DanceSafe was risky for *them*. My inexperience was a liability, especially with health advocacy, where a mistake in advising a curious raver could have disastrous consequences on their body or mind. I know now, looking back, that I *did* make mistakes. I mistakenly referred to the drug 2CB as a liquid, when it's actually a pill or powder. Ravers asked me on various occasions about the drug PMA, which was red-flagged on our poster as an adulterant, and I had no idea what it was. I'm not sure what the consequences of my errors are, but I do know that each one damaged the carefully built ethos of the organization.

Ethnographers who engage advocacy—who intend to actively *perform* advocacy—must understand their personal limitations before they enter the scene. Certainly, self-reflexively taking stock of our positions and identities is important. But ethnographers would be wise to also identify their *novice* status as well. Overly concerned with the *research* part of my project, it was easy to forget that I am an invited participant, a representative, and a beginner in this organization. And my research and educational credentials don't mean much in the world of raving.

At the same time, ethnography is about *becoming*. My learning curve provided an extra set of data to analyze. I reflexively examined my role in the organization as I continued to grow and learn. My mistakes became personal lessons, all in an effort to gain the wisdom of being a veteran advocate. Toward the end of my project, I felt confident that I had effectively learned how to advocate as a DanceSafe volunteer, and was active in recruiting and training new members into the organization, members who will eventually take over the volunteer program and its mission. I finished my project, having given back to DanceSafe both my service and commitment, returns on the risky investment they placed in me. And I left with a new appreciation and understanding of health advocacy, drug prevention, and the underground culture of raving.

In the last analysis, I'm glad that DanceSafe took a risk on me.

Don't Take My Picture!

Photography as Risky Data

Karen A. Stewart

I am standing in the middle of the Nevada desert, camera in hand, and I have a decision to make. *Do I take a photograph of the people camping next to me?*

Earlier in the day, the answer would have been simple. *Yes. Take their photo. They're fun. They're nice. They'll consent. Document your neighbors.*

That was when they were "just" the neighbors.

But now my neighbors are rolling around naked on a tarp and drenching each other with beet juice. Apparently, they have decided to dye their skin purple. I don't know why they are doing this, but now is clearly not the time to ask. I don't want to get too close and end up purple, either.

This is a strange research moment ...

But isn't this what I expected? After all, I am at the annual Burning Man Festival, an event with a reputation for "radical self expression and radical self reliance,"[2] and for days I've been observing and documenting a wide range of performance art. This moment shouldn't be any different. But it *is*; at least to me. It's different because the scene is abruptly changing before my eyes and I no longer understand what I am seeing. My laid-back neighbors are no longer laid back. They are naked and caught up in the creation of their performance—a performance I am witnessing without a context. And I don't have time to process this new scene before I must decide whether or not to photograph it. The performance is passing. My neighbors are rapidly becoming more purple than pink. It will be over soon.

Do I take a photograph of the people camping next to me? The naked, purple people camping next to me?

I tell myself to decide now—and I go with "Yes." Take their photo. They're fun. They're nice. Ask for consent later. Document your neighbors.

When I stand behind the camera, I feel an ethical tension. The camera clearly marks me as researcher—a privileged observer, recorder, and voyeur who frames, reduces, and objectifies her research subjects. But I also know I am capturing unique moments of human expression and bearing witness to passion and play—modes of expression easily dismissed by dominant arenas of cultural production. The camera allows me to capture these moments and to share their importance with new audiences—a process made especially effective by the power of visual data.

I do not dismiss this tension. I have been trained in the practice of new ethnography, a highly reflexive approach to ethnographic research that challenges ethnographers to constantly consider their relationship to their research topic and the people it involves. As a counter-argument to ethnographic methods based on positivist principles, new ethnography is also a reminder that data are never truly objective. New ethnography acknowledges the limitations and biases inherent to the process of data collection and presentation and calls for researchers to bring these biases out in the open.

I choose to operate within this spirit of reflexivity, so I carefully contemplate each click of my camera. As the researcher, I am ultimately responsible for creating, interpreting, and circulating my images—and although I cannot completely control how audiences will read and perceive the images I create, I can make the effort to respectfully present the material and the people contained within.

Theoretically, methodologically, and emotionally I am invested in this approach to my work—and I can justify this approach when I write my methods sections. But underneath it all I have some doubts. Not about the importance or validity of ethnography practices based in reflexivity, but in my ability to actually execute them. Reflexivity requires time to think—to process and contemplate research decisions—and as I become more and more invested in visual ethnography, the one thing I am quickly realizing is that in the field, time is a luxury I often don't have.

Decisions need to be made quickly and constantly—click or don't click. Decide now. Contemplate later. The moment is passing.

———

I take the photograph and instantly nine purple heads turn in my direction. One of the naked men jumps up from the tarp, points to me and roars, "DON'T TAKE OUR PICTURE!!!"

I'm in the middle of clicking off my second shot when he does this, so I capture his admonishment with my camera. I feel badly that I do. Technically, this is a public performance, and although they don't mind me watching, I realize now they aren't comfortable with me taking photographs and recording them.

My actions are violating the intimacy of their performance space. *Should I have realized this before?* I stop taking pictures and return to the position of nonmediated observer.

The admonishment, though, stays with me for the remainder of my fieldwork.

———

Burning Man is challenging to photograph. On the one hand, event organizers encourage photography because they recognize it as a legitimate form of self expression and social interaction, both of which are acceptable forms of festival participation. But on the other hand, participants are incredibly media savvy, and they understand all too well how easy it is for photographers to treat the event as spectacle, resulting in the taking and circulating of images without consideration for the people included in the shots.

Media Mecca, the official public relations organization for the event, requires professional photographers to register their equipment and tag their cameras. They make a valiant effort to tag *every* video camera—amateur or professional—that enters the gate as well. They also keep tabs on images from Burning Man that are put into public circulation after the event, watching for exploitive images of festival participants.

Nonofficial participants also work as photography gatekeepers. It is not uncommon for someone to yell at you while you are taking photos—telling you to put your camera down, stop look-ing, and start *participating* (a festival catch-phrase reflecting a philosophy where doing and experiencing is valued over passive or voyeuristic observation.) Others, like the Bureau of Erotic Discourse (B.E.D.), find creative ways to incorporate the concept of respectful photography into their festival discourse. B.E.D is made up of a group of volunteers who educate participants on the importance of clear and respectful communication in romantic and sexual situations in an effort to increase awareness about sex-ual assault. Along with their educational messages about asking before touching and setting intimacy boundaries, they discuss the need to ask permission before taking photographs of people.

This layered exposure to accountability messages I experi-ence in the field reminds me that conceptually, reflexivity is not just a methodological framework or an extension of institutional review board protocol. Audiences also understand the potentially negative consequences of becoming "subject," and they are asking for researcher accountability as well.

I think of all these arguments when I click my camera. And I recognize that if I am to hold myself accountable to me, my methods, and the participants in my research, I must keep work-ing to find ways to navigate the compression and compaction of constant decision-making fieldwork inevitably involves.

It is within this navigating process that I feel my work is risky, because it matters to me that my efforts don't fall short.

A few weeks after Burning Man ends, Beet Camp (the rather obvious name I now know my purple neighbors go by) posts a request on an online networking site asking if anyone has pho-tographs from their performance they would be willing to share. Given their earlier admonishment, I'm surprised to see the post. But after reading the request, I realize they are asking for photos because they, too, see value in a photographic memory of their performance and they also want something visual to share from their experience.

I email my two photos with a thank you for the opportunity to photograph them.

One of the Beets e-mails a reply. She is surprised and happy to receive the photographs and she also sends her thanks for sharing. Our exchange ends on a warm, positive, and reciprocal note. *I tell myself, "This is the way photographic research should be."*

Risky Business

H. L. Goodall, Jr.

One consistent literary theme in ethnography, or perhaps it is just a consistent storyline, or maybe even a consistent heroic myth, is that what we do "in the field" is risky business. I wonder about that.

From Malinowski at least through Clifford Geertz, the ethnographer at work away from home is crafted as one part grand adventurer and one part reflective academic, and the element of risk is a built-in narrative device designed to keep readers interested. For although it is true that most of us read ethnographies out of a curiosity to learn about cultures different from our own, we also read past the facts out of a different sort of curiosity to see "what happens next." The mystery, riddle, or question that guides field research, and the storylines that emerge from the field, therefore, must be sufficiently cast with an element of uncertainty—of risk—or else we bore the reader and kill the story.

But there is Risk (capital R) and there is risk (small r).

I think a lot of what we like to frame as "risky" in fieldwork is small "r" stuff. Most of us do not put ourselves in harm's way—risking life and limb—so much as we risk putting ourselves in the path of a tenurable career. What we call "risky" could just as easily pass as "sexy" or "sensational." We go on the road with rock bands or interview celebrities or politicians or executives; we hang out with addicts of every kind; we study illegal immigrants, or street gangs, or strippers, or the police. We describe our secret longings, our sexual identities, our childhood, and our academic lives. Yes, there is an element of risk in all of these scenarios—risk to our careers—but unless we do something really boneheaded, we are unlikely to die.

Of course there are exceptions. Consider the anthropologists who volunteer for the Pentagon's Human Terrain project in Afghanistan and Iraq. So far, two of them, Michael Bhatia and Nicole Suveges, have met death in bomb blasts and another one, Paula Lloyd, was set on fire by the Taliban.[3] That is Capital R risk. And really, there is nothing vaguely sexy about being seriously wounded or killed in a war zone.

Nor will that sort of funded fieldwork help an academic career, given the taint of both military and CIA involvement with the Human Terrain project or other attempts to embed social scientists and journalists with troops. The ugly specter of one of Vietnam's darkest legacies, that of anthropologists and journalists who provided military and intelligence officials with cultural and logistical information that led to the death of civilians and destruction of villages, hangs over it.[4] Different war, similar circumstances, maybe different rules. Maybe. But Big R risk just the same.

So I make no claims about being a risky ethnographer. The risks I have taken have all been pretty small, although at the time they felt large. I once illegally entered a government facility and was apprehended. Could have gone to jail, but didn't. I played in a lot of dicey bars and clubs when my band, Whitedog, toured the Southland. In some of them, fights broke out. I stayed safely away from them, observing rather than participating in them. I've hung out with some strange characters in some even stranger places, but, so far as I can tell, I am not any worse the wear for it. And I have collected a lot of stories. It's been a good life.

I imagine that all—or at least most—of you who are at this very moment reading this chapter could say the same thing. You, too, have put yourself "out there" in the field.

You've been in some odd places and you've worked with unusual people who, given the chance, could have taken the interview or the field experience in a very different direction.

Maybe you've traveled to exotic environments in your own hometown or abroad only to find yourself without a clue about what to do next, feeling both lost and alone.

Maybe you've looked in the mirror after a particularly telling night of fieldwork and wondered what the hell you ever thought you were doing *there*.

And no doubt you have—as we all have—had more than a few dark nights of the ethnographic soul where everything you thought you were, whatever identity you thought you had, and please God whatever you thought you were doing, came suddenly and irrevocably crashing down.

So it goes.

On the other hand, what constitutes risk is less about what took place in the field than what takes place on the page. How we *story* the experience. And what we decide to reveal. The risk at this level is about what we disclose to readers about ourselves and others, and how what we write about may figure into our careers.

So, for example, I know there are details I've left out of many of my accounts. Didn't want to reveal, disclose ... didn't want to take the *risk*. Sometimes my sins of omission involved keeping things I knew about others quiet, too. Discretion is always the better part of a tenure case.

So it went.

At least for me.

But years do pass and things do change after the brass ring is yours to wear. The line, if there is one, between Big R and little r risks become blurred. The once all-important consequences of gaining tenure and a full professorship, for me, have redefined what risk means. I'm still not in the "life and limb" Big R category, but my writing and teaching has certainly taken a political turn that carries with it a risk to further career advancement that comes with public exposure.

Because I write critically about cold war culture and its reemergence in the current global "war on terror," because I write about the CIA, the Department of State, and the Pentagon, because I contribute white papers and posts to a widely read blog about counterterrorism and public diplomacy as well as participate in seminars on countering ideological support for terrorism, and despite the fact that I have served as a funded U.S. Department of State international speaker on those issues, I can no longer be classed along other "safer" colleagues—particularly when it comes to being considered for a senior administrative role.

I'm the kind of academic man who now makes other kinds of academic men and women nervous—especially if they consider themselves politically conservative and if it is their business to deal with conservative fundraisers. Certain donors, well, let's just say I'm not perceived to be the right guy to be cultivating a relationship with them.

It's not my research that is risky. It is that *I* am.

Notes

1. See *Going Tribal* as a contemporary example of the "ethnography as adventure" research approach: http://dsc.discovery.com/fansites/going-tribal/about/about.html (accessed June 13, 2008).

2. For more information about the Burning Man Festival, visit http://www.burningman.com/

3. See http://chronicle.com/news/index.php?id=5455&utm_source=pm&utm_medium=en (accessed November 18, 2008).

4. See http://en.wikipedia.org/wiki/American_Anthropological_Association (accessed December 6, 2008).

References

Flaherty, R. J. (Producer/Director). (1922). *Nanook of the North* [silent film]. Les Frères Revillon and Pathé Exchange [Production Companies].

Tracy, S. J. (2000). Becoming a character for commerce: Emotion labor, self subordination and discursive construction of identity in a total institution. *Management Communication Quarterly*, 14, 90–128.

Tracy, S. J. (2005). Locking up emotion: Moving beyond dissonance for understanding emotion labor discomfort. *Communication Monographs*, 72, 261–283.

Tracy, S. J. & Tracy, K. (1998). Emotion labor at 911: A case study and theoretical critique. *Journal of Applied Communication Research*, 26, 390–411.

Chapter 10 ||| Racializing Ethics and Bearing Witness to Memory in Research[1]

Cynthia B. Dillard
(Nana Mansa II of Mpeasem,
Ghana, West Africa)
The Ohio State University

Bearing witness

Our ability to remember is at risk in a culture where only the present moment matters. ...We have to value conversation and storytelling, because our memories and histories are shared and kept alive through these practices.

—hooks and Mesa-Bains, 2006, p. 112

As Vic and the seller were finishing their transaction, the old woman reached over and touched Vic's arm, her face now absolutely perplexed, nodding in my direction: "What *is* she (me)? Is she a white woman?" I nearly fell over, a rush of emotions running through me, from absolute horror to disgust to disbelief to sadness. Vic giggled and explained to the woman (who had still not quit starring at me) that I was not a white woman but a black American. But that evening in my researcher's journal (and through confused, angry, and sad tears that could've filled a river), I wondered aloud as I wrote: "How could she see *me* as a white woman?" "Couldn't she see the African woman I could see in myself?" "Didn't she know what had happened to millions of Africans who'd been forcibly taken from the shores of Ghana and other West African countries?" "Where did she think we had gone?" "Had she never imagined that some of us would return?" "How can this sister/mother see me this way?" In reflection, what frightened me most about her question was that, at that very moment, I couldn't answer it myself:

> What had been the rather solid taken-for-granted nature of my African American identity—an identity that I'd used to make sense of myself—melted down like butter on a hot summer's day in that moment in Ghana. Something very rich that I loved dearly had become useless fat on the sidewalk, no help whatsoever in explaining and understanding what she saw, or who I was. But I know there is wisdom in her question or it wouldn't have come to teach me a lesson. If I'm to "be" a researcher in this space, I will have to struggle with the butter on the sidewalk, the shifting ground of African identity through Ghanaian eyes. Neither here nor there (Ghana or the US), neither African nor American, neither recognizably Black nor white. Maybe it's not either/or: Maybe it's both/and? Somehow, it feels like it's beyond these dualities. They seem too simple. Regardless, it hurts to do this work. (Journal, 1/22/98)

Talking Back: It's beyond Intellectual

The narrative above is a story taken from my book *On Spiritual Strivings: Transforming an African American Woman's Academic Life* (2006), very much in the spirit of the conversations called for by hooks and Mesa-Baines in the quote above. I share it as a way to both stand in solidarity with and to bear witness to the power of memory to inform research ethics—our system of moral principles that undergird what we believe to be right or wrong and which shape and influence the morality of our motives and our practices. And as an African ascendant feminist researcher, this is a revolutionary task, one that requires courage and daring to boldly "talk back" (hooks, 1989): To ourselves, to the academy, to various cultural spaces and places in the world, to one other, to those who are culturally distinct from ourselves. In such ethical racialized voices (particularly in those of many African American women scholars) is an underlying and unasked question that DuBois (1989) raised years ago: "unasked by some through feelings of delicacy; by others through the difficulty of rightly framing it. All nevertheless flutter round it, the real question ... How does it feel to be a problem? I answer seldom a word" (pp. 1–2).

This question of being framed as "the problem" accurately describes the deeply raced, gendered, cultured, sexualized, often bitter negotiations that are the everyday landscape for scholars of color in our academic lives, historically and contemporarily. This landscape described by DuBois above is familiar territory for me, whether in Ghana or in other contexts, and for other scholars of color, echoing his notion of the sense of double consciousness:

> the sense of always looking at one's self through the eyes of others, of measuring one's soul by the tape of a world that looks on in amused contempt and pity. One ever feels [her] twoness—an American, a Negro; two souls, two thoughts, two unreconciled strivings; two warring ideals in one dark body, whose dogged strength alone keeps it from being torn asunder. (DuBois, 1989, p. 3)

But what is also highlighted in DuBois's ideas is not only about the need to interrogate oppressive and sometimes unintelligible research and teaching contexts, but the more difficult task he spoke of (DuBois, 1989): his idea of reconciling and "merging one's double self into a better and truer self" (p. 3). And a central wrestling I find in attempts at that reconciliation take us back to the story of the elder Ghanaian woman and my overwhelmed response to her characterization of my racial/ethnic identity: "*Somehow, it feels like it's even beyond these dualities. They seem too simple. Regardless, it hurts to do this work.*" So, I would like to look at further complexities and possibilities of identity (leaning on DuBois's notion of double consciousness) when located *not* in the white racial landscape of the United States but against the varied racial, cultural, and (inter)national contexts explicated by many scholars of color.

One way to read this exploration might be as a critique of the limitations of DuBois's notion of double consciousness in capturing the complexities and the possibilities of identities beyond the binary of black and white, beyond nation state, ethnicities, or other racialized ethics and constructions of difference. However, more importantly, I am suggesting that the discussion of identities can also be informed by the often ignored notions of the spiritual in DuBois's work, and how spirituality might mediate our contemporary meanings of racial and other identities. It seems to me that beyond our wrestlings with the biological and cultural explanations of identity, recognition of the spiritual nature of identity extends our notions beyond their overreliance on race as an identity—and toward the possibilities of moving through and maybe beyond race to a more equitable and subjective identity as spiritual beings.

Re-Membering: Toward an Ethic of Spirituality

Central to my thinking about race and research is an often unnamed element of identity, one that for me is inherent in the acts of research and teaching. That is, that both teaching and research are *deeply embedded in the act of memory, of re-membering*. And as human beings, we have an unlimited capacity for memory, all kinds of memory. Sensory memory, of things touched and felt, sensual and alive. Physical memory, of pleasure and pain, of bodies stretched and moved in ways we had not thought possible. Spiritual memory, of knowing the energy of God/dess and seeking to find ways to ease our separation from the Creator and from one another. Emotional memory, the feelings of sadness, happiness, envy, and hatred, to name a few. And we have cultural memory, memory of our unique and collective ways of being on this earthly journey. In research by scholars of color and others, we see that cultural memory is at least part of what is raised up in our on-going quest to be "seen" and "heard" and "unlimited" in the myriad ways we approach our questions, our scholarship (see Alexander, 2005; Coloma, 2008; Daza, 2008; Strong-Wilson, 2008; Subedi, 2008; Subreendeth, 2008 for examples). In common, memory can be thought of as a thing, person, event that brings to mind and heart a past experience—and with it, the ability to "re"-member, to recall and think of *again*. The *American Heritage Dictionary* (2000) goes so far as to say that to remember is "to bear in mind, as deserving a gift or reward" (p. 597). And the very intimate nature of various research narratives like those cited above suggests that memory is also about an *awakening*, an opening to the spirit of something that has, until this moment, been asleep within us.

For many researchers of color, embracing an ethic that opens to spirit is fundamental to the nature of learning, teaching, and by extension, research. We seem to inherently recognize that such spaces and acts—and our memories and ways of being with/in them—are always and in all ways also political, cultural, situated, embodied, spiritual: They are *alive* and present within us. However, all too often we have been seduced into forgetting (or have chosen to do so), given the weight and power of our memories and the often radical act of re-membering in our present lives and work. And if we assume, as I do, that the knowledge, wisdom, and ways of our ancestors are a central and present part of everything that has existed, is existing, and will exist in what we call the future, then teaching and research must also undertake an often unnamed, unrecognized, unarticulated, and forgotten task that is important for individuals who yearn to understand ways of being and knowing that have been marginalized in the world and in formal education. Simply put, *we must learn to re-member the things that we've learned to forget.* Whether through wandering into unfamiliar/always familiar contexts, making conscious choices to use/not use languages and cultural wisdom, or strategically choosing to cover or uncover, in returning to and re-membering, an awakening in research and teaching is possible and powerful.

Toward a Definition of Racial/Cultural Memory

I began to see how important the telling of this particular story could be for Africans all over the world, many who consciously or unconsciously share this race memory, this painful experience of the Middle Passage. ... But if this part of history could be told in such a way that those chains of the past ... could, in the telling, become spiritual links that willingly bind us together now and into the future, then that painful Middle Passage could become, ironically, a positive connecting line to all of us, whether living inside or outside the continent of Africa.

—Feelings, 1995

Human beings have an unlimited capacity for memory, whether historical, sensory, spiritual, physical, or emotional. However, both our pedagogies and qualitative research methodologies, although varied and complex, often fail to consider the role of race/cultural memory as situated in the research/teaching endeavor; that is, memory that makes a demand on our present actions, thoughts, and feelings as we engage in the process of teaching and research. Such an exploration is important because what often "matters" in the ethical practice of research and teaching is not so much our technical expertise or our ability to ask "good" questions, but our cultural and political expertise: *Our ability to know and decide when and how and to whom questions should be asked*. I am suggesting here that such "expertise" is deeply embedded in the reflections and interpretations of the racial/cultural, political, and spiritual memories of the teacher/researcher and is thus worthy of exploration.

What is racial/cultural memory? What do such memories mean for the teacher/scholar (of color and conscience), and how might we more explicitly and systematically engage them, re-member what we have forgotten as a way toward healing not just ourselves but those with whom we teach and research? In Feelings's (1995) quote above, he suggests first that such memories, from a spiritual framework, have the potential to connect those on the continent of Africa to those in the diaspora, the result of the traumatic acts of the trans-Atlantic slave trade. This is a central characteristic of racial/cultural memories for African Americans and for others living with/in diaspora: *They are memories that acknowledge an ever present link between the diaspora and the continent, a heritage "homeplace."*

It is not accidental that many scholars of color take up the exploration and research into/about connections to or with/in some version of an ancestral, heritage, or cultural homeplace. Second, Feelings suggests that *racial/cultural memories are intimate*: They are memories that, good or bad, make you ache with desire "to find the marriage of meaning and matter in our lives, in the world" (Mountain Dreamer, 2005, p. 42). I believe this may be true for Whites and others who have not carried or been politically or culturally marked or "racialized"—and it is worthy of being explored by white researchers. Regardless of race, such intimacy is inextricably linked to racial and cultural identities; that is, memories are part and parcel of the meanings of identity for Asian, African, Latin American, Native or other ascendants with/in diaspora, of the meaning of who we are and how we are in the world. Husband (2007), in his work on African American male teacher identity suggests that cultural memories are those memories of experiences and/or events related to collective and or individual racial/cultural identity "that are either too significant to easily forget or so salient that one strives to forget" (p. 10). Husband goes on to describe the fundamental nature and character of racial/cultural memories:

> In the case of the former, cultural memories can be thought of as memories of events as racial/cultural beings that are/were so remarkable that we consider them to be defining moments in our life histories. ... Pertaining to the latter, race/cultural memories are those related to our racial/cultural identities that are so potent [often painful] that we tend to suppress [them] in order to function as human beings. (p. 10)

What we see here is that the intimate nature of racial/cultural memories and their work in identity creation is inseparable from what it means to be vulnerable in our work, from reaching down inside of one's self and across towards others to places that may "break your heart" (Behar, 1996)—but, like these brave researchers, *choosing to go there anyhow.*

That brings us to the final part of a definition of racial/cultural memories: *They are memories that change our ways of being (ontology) and knowing (epistemology) in what we call the present.* They are inspirational, breathing new life into the work of teaching, research, and living. They are memories that transform, a place within and without that feeds our ability to engage new metaphors and practices in our work (Dillard, 2000).

So racial/cultural memories are those memories that may connect us to our heritage/cultural knowledges, to events and to people. They are intimate, personal, and shapers of identity. And they are memories that can change our present. They are the substance of things hoped for that DuBois (1989) spoke of years ago and that I pondered in *On Spiritual Strivings* (2006), ideas that have so captured my interest that I continue their examination here. They are about re-membering as an act of *coming full circle*.

Racial/Cultural Memories: Full Circle Research as Re-membering

Re-membering refers to the process of bringing to mind a particular event, feeling, or action from one's past experiences and the process of actually putting those memories back together in the present ("re-membering"). To re-member, one engages in reflection (Freire, 1970), a process of thinking about such remembrances of the past so as to seriously consider them, and to consider their meaning in present circumstances. According to Freire, this is also a transformative process.

Looking back, how do these racial/cultural memories make demands on present projects? How might these engagements with the "present" circumstances be interpreted in ways that move beyond simple nostalgia to actually *transform* political, cultural, and spiritual consciousness and our notions of identity (Dillard, 2000)? I suggest that what scholars of race and cultural memory do is show us what such mediation (between racial/cultural memories and present cultural contexts and engagements of teaching and research) look like and why they are critical and fruitful sites for developing consciousness that enables us to engage in inquiry and teach in ways that truly respect diversity in all its facets. And coming full circle is a spiritual concept that seems to embody the ontological and epistemological ideas within, against, and through such mediation, that opens up a conceptual and metaphorical space to explore these racial/cultural memories with an eye toward the deeply embedded spiritual nature of the endeavor we call research.

I turn here to Lakoff and Johnson's (1980) work on metaphor as a way to begin:

> Metaphor is pervasive in everyday life, not just in language but in thought and action. … The concepts that govern our thought

are not just matters of the intellect. They also govern our everyday functioning, down to the most mundane details. Our concepts structure what we perceive, how we get around in the world, and how we relate to other people. Our conceptual system thus plays a central role in defining our everyday realities ... and what we do every day is very much a matter of metaphor. (p. 3)

Walker (1988) offers three metaphorical and concrete ways that racial/cultural memories influence the transformation of consciousness and thus can shift the experience and everyday existence of those of us who teach and research, providing a new racialized ethics of both. She suggests that engaging racial/cultural memories gives:

1. a new set of connections and recognitions;

2. a new site of accountability; and

3. a new source of power.

The first thing that seems clear is that re-membering allows a new connection to the reseachers' heritage, cultural, spiritual knowledge, and ways of being as well as a recognition and centering, however slippery or tentative, to the researcher's named/self identified ethnic and national homeplace. It provides a link in the chain that, as a person of color, we all too often could and did not explore in history class, given our often subjugated histories. But it is through the often thoughtful and systematic attention to these identity-based connections/recognitions that we can see more clearly the ways that white supremacist patriarchy, sexism, racism, homophobia, etc., and the current conditions of people of color throughout the world are manifest and maintained.

The second thing about of Walker's idea of the possibilities of transforming consciousness through racial/cultural memory—and another manifestation of coming full circle—is that doing so provides a new site of accountability: One sees oneself as responsible to and for others in new, more powerful ways. From committing to the work of teaching about diversity despite racism and resistance, to making strategic decisions about the conduct of research, to continuing to center particular identities as a way to become more fully human (Freire, 1970), such commitments render all scholars who chose to engage these racial and cultural memories in their research accountable to the whispers of the ancestors and their ascendants.

Finally, engaging racial/cultural memories provides a new source of power as a full circle moment. It allows us to see the "weight" of African brilliance, the realization of how powerful we can be when all of us—mind, body, and spirit—are awake in heritage knowledge and grounded in theoretical and experiential conditions that open a space for all parts of us to be awake and engaged in the research process. This new source of power is also an important recognition that there remains much work to do in the process of learning to re-member the things we've learned to forget, particularly for scholars of color, given the reified ways of white supremacist thought and actions: That is the work that the ancestors have left for us to do.

A new set of connections and recognitions. A new site of accountability, one that moves us to more expansive ways of thinking and being. New sources of power. A new way of coming full circle—and a new meaning and purpose for doing so. What I am suggesting here is that acknowledging and examining racial/cultural memories are central to the full-circle process of learning to re-member (that is, put back together) the things we've learned to forget. But I believe that the usefulness of racial/cultural memories and their power to transform consciousness and research practice might be taken up by all racial or cultural groups:

> I believe it is a human trait—and for all I know, even a nonhuman animal one—and that what the Black, the Native American, and the poor white share in America is common humanity's love of remembering who we are. It is [only] because the language of our memories is suppressed that we tend to see our struggle to retain and respect our memories as unique. (Walker, 1988, p. 63)

The work of remembering what we've learned to forget is work for all to do in order to heal the depth of conflict and differences between us and "the metaphors we live by" (Lakoff & Johnson, 1980).

Note

1. An earlier version of this paper appeared in slightly different form as "Re-membering Culture: Bearing Witness to the Spirit of Identity in Research" (2007) in *Race and Ethnicity in Education*, 11(1), 87–93.

References

Alexander, M. J. (2005). *Pedagogies of crossing: Meditations of feminism, sexual politics, memory, and the sacred*. Durham, NC: Duke University Press.

American Heritage Dictionary of the English Language. (2000). Boston: Delta Books.

Behar, R. (1996). *The vulnerable observer: Anthropology that breaks your heart*. Boston: Beacon.

Coloma, R. (2008). Border crossing subjectivities and research: Through the prism of feminists of color. *Race, Ethnicity and Education*, 11(1), 11–28.

Daza, S. (2008). Decolonizing researcher authenticity. *Race, Ethnicity and Education*, 11(1), 71–86.

Dillard, C. B. (2000). The substance of things hoped for, the evidence of things not seen: Examining an endarkened feminist epistemology in educational research and leadership. *International Journal of Qualitative Studies in Education*, 13(6), 661–681.

Dillard, C. B. (2006). *On spiritual strivings: Transforming an African American woman's academic life*. Albany: State University of New York Press.

DuBois, W. E. B. (1989). *The souls of black folks*. New York: Bantam.

Feelings, T. (1995). *The middle passage*. New York: Dial Books.

Freire, P. (1970). *Pedagogy of the oppressed*. New York: Continuum.

hooks, b. (1989). *Talking back: Thinking feminist, thinking black*. Boston: South End Press.

hooks, b., & Mesa-Bains, A. (2006). *Homegrown: Engaged cultural criticism*. Cambridge, MA: South End Press.

Husband, T. (2007). Always black, always male: Race/cultural recollections and the qualitative researcher. Paper presented at The Congress of Qualitative Inquiry, May 3–6, University of Illinois, Champaign-Urbana.

Lakoff, G. & Johnson, M. (1980). *Metaphors we live by*. Chicago: University of Chicago Press.

Mountain Dreamer, O. (2005). *What we ache for: Creativity and the unfolding of the soul*. San Francisco: Harper Collins.

Strong-Wilson, T. (2008). *Bringing memory forward: Storied remembrance in social justice education with teachers*. New York: Peter Lang.

Subedi, B. (2008). Contesting racialization: Asian immigrant teachers' critiques and claims of teacher authenticity. *Race, Ethnicity and Education*, 11(1), 57–70.

Subreendeth, S. (2008). Deconstructing the politics of a differently colored transnational identity. *Race, Ethnicity and Education*, 11(1), 41–56.

Walker, A. (1988). *Living by the word: Selected writings 1973–1987*. San Diego, CA: Harcourt Brace Jovanovich.

Chapter 11 ||| The Death of a Cow

Jean Halley
Wagner College

In this chapter, I explore the death of beef cows. I contrast these deaths with the death of my beloved childhood cat and with the sadness—a kind of dying—in my childhood. I look at the violence of these deaths, but also simply at the ways the deaths are a movement from one state to another, not only for the dying, but for all those involved in and surrounding the death. I try to capture the feel, atmosphere, and experience of these changes. And I use the data or evidence of my life experience along with the lives of cows to tell this story. This chapter is part of a larger project, a book in which I juxtapose the social history of beef ranching with the story of my childhood family, one side of whom were cattle ranchers.

The experience of living is the experience of change. Dying is perhaps a more significant change than many, but it is still only one change in the midst of an infinity of tiny and large changes making up our days. I contrast this movement, this change, with the ways in which we—cow, cat, all of us—are also momentarily caught, contained in emotional, physical, and body spaces. In other words, we are held in life, in our bodies and in our life situations. There is no getting away from my own physicalness or my own life story, or my own emotional pain and joy. Even so, each of these things constantly changes, moves and transforms to something else. In its new form, the matter—be it me or a cow or a cut of meat—is both different and still the same. For even death does not stay still. Everything moves, everything changes.

Death as Production

Historically in the United States, the slaughterhouses have made most of the money to be made in beef. This is true even though the slaughterhouses were merely one stage in the production of meat. Some people bred and raised the cows; others slaughtered them and packed their meat to be sold; at the final stage, the consumer bought and ate the flesh. Jimmy M. Skaggs (1986) writes that the process was like an hourglass with lots of people in the beginning raising cows—the ranchers—and lots of people at the end eating cows—the consumers—but not many slaughtering them. The slaughterhouses had and continue to have a stranglehold on the industry. A small number of people have made and continue to make an immense amount of money off the backs of cows, literally, and less literally off ranchers. Indeed, Karen Olsson writes, "Four giant competitors—IBP, ConAgra, Excel (owned by Cargill) and Farmland National Beef—dominate the beef industry, together controlling over 85 percent of the US market" (2002, p. 12).

Similar to their counterparts in other industries, ranchers who supply the cows to these four companies, need to produce as much of their product—cow-to-be-meat—as possible with as little lost labor or other resources as possible in as short a time as is possible. To survive as a profitable business, they must raise their cows to make as much desirable meat as possible in as short a time as possible. The bigger the cow and the faster growing the cow the better. Yet there are other factors. American meat eaters want meat of a certain flavor and look. So cattle ranchers have slowly bred and raised bigger cows faster over the past century. This has a number of implications for the cow. Cows' lives have become significantly shorter. And they have slowly been ballooning out into larger and larger animals. Remarkably, this is the case even though they have less time to grow before slaughter.

When it comes time to be slaughtered, cows are either sold from their most recent owners, probably the people who own the feedlot or the slaughterhouse itself fattens the cows before slaughter. The cows need to be at a certain standard of health before the federal government allows them to be slaughtered. My grandfather owned a sale-barn. So he was a conduit from the people raising the cows to the people slaughtering the cows. Of course, he also raised cows himself. He made money by selling his own cattle as well as by auctioning other ranchers' cattle.

I remember walking above the cows on raised wooden pathways at my grandfather's sale-barn. I saw the cows from above. I walked up above these enormous pens filled with manure and mud and mooing animals, I walked and looked down on cow. But when you are around cows, you do not just see them. Perhaps the most dramatic experience of being with cows is the smelling of them. They have a very strong and very particular odor. The kind of odor—like breastfed baby poop or wet dog—that is definitively cow. Of course, like the poop of babies fed formula versus breastmilk, the odor changes depending on what you feed the cow. And our cows in the United States eat corn, lots of corn.

In killing cows, transforming this living, breathing, eating life into meat, the process has been routinized, much like the making of most other products in our postindustrialized world. Each step of a cow's death has been broken into its smallest component and done over and over again to thousands of cows. For instance in the 1990s, the John Morrell plant in Sioux Falls, South Dakota, then the only remaining tri-species plant, slaughtered "several thousand cattle, hogs, and sheep each day on three separate killing floors" (Eisnitz, 1997, p. 117). At the time of her research, journalist Gail A. Eisnitz found that

> one hundred and one million pigs are slaughtered each year in the United States. Thirty seven million cattle and calves. More than four million horses, goats, and sheep. And over eight billion chickens and turkeys. In all, annually in the United States farmers produce 65 billion pounds of cattle and pigs ... 46 billion pounds of chickens and turkeys. (p. 61)

That is a lot of killing.

Federal law mandates that the killing happen at slaughterhouses in the following manner. First, the cow is herded and probed through a chute in a "knocking box," or they are herded one by one into a restrainer on a conveyor belt. The conveyor belt carries the animal to a person whose job it is to stun the cow, the aptly titled "stun operator" or "knocker." This person has a compressed-air gun with which he or she shoots the animal in the forehead. The gun "drives a steel bolt into the cow's skull and then retracts it. If the gun is sufficiently powered, well maintained, and properly used by the operator, it knocks the cow unconscious or kills the animal on the spot" (Eisnitz, 1997, p. 20). The also aptly named "shackler" shackles the animal. This person's job is to put a chain around one of the cow's hind legs for cow after cow after cow. The chain is attached to a powerful machine that lifts the cow by its leg up into the air, then carries the cow, hanging upside down, through the next stages of the slaughtering process.

Next a person called the "sticker" cuts the cow's throat; "more precisely, the carotid arteries and a jugular vein in the neck" (Eisnitz, 1997, p. 20). The sticker makes a vertical, not horizontal, incision in the animal's throat, near where the major vessels issue from the heart, to cut off the flow of blood to the animal's brain. "Next the cow travels along the 'bleed rail' and is given several minutes to bleed out. The carcass then proceeds to the head-skinners, the leggers, and on down the line where it is completely skinned, eviscerated, and split in half" (p. 20).

The federal government passed the first version of this killing process into law with the Humane Slaughter Act (HSA) in 1958. Congress expanded the HSA in 1978. "Among the HSA's most important provisions is the requirement that all animals be rendered unconscious with just one application of an effective stunning device by a trained person before being shackled and hoisted up on the line" (Eisnitz, 1997, p. 24).

The Jungle

The story of what actually happens to cows at the kill is another story. But that story requires yet another story before its telling.

In 1906, Upton Sinclair published his famous novel about an immigrant family new to Chicago and carrying the "American Dream." As we watch this family struggle to survive, the "American Dream" is unraveled, and the American reality for new immigrants and the working poor is revealed. Sinclair wrote *The Jungle* out of his profound political commitments. Sinclair was a lifelong radical and activist, and a "significant presence within early socialist groups in American: In 1905, he cofounded the Intercollegiate Socialist Society with Jack London, Florence Kelley, and Clarence Darrow; in 1906 he established a socialist community, the Helicon Home Colony, in Englewood, New Jersey" (Spiegel, introduction to Sinclair 2003 [1906], p. v). Writing was one important venue for the expression of Sinclair's politics. "His work is identified with that of the writers Theodore Roosevelt dubbed 'muckrakers.' In all, he published more than ninety books and pamphlets and countless articles" (Spiegel, introduction to Sinclair, 2003 [1906], p. vi).

Through his perhaps most famous work, *The Jungle*, Sinclair revealed the underbelly of U.S. capitalism. Sinclair lived in

> an age of capitalist Titans, of magnates whose wealth, power, and hubris seemed unlimited: A single man owned a million acres of the Texas Panhandle, an American coal tycoon attempted to buy the Great Wall of China, and in the Midwest a combination known as the Beef Trust tightly controlled the production and sale of meat through pervasive wage and price fixing and the unrelenting exploitation of the stockyard workforce. (Spiegel, introduction to Sinclair, 2003 [1906], p. xv)

Sinclair intended to expose the terrible treatment of workers in the meat industry, particularly after the meatpacker's strike that failed to change the conditions of these workers in 1904. But the American public responded to the *conditions* under which their meat was processed from living animal to the product they bought and ate:

> *The Jungle* revealed slaughterhouse conditions so shocking and meat so filthy that meat sales plummeted more than fifty percent and President Theodore Roosevelt personally crusaded for enactment of the Federal Meat Inspection Act of 1906. That law and subsequent legislation established standards for plant sanitation and required federal inspection of all meat shipped interstate or out of the country. (Eisnitz, 1997, p. 21)

Although the American public *did* respond to the filth in their meat, they did not respond to the abuse of workers who produced their meat or to the violence against the animals that became their meat. As Sinclair himself said, "I aimed at the public's heart, and by accident I hit it in the stomach" (Spiegel, introduction to Sinclair, 2003 [1906], p. vi). Indeed, reading *The*

Jungle, one often feels sick to one's stomach. For example, Sinclair describes the deceptive and unsafe practices of the Chicago meat industry and its complete lack of concern for the public's health. Every part of every animal was used to make some product to sell to the unsuspecting consumer. Even sick animals were used. Sinclair wrote:

> It seemed that they must have agencies all over the country, to hunt out old and crippled and diseased cattle to be canned. There were cattle which had been fed on "whiskey-malt," the refuse of the breweries, and had become what the men called "steerly"—which means covered with boils. It was a nasty job killing these, for when you plunged your knife into them they would burst and splash foul-smelling stuff into your face; and when a man's sleeves were smeared with blood, and his hands steeped in it, how was he ever to wipe his face, or to clear his eyes so that he could see? It was stuff such as this that made the "embalmed beef" that had killed several times as many United States soldiers as all the bullets of the Spaniards; only the army beef, besides, was not fresh canned, it was old stuff that had been lying for years in the cellars. (Sinclair 2003 [1906], p. 110)

These, along with Sinclair's other assertions, were all but one independently verified when his book was published.[1] Understandably, when discovering the real origins of their dinner, the public was outraged. However, Sinclair made vivid more than just the health hazards birthed by the industry. Nonetheless, in contrast to the rapid enactment of the Meat Inspection Act and the federal Food and Drug Act passed the same year the book came out, no legal or other formal changes were made on behalf of meat industry workers. And the HSA did not come about until 1958.

The HSA addresses, of course, the death of cows and other animals. Yet there is more to their lives than dying. Death is only one among other changes in the life of a beef cow. Another important change is that of calf to adult cow. In a capitalist economy, the most important part of this change is that of small cow to large cow, less cow to more cow. And maybe caught in pressing, pressing of more life into life, pressing of more cow into cow, more meat into the skin wrapping and bone rack of animal, there is only one way out, only one way, and that is back to the place from which we came, back to sadness, back to dying. Maybe it is silly to dwell any longer on cows, stupid creatures. But they are gentle and alive. And they do offer themselves to us, unknowing. They make the sacrifice of dying. And then they live again, allowing their flesh to become ours. It is a kind of passion, a fully giving of one's self.

Somewhere around fourteen to sixteen months old, fattened cows are loaded into cattle trailers and carried to their last stop, the slaughterhouses. Cows must walk the last few steps of this journey. In fact, in this walk, they have always taken part in their own dying. The distance they walked decreased significantly over the past two hundred years. They used to walk for miles, for days, even months to the place of their slaughter. Albeit a shorter walk, cows still walk to the site of their death. Indeed, there is a law requiring that the animal do so. This is not, of course, meant to benefit the cow. Humans have devised this test to be sure the cow is healthy before transforming its flesh into food. A cow that cannot walk, a "downed cow," could be a sick cow whose flesh is unfit for human consumption. Healthy cows tend to spend a lot of time on their feet. And obviously, almost all healthy cows can walk.

Given our profit-driven society, that cows must walk to their own slaughter has made things pretty rough for the cows. The Humane Society of the United States (2008) offers video footage at their website from numerous undercover investigations involving their "Factory Farming Campaign: Working to Reduce the Suffering of Animals Raised for Meat, Eggs, and Milk." Among its investigations, in 2008, the Humane Society looked into the sale and slaughter of dairy cows that were no longer producing enough milk to make them profitable.

Typically, dairy farmers sell unproductive cows for slaughter. The Humane Society secretly inspected numerous auctions and slaughterhouses where they find that downed dairy cows "too frail to walk may be dragged to their death or left suffering for hours" (2008). In the video footage, one views downed animals being beaten until they drag themselves on broken limbs to their own slaughter. And in the end, potential profit carries more weight than the law that the animals must walk. Machines drag animals, seemingly too sick to be forced to move. Workers attach a chain to the leg of one dairy cow. In the footage, they proceed to drag the cow's full body weight by her overextended leg to the slaughterhouse. One witnesses other animals being kicked, beaten, and shocked as workers attempt to force the downed animals up. One worker repeatedly and forcefully probes a downed cow in her eye. Another worker rolls a downed cow bellowing and crying in front of a farm vehicle. Before stopping this rolling, the worker drives over her head. After beating another downed cow to no avail, a worker tries to force her to her feet by spraying water down her nose so that she feels that she is about to drown.

Along with the issue of cruelty to these animals, as the Humane Society points out, if downed and sick animals are being slaughtered and processed for meat, consumers are probably (unknowingly) eating diseased meat from such sick animals (2008). Indeed, children at school seem to be the consumers of some of this meat. One of the slaughterhouses found to abuse and slaughter downed cows, the Hallmark Slaughterhouse, provided meat for the Westland Meat Company, itself a top supplier to the National School Lunch Program. The Humane Society believes that the National School Lunch Program has received and served a significant amount of meat from downed, and potentially sick, cattle.

At the slaughterhouse, all the cows' efforts bear fruit. And they become meat. They are stunned, bled, and eviscerated. Then they are graded, checked for disease, and broken down into cuts. And, given that at some beef plants, 390 animals are killed every hour, that is a lot of killing. And a lot of meat.

And so the cows offer themselves to be eaten. They become us. The body and the blood. It is a kind of passion, a kind of giving. And maybe no one, not cows, not us, maybe no one really owes anyone their passion. But they give it anyhow. I am one of those who gives passionately. The catch is that passion, given or received, brings something with it, some weight of its past it carried into new form. Passion is not freedom. It is a heavy kind of love.

I know about this. I love, at least a few people, with everything. They are my everything. But if this loving is giving, it is a funny kind of giving. Really, in it, in giving this love, I try to leave myself. I try to step away from the unbearable place that is me. I try to enter into them, and become anew. Passion can be dying. But passion can also act to kill, to press into, to push aside and away, bloating, exploding the walls of another.

But Here

My sadness leaves me no choice. It pushes all else aside. It is the hardest thing to name and yet demands naming. It is a dry, dusty washed-out-by-too-much-sun place. It is a place that swallows all else, all other desires, all color, all beauty. All gone to this still quiet.

We all risk returning to this emptiness that makes one long for dying because at least in dying there is a strength. Color and presence live on in dying. But here, but here, how can I tell it? I am again my horse before a storm, rushing along fence lines, frenzy whirling in the air, gripping me from inside out. I rush, seeking words to release me.

And yet, somewhere I know there is no release. My horse, too, lived forever in-between fences. His escapes were momentary. He was always caught, always brought home, always, to that place between wires. That is where I too live. It is no place and yet it fills everywhere, inside of me.

This. This is the ghost of my family. Somehow, of that, I feel a kind of sureness, even as the sureness slips away. This is the ghost. My grandfather, my father's father, whoever he was, was a man willing violence, willing rupture of another. And there lived the ghost. He was a man who got rich. A man who hated "niggers," who pulled my hair, who touched my breasts before breasts pushed forward. He voted Republican, drove crazy-like, beat his sons with a belt or worse when they misbehaved, and supposedly loved my grandmother, whatever that means. Or at least, that is the story as I now know it. They say my grandfather was sane. He was the wire fence line, dividing this from that, cutting through, controlling all things.

My father, like my mother's father, was out of control. He was insane. He was the waste left behind my grandfather's life. He was the violence ricocheting here and there, controlling nothing, moving wildly. But that, too, of course, is a kind of control. And so if my grandfather held the gun, steady and shot, my father, the bullet, ran until it found me. And I live with it, embedded inside. It will not let me go. Nor I, it.

Yet there is no quick way out, anyhow. The fences go to infinity. They live on with or without me. And I cannot leave, anyhow. My grandfather, dead fifteen years, is still here, of course. Everything stays.

And me too, just when I think I have turned away to somewhere else, no fence no land no frenzied horse no sun-bleached colorless sky no boy scarecrow hanging on a fence no girl wet with his release no story clinging to her no toilet whirling cat gut away no more, no more, just then I turn, and there it is again. Just then I turn and find the fence to meet me.

Barbed Wire

My grandfather worked among cows. His life was made of power and violence and a certain kind of success. And among other things, his spent his days containing cows, growing more cows and bigger cows, selling cows and starting over, containing more cows. As with most things growing and becoming, becoming cow, becoming meat entailed containing. Beef growing is contained most closely by skin stretched tight. Beyond skin, containing cows entails fence and fence entails wire. In its beginning, cow meat is often held by wire, barbed wire. And as with most everything, what holds us, what presses in on us, is as much us as we are who press out against our walls.

Barbed wire was invented in 1874 after Joseph F. Glidden was struck by a device on sale at an agricultural fair—nails stuck into a wooden board to be attached to the head of wandering livestock (Netz, 2002, p. 17). Whenever the animal tried to press herself into a limited area, she would cause herself intense pain. The board with its nails replaced the presence of human beings. It was a punishing, portable wall. Through the pain it caused, the board demanded obedience. Glidden, recognizing its potential, developed this innovation. He took the nails off of the animal and put them on an actual wall, or really a fence (Netz, 2002, p. 18). The fascinating part of this invention was its frailty. The fence, made of strands of wire with nails or barbs attached, barbed wire, is insubstantial. The fence is frail. For strength, when it comes to pain, is often unnecessary. This is not because animals will not fight. We all fight. We all fight for our freedom in one way, or another. And, oddly, for some, the tighter we are held, the closer the walls, the more we desire freedom, the more we desire that which is far away. The more we desire.

The Walls in My Dream

And the basement went on and on and on, walls moving into halls and rooms, tunnels curving here, winding there, it unfolded back and again back in time, through years, then more years. And all the while, menace pressed in on us like a hand, reaching. It was always almost there, always almost grabbing hold, lurking panting pushing in on us, like a bad horror movie. Danger pressed against the windows that kept appearing in my mind. I was afraid. How many ways are there to say it. I was afraid. I tried to find a place where we could rest, the we that we were, always changing. Yet most important, my child, my son, my love kept slipping out of my reach. And then, I became the hand, only frantic, edging against panic, stretching to find him again, stretching to enclose him against, in, within me. In the dream, I tried to find a place where we could rest. I made resting places on the way as we ran on through time and basements of my past woven together, reaching across spaces, places too large to ever really cross. Finally, in the end, I made a bed in a cement unfinished basement room, a bed on the floor from sofa mattress pads and old blankets and memories and things. I tucked my child in. To sleep, my child, to sleep amid my fear. As the basement ran on, around us.

Maybe no one really owes anyone their passion. Even so, I am one of those who gives it. And in my life, no one ever loved me with passion except perhaps my cat, Thomasina. Thomasina was the only one that gave me her full allegiance. She loved me. It was final, forever and always. She, really, loved me. She gave me her body, warm and soft, small, gray, wrapped around my neck at night, gently, loudly purring. She gave me her full presence. And when I was away, she cried, for hours and through the night, loud calling, calling outside my mother's bedroom door. She insisted I be returned to her.

And now, she is gone. It was only her small cat body that kept me from the vastness of being totally alone. And I wonder how I can spend a lifetime this way. No matter what, unwanted. No matter what. How can I live a whole life this way. It will always be too long, too many days, too much hurt.

Thomasina died. But I know, I know it wasn't really because she was old. Her arthritis was making her ache in the freezing, bitterness of winter in Montana, at least nine months of cold, maybe more. By then, by the time Thomasina's arthritis chilled her limbs to stiff and aching, I was away. Her last winter was my semester abroad in Alicante, Spain. Even being in Spain, even being in college, that time when they say everything is good, even so, I longed to come home. And it was then that my mother said that Thomasina could not fully move her body. Instead she dragged her stiff back legs through the house to a resting place where she would stay until her hurting body's needs made her move again.

So that's when, that was when we decided to kill her. We decided that we would leave her to living for one more summer, one more summer in Montana with its gentle, sweet warmth, long days, free of suffering. Summer in Montana is a romance that the world has with itself. We decided that we would kill her at the end of summer.

And yet I know that she was really the only one that loved me more than anything; she loved me with intensity and faithfulness, focus. She really loved me. And so I decided to have her killed. It was because, really because, her love was unbearable. That's why. It was unbearable in the threat of its leaving. Because the leaving always comes. And in its passing, there is left behind, only the brilliant raw pain of myself. I could not bear for her to leave. I just couldn't.

It is ironic. Vegetarian, pacifist that I am. I am adamantly against killing. And yet I consciously decided to kill the one that loved me most.

So we chose a day for her dying. And even so, even being the one who decided, I could not endure her. The night before her death I spent with a man I hardly knew. My time with Thomasina was perfunctory. It was time I had to spend. And then I stroked her. And then I left. And the next day I got my brother to make photographs of her and me together one last time. Odd that there was no film in the camera, a mistake that made sure there were no traces left behind. She was really gone. And then we, my brother and sister and I, drove her to the veterinarian. My mother could not be there. And so we drove her, the three of us who knew so much about leavings from the place of being left. And then I held her on the veterinarian's shiny steel table. I held her down and still.

She died crying. And we laughed because she had done so much crying. We laughed, and she died. Maybe she knew that her leaving was really my leaving. I was gone again. It merited long cries, as many as she could manage before we each were gone. I had to do it. I had to go. I could not bear for her to leave. It was one more leaving I could not allow.

———

Yet, you know that nothing ends. And dying is not always what it looks like. We often tell each other that dying is the end. But it's not. Even death is funny that way. Nothing really ends. There is always a resurrection. Life always pushes for life, again. We all do. We all push, for life, in one way or another. Even in the placidity of cow-being, life pushes for life. Some animals fight in a way that is wild. Some animals fight in a way that is breathless. But that is not the only way. Cows fight, too; cows fight by waiting.

From the perspective of the meat industry, there are a number of problems with the HSA. Ultimately, all the problems result in a loss of profit. And we must remember that the meat industry is not in the business to feed the hungry masses or to hearken back to a safer, saner time when we all lived on farms, or even to supply good work to those in need of it. The meat industry is, of course, all about profit. Not the animals, not the food made from their flesh, not the human beings who kill the animals and pack their meat, or the ones who eat it. It is, pure and simple, about profit. Following the HSA's mandated procedure for killing animals takes too much time. There is time involved in properly stunning an animal. There is time involved in correcting an improper stun. And there is time involved in keeping the line slow enough to protect the workers. Indeed, often in an attempt to speed up production, animals simply do not get stunned properly, if they get stunned at all.

With stunning, lost time is a central issue but not the only issue. There is a common belief in the meat industry that stunning an animal to the point of stopping its heart will make the meat less valuable. "It's an industry myth that an animal's heart has to keep beating in order to pump all the blood from its muscles. When the blood is retained in the meat, it provides a good medium for bacteria to grow, and that reduces the meat's shelf life" (Eisnitz, 1997, p. 122). Eisnitz interviewed Bucky White, a meatpacker at the John Morrell plant in Sioux Falls, South Dakota. About stunning cattle, Bucky White said, "We got a superintendent who claims the big bolt kills the cattle 'too dead' and they don't bleed properly ... I've headed [skinned the heads of] and stuck cattle for twenty-one years, and I've never heard of cattle being too dead" (p. 122). Here Bucky White's spouse, Margie White added, "They're climbing up the walls and kicking you ... but they're too dead" (p. 122).

Fully stunning animals, of course, is good for the animal about to be slaughtered and good for the workers processing its meat. The animal is then processed with minimal suffering. And workers stay safer, sticking, skinning, and cutting large animals that are dead rather than fighting the meatpackers as they work. In the early 1980s, many studies demonstrated that "killing an animal by stopping the heart instead of just stunning it has no effect on the amount of blood retained in the meat" (Eisnitz, 1997, p. 123). Nonetheless, the meat industry clings to the idea that animals should not be stunned to the extent that their hearts stop. Because of this worry over "too dead" cows, management often keeps the stun gun current turned down. Bucky White explained to Eisnitz "that the captive bolt knocking guns they used have two sizes of bolts. Plant management requires that the smaller, less effective bolt be used" (p. 122).

Eisnitz asked Bucky White how often alive and conscious cattle come through the stunning process: "The way I look at it," White said, "out of the 1,228 beef I stuck today it would have been okay if a few were still alive. But it's all day. Constantly, all day, I get live cattle" (Eisnitz, 1997, p. 121). In response to Eisnitz asking him how he can tell that the cattle are alive and conscious, White said, "The live ones you could tell 'cause they're bellowing, blinking, looking around" (p. 121). Because the animals are alive, they fight and this is dangerous for the workers attempting to process the animal's flesh:

"A month ago Bucky got kicked in the mouth," Margie said.

White pointed to his lip. "Right here, just about drove my tooth right through. Then I got kicked behind the ear."

"Two weeks ago he got it right above the eye," Margie said.

"So in the last month," [Eisnitz] asked, "how many times did you get nailed?"

"Got kicked in the mouth, the eye …"

"Under the arm," Margie said, "And just yesterday, underneath the other arm, it's black and blue." (Eisnitz, 1997, p. 122)

Eisnitz also met with then United States Department of Agriculture (USDA) meat inspector, Kevin Walker about his experience at a slaughterhouse in Bartow, Florida, Kaplan Industries. Before their meeting he had contacted her by mail with his concerns. He claimed that cattle were being skinned alive at Kaplan Industries.

"This is not only extremely cruel," he wrote, "but also very dangerous for the plant personnel who have to skin these kicking animals." Plant management knew about the problem, he said, but didn't want to correct it because that would mean slowing down the production line. "I have contacted a number of federal agencies but have been told there is nothing they can do. They also told me that the problems I described exist all over the country, that they are just a little worse at Kaplan's." (Eisnitz, 1997, p. 18)

Eisnitz, the chief investigator for the Human Farming Association, was initially skeptical about Walker's claims.

> Who in their right mind would attempt to skin conscious cows, particularly right under the nose of United States Department of Agriculture (USDA) meat inspectors? Sometimes involuntary

reflexes in stunned or dead animals can look like conscious kicking. (Eisnitz, 1997, p. 18)

Eisnitz decided to look into the matter.

Clearly, animals alive and conscious violates the HSA. However, oddly enough, the very group who is supposed to enforce the HSA, the USDA, opposes the act. Indeed, the USDA is itself allied with the meat industry. Further, there are no penalties—no fines or possible prison time—for violating the HSA. USDA meat inspectors are merely supposed to shut down the kill line until the slaughterhouse remedies the violations. Of course, shutting down the kill line, even momentarily, cuts into company profits. The danger of even a brief loss of time in production is meant to keep the meat industry complying with the law.

Unfortunately, Eisnitz found that rather than forcing a shut down, the USDA simply ignores nearly all violations of the HSA. Eisnitz interviewed numerous workers at various levels of work inside U.S. meat-packing businesses and found that the slaughterhouses are consistently violating the HSA. Again and again, different people involved in meat packing with different companies reiterated similar stories. Cows are being skinned alive and conscious. Conscious pigs are regularly immersed in scalding water and boiled alive. Awake and aware chicken are normally bled out and scalded in boiling water (to loosen their feathers). And because the HSA does not protect poultry in the United States, the USDA does not have to bother ignoring the brutal poultry slaughtering process. Scalding live chickens in boiling water is completely legal.

Eisnitz found that the Kaplan company was killing around six hundred cows every day. "Not as many as some of the nation's newer high-speed mega-operations, but still high enough to make it the largest beef slaughterhouse in Florida" (Eisnitz, 1997, p. 19). Yet, according to Walker, the facility was in poor repair and simply could not even handle the slower line times such as when they slaughtered only fifty to seventy cows an hour. "As a result, when the line speed was increased—particularly when the foreman was trying to push through as many cattle as possible at the end of the work day—plant employees just couldn't keep up" (p. 28). Rushing at their work, stun operators would sometimes miss and knock the animal at the side of its head instead of straight on. Some of the improperly stunned cows respond by breaking free and running wildly through the plant. Most however, "regained consciousness after they'd been shackled and hoisted onto the overhead rail" (p. 28). These animals, hanging by one leg, fight, twist and turn, trying to break free. Walker told Eisnitz that in "addition to kicking and thrashing as they hung upside down … they'd be blinking and stretching their necks from side to side, looking around, really frantic" (p. 28).

Conscious animal or not, the overhead moving rail continues either way, and with it the cow moves to the next stage in the process, to the sticker. When the cow is conscious and fighting, and particularly when the line is moving fast, the sticker sometimes does not manage to cut the cow's throat in such a way that it bleeds out fast. Nonetheless, within seconds after being cut, the cow arrives at the head-skinners who skin the hide off of the animal's head. Eisnitz quotes Walker as saying, "A lot of times the skinner finds out an animal is still conscious when he slices the side of its head and it starts kicking wildly. If that happens, or if a cow is already kicking when it arrives at their station, the skinners show a knife into the back of its head to cut the spinal cord" (Eisnitz, 1997, p. 29). Eisnitz writes, "This practice paralyzes the cow from the neck down but doesn't deaden the pain of head skinning or render the animal unconscious; it simply allow workers to skin or dismember the animal without getting kicked" (p. 29).

It is an understatement to say that skinning the hide off of a conscious animal is cruel. Even so, cruelty to the animal is not the only issue. Live cattle struggling and fighting as they are being processed into meat present an extremely dangerous situation for the workers, the meat packers, processing them. The workers are themselves crowded together and unprotected, many carrying knives. It is a perfect set-up for accidents. Walker told Eisnitz,

> Sometimes animals would break free of their shackles and come crashing down headfirst to the floor fifteen feet below, where other men worked. … It's a miracle that nobody's been killed. There were three in one day, one right after another. One hit a worker, just a glancing blow, broke his leg. I almost got crushed by a falling bull. (Eisnitz, 1997, p. 29)

At the National Beef plant, almost four hundred animals die every hour. They are set free, to become something else. They become us. You know, everything passes. Everything passes away, leaving a shadow of itself behind, transformed into something else.

And cows become us. Of course, in the food chain, we aren't the only ones eating cow. In fact until August 1997, even the cows ate cows. And they still eat meat, just meat from more distant relatives. "When a cow is slaughtered, about half of it by weight is not eaten by humans: the intestines and their contents, the head, hooves, and horns, as well as bones and blood. These are dumped into giant grinders at rendering plants, as are the entire bodies of cows and other farm animals known to be diseased" (Lyman, 1998, p. 12). Yet not only farm animals are "rendered." Euthanized pets such as the six or seven million cats and dogs put down in animal shelters each year and road kill are all transformed, rendered into something else. The whole mix, forty billion pounds of dead animals each year, is ground up and steam-cooked. Then the lighter fatty material floats to the top of the mix and is separated out to be used for making candles, waxes, cosmetics, soaps, lubricants, and whatnot. The renderers dry and pulverized the heavier protein material into a powder. This "protein concentrate" is used as an additive in almost all pet food as well as to livestock feed.

So. We eat cows. And the cows used to eat cows. They eat other meat now in the form of protein concentrate. Who cares really? Well, the problem is not just the meat eating meat before we eat the meat. There are a number of problems with meat. But not only problems; meat is not only laden with problems. Meat is also food. It is a gift of sorts from the cows, and the labor and the land. And those who eat meat devour it and are, at least a little bit, renewed. And the cows die unto us, and eventually we to the land, and the land feeds. And we begin again.

Note

1. The only assertion in his book that could not be verified involved Sinclair's report of workers who accidentally fell into open vats of hot water in the tank

rooms. He wrote, "When they were fished out, there was never enough of them left to be worth exhibiting, sometimes they would be over-looked for days, till all but the bones of them had gone out to the world as Durham's Pure Leaf Lard!" (Sinclair 2003 [1906], p. 113).

References

Eisnitz, G. A. (1997). *Slaughterhouse: The shocking story of greed, neglect, and inhumane treatment inside of the U.S. meat industry.* Amherst, NY: Prometheus Books.

Humane Society of the United States. (2008). Factory farming campaign: Working to reduce the suffering of animals raised for meat, eggs, and milk. Available online at http://video.hsus.org/ (accessed July 16, 2008).

Lyman, H. (1998). *Mad cowboy: Plain truth from the cattle rancher who won't eat meat.* New York: Simon & Schuster.

Netz, R. (2002). Collections of confinement: Thoughts on barbed wire. *Connect: Art, Politics, Theory, Practice*, 12(1), 15–22.

Olsson, K. (2002). The shame of meatpacking. *The Nation*, September 16, p. 12.

Sinclair, U. (2003 [1906]). *The jungle, with an introduction and notes by Maura Spiegel.* New York: Barnes & Noble Classic.

Skaggs, J. M. (1986). *Prime cut: Livestock raising and meatpacking in the United States, 1607–1983.* College Station: Texas A&M University Press.

Chapter 12 ||| Rethinking Words, Concepts, Stories, and Theories

||| Sensing a New World?[1]

Ian Stronach
Liverpool John Moores University

What new world? Well, there's the politics of new local/global relations[2] in the postmodern. There's the "transnationalization of production" (Burbach, 2001, p. 25). There's tension between notions of liberty and freedom and those of justice and equality, values whose foundations are now in a multi-layered disparity over various local and global determinants. And there's the need to consider much more the relations between these concepts, how they connect and disconnect with each other—some new sense of adjacency, perhaps. That would be the "rethinking" in my title.

So this is an attempt at a postmodernism of the postmodern, taking these concepts to be antagonisms and at the same time necessary adjacencies. They are "lean-to" concepts in ways that we need to articulate: They only stand up by leaning against each other. This article, then, has two critical ambitions. The first is rather grandiose—a politico-philosophical excursion into the *co-construction* of contemporary meaning, including some of the values that invest such meaning. More modestly, the second might be regarded as a prosaic hopping around and pecking at the differences between words like global, local, social, individual, freedom, justice, and so on. In so doing, I want to consider a number of discursive phenomena. These are "word-crashes," "semantic collisions," "narrative near-misses," and a somewhat engineered mid-air theory "incident" involving Jean-Luc Nancy and Friedrich von Hayek.[3] In many ways, all of these are quite ordinary contemporary discursive events, things that we have been doing behind our own backs, as it were, but also things that we have not been thinking about as such. This is advocacy for looking more closely at these contemporary percussive epistemological moves, as well as the ontological ghosts that haunt them.

"Word-Crashes"

I have never found a concept that was grasped in a word.

—*Derrida, 2005*

Word-crashes are not a new phenomenon. After all, it was James Joyce who crashed "chaos" into "cosmos" to give us "chaosmos." And, much earlier, we might want to recall Sterne's fondness of "cross accidents" ([2003 [1759], p. 11). But they are now very prevalent, as the following examples suggest:

local/global – "glocalization" (Friedman, 2006, p. 420)

anglo/global – "anglobalization" (Friedman, 2006, p. 186)

occident/accident – "o/accident" (Nancy, 2000, p. 22)

chaos/error – "chao-errancy" (Deleuze, 1994, p. 69)

equality/liberty – "égaliberté" (Balibar, cited in Žižek, 2008a, p. 8)

amour/amitié – "aimance" (Derrida, 1997, p. 69)

farce/fascism – "farscism" (Stronach, Halsall, & Hustler, 2002, pp. 167ff)

Of course we can disregard this as ugly word-play, or gobbledegook, to use the politician's favorite term for complexity. Or we can see it skeptically as authors trying to neologize themselves into a conceptual after-life. In particular, we have to be suspicious of the place of translation, which is inevitably also the space of mistranslation, as Derrida has taught us (2001; Stronach, 2007), and as disciplines like anthropology constantly remind us when in reflexive mode: "The pupils sang in a language that was neither French nor their own tongue. It was a curious gibberish which the villagers took for French, and the French for the native language. Everyone clapped" (cited in Droogers, 1980, p. 186).

On the other hand, we might want to consider such word-crashes as somehow symptomatic. If you look closely at a word-crash like "glocalization," it can be seen that the two old words remain visible, along with the new coinage. It is as if they resist dialectical synthesis, a reduction to a new one. The contradiction is kept on the surface, in play—maybe as a new kind of hybridic triangulation? In such a creativity, we might want to regard Derrida's "différance" as a kind of "ur-word-crash."[4]

At any rate, we can see that here we have a kind of semantic arithmetic where one and one always makes three, an Unholy Trinity where the overarching contradiction of "global locality" (Wilk, 1995, p. 111, citing Appadurai) inaugurates a "structure of common differences" in a globality that is a "disconnecting succession to foundering imperialism" (Nairn, 2007, p. 4). Things fall apart, but always together. Things come together, but always apart.

"Semantic Collisions"

Taking the latter "symptomatic" line, we can regard "semantic collisions" as related phenomena. These are even more numerous in accounts of the contemporary, and also involve an irresolution that keeps contradiction in play:

"benevolent hegemony" (Fukuyama, 2007, p. 95)

"liberal empire" (Ferguson, 2005, p. 2)

"preventive war"

"radical centre" (Tony Blair)

"war on terror" (George W. Bush et al.)[5]

Nor are these oxymorons just creatures of the Right:

"pacifist militarism" (Žižek, 2008b p. 3)

"postmodern Marxism" (Burbach, 2001, p. 83)

"postmodern Marx," "market socialism" (Carver, 1998, p. 134)[6]

"liberal fascism" (Marcos, 2000)

"neoliberal theology" (Hobsbawm, 1994a, p. 431)

"market stalinism" (Graeber 2002, p. 62; de Sousa Santos, 2006, p. 2)

"paz violenta" [violent peace] (Rus, Castillo, & Mattiace, 2003, p. 83)

"policy hysteria" (Stronach & Morris, 1994, p. 5)[7]

Again, we might read all of these as trivial concept-mongering, but it is interesting that each conceptual innovation chooses to highlight the same determination to keep a contradiction in play, to emphasize that meaning is to be found *between* these words, or, as I will argue, in their "*with*" relation in regard to the other. It is this sense of coproduction of meaning, of coexistence, of new kinds of association that I want to develop in this chapter. And some have already pointed in this direction. Nash argues that in a "postmodern world of pluriethnic and pluricultural coexistence we need a 'new vocabulary'" (2001, p. 220), and Badiou calls for "new writing between philosophy and literature" and "adventurers of the concept" (2005, pp. 4, 6). Jean-Luc Nancy might well interpret such semantic collisions and word-crashes as attempts to point beyond the words themselves to the event of their happening together—both a "fold" and a leap (Nancy, 1996, p. 107), an unsettlement of the asynthetic, an "incompatability within the fold" with which we might endeavor—among other things—to "have language bear the weight of what it is not" (p. 111).[8] Finally, Baudrillard asks the radical question, "Might we not transpose language games on to social and historical phenomena: anagrams, acrostics, spoonerisms, rhyme, strophe and catastrophe?" (1996, p. 37). These are all incitements to paradox and serious play.

If such or suchlike is the case, then it seems that we need to move from theories based on nouns and their proper definition (truth, meaning, value, etc.) to a consideration of the meaning of prepositions—"between," "with," "against"—and the meaning of their juxtapositioning. Is it the case that the task that lies ahead (a dodgy preposition, of course) is to found-unfound a philosophy of prepositions rather than a philosophy of nouns? Again, philosophers of difference would want to answer "of course" to such a suggestion, and much of the work of Derrida, Deleuze, and Nancy has undertaken such excursions into these regions. But that task, as Nancy suggests, has yet some way to go. So we need at least to gesture, at this stage, toward a kind of epistemological liminality, a world of intrication and imbrication,[9] where living in contradiction, paradox and oxymoron is, ironically only, the new stasis.[10]

At any rate, we can now argue that both word-crashes and semantic collisions, read as symptomatic of the contemporary, offer a key to the nature of the collision—as "with" (Nancy, 2000), "without" (Blanchot, in Derrida, 1997, p. 251) [or "against"]—all within some notion of "agonistic democracy" (Higgins, 2004, p. 188). This is language "out of joint" (Derrida, 2001; Jameson, 2008 [1999], p. 41; Nancy 1993a, p. 11) that requires us to say more about the nature of "co-ipseity," as Nancy puts it (Nancy, 2000, p. 44), and this "co-ipseity" or "co-appearance" may extend from persons to words, concepts, stories, and theories. It may also manifest itself in new and more horizontal practices of the singular and the plural—as in networks, the web, and direct action groups.[11]

"Near-Miss Narratives"

I intend to take a performative turn in this section of the chapter, by relating (correlating?) two very different and quite unrelated stories which, coincidentally (but what does that mean?) I happened to read at around the same time.

> Stalin died on March 5th 1953. The next day, an old woman in Kazakhstan went to her local shop. To her astonishment, the shop had sugar for sale. She bought a kilo and carried it in triumph back to her daughters. They were horrified. "We threw ourselves at poor Mama, and became hysterical." No-one else had dared to buy any. (Figes, 2007, p. 529)

You see the daughters' logic: death of Stalin>sugar>cake>celebration>gulag. They live, after all, in the "collectivist nightmare" of Stalinism, perhaps the nadir of the modernist project of the Enlightenment (Skidelsky, 1995, p. 180).[12] They live a semantic collision of sane paranoia: It's mad to be sane in a crazy world.

This expresses the collective reach of the totalitarian state, down to the last bag of sugar in the village shop.[13]

I juxtapose a second story, and consider what happens when the two stories begin to interact. What I have in mind is a reading of the apparent "blank" of "co-incidence."

> It's February 2008. The place is Berwick-on-Tweed. Close to the border with Scotland, it is a small English county that's about to be absorbed by a larger county. It holds a poll on opting instead to leave England and join Scotland.[14] 61% are in favour. The right-wing press in England sum up the situation: "Scots plan to capture 20 miles of England." (Gunn, 2008)

Such a story—including its instant balkanization by the media—is a brilliant and ineffably postmodern collision of past, present, and future. There is a grain of history in there: Scotland ceded Berwick to England as a concession that sealed the end of its successful War of Independence in the 14th century.[15] There is a much greater grain of the contemporary—the Scottish parliament abolished fees for university students and offers free care for the elderly: It's currently cheaper to grow up and grow old in Scotland. Finally, there is an interesting future dimension. Scotland—outside the EU—might not be a viable economic entity, but the EU and the euro offer to even small countries a fairly level playing field in terms of trade, a stable currency, and political security. Such a phenomenon can be seen as the "return of Scotland" (Nairn, 2000), in defiance of Trevor-Roper's epitaph—"Scotland is over." In any case, as Nairn later says, "All nations are becoming mongrels, hybrids or foundlings, in the circumstances of globalization" (Nairn, 2007, p. 1).

In contrast to the modernist nightmare of Stalinism, we have secession as a kind of postmodern romantic elopement. The collective individual that we call "the English" wakes up to find one of its toes has voted to join another body. It instantly accuses the Other of wanting to steal its proverbial toe. What is this if not an illustration of Jameson's "postmodern present" wherein are exercised "neo-ethnic pluralities of free choice" (Jameson (2008 [1999], p. 53)? Žižek, too, might offer support. He defines the nation-state as a "precarious, temporary balance between the relationship of a particular ethnic Thing [...] and the (politically) universal function of the market" (Žižek, 1998, p. 9).[16]

It is important to see the strategy that "contrasts" the stories, as it were, in front of itself. It suggests a hidden meaning of *co-incidence*, and the miles-apart stories then become "near-miss narratives" in which each infects/deflects/inflects the meaning of the other. An easy reading contrasts:

centralist – decentralist

horror – farce

coercive – voluntarist

amusing – terrifying

Each opposition essentializes the other: It makes rather than marks difference. They do not border each other so much as they invest the heart of the other with its parodic opposite. They oppose each other like an invisible, unwordable force, a discursive magnetism that at-tracts and dis-tracts the other. Nor is that the only axis of comparison—the stories readily form a sequence: modernist tragedy>postmodern farce (a certain ghost of Marx in there). At any rate, neither story holds still with the other. We can even make the stories coalesce, although it is a more tricky game. After all, the Kazhakhstan bag of sugar can match the Berwickstan bags of sugar (no tuition fees, free elderly care), and both are assuredly political stories, as well as sharing a certain hysteria in response to their central events (daughters/media).

In these movements of opposition, sequence and coalescence the stories won't hold still across the "empty" span of their (dis)connection; they insist on being "with" and also "against" the other in acts of mapping and spacing. In so doing, they recall an observation of Georges Perec (1999 [1974], p. 13):

> To describe space: to name it, to trace it, like these portolano-makers [medieval mappers], who saturated the coastlines with the names of harbours, the names of capes, the names of inlets, until in the end the land was only separated from the sea *by a continuous ribbon of text*. (emphasis added)

The boundary as a "continuous ribbon of text" between land and sea is a rich association: after all, what is a lighthouse if it is not an exclamation mark?(!) The textual ribbon is a separation and a continuity. Both. Land and sea. In terms of that association, we could add to Perec's thought because that "continuous ribbon of text" acts as a multiple register of both land (cape, point, cliff, beach) and sea (inlet, bay, bight, sound), each continuous in its separation, and separate in its continuity.[17] And there is even a third language in there, where words like "seashore" effect their own disguised collision in an explicit double recognition. It is a ghostly business, but these, too, are "lean-to" registers.

Such an analogy enables us to return to the two stories and see their "multiple register" that we must name to map and space them, the one *from/with/against* the other. It is a dynamic nexus. "Near-misses," then, are also "indirect hits," capable no doubt of collateral damage. Their "withness" and association, their "co-ipseity" traces an epistemological strand of oppositions, sequences and commonalities with an accompanying ontology of "co-appearances." A process of circulation "assembles them as it spaces them [that continuous ribbon again]; they are linked as far as they are not unified" (Nancy, 2000, p. 33)—like the words, concepts, and stories of this account so far.

From an ontological perspective, we can also see the two stories as a vivid illustration of that complex notion of the Neitzschean "eternal return." We cannot return to the stories except in difference: "Eternity occurs as the truth of its passing" is an underlying paradox (Nancy, 2000, p. 4), as each reads into and out of the other in an unending sequence of differences, disembedding the Same, enmapping the Difference, in the manner of Deleuze— "Returning is being, but only the being of becoming"; "In other words, identity in the eternal return does not describe the nature of that which returns but, on the contrary, the fact of returning for that which differs" (Deleuze, 1983 [1962], p. 48, 1994, p. 50). Such a return brings out the nature of a un/certain "with" relationship: "if Being is being-with, then it is, in its being-with, the "with" that constitutes Being: the with is *not* simply an addition" (Nancy, 2000, p. 30; emphasis in the original).

Once again, one plus one is three: The stories multiply rather than add and in so doing they ethicalize the other. Neither meaning nor value holds still. There is a "relationless relation to the other" (Critchley, 1998, p. 265). In according greater priority to the notion of "with" and subordinating the notion of "between" as a kind of hidden pseudo-entity (a conceptual something between things, even if a liminal stage), Nancy develops a notion of "Mitsein" (2000, p. 31) rather than "Dasein," drawing on but changing Heidegger's original emphasis on the latter. His broad argument is that notions of "co-ipseity" have been neglected in Western thought, where a certain individualism (and also a certain collectivism) have predominated. Indeed his project is to abandon that polarity between individualism and collectivism, seeing formulations from Aristotle's "logos" of the *polis*, through Rousseau's "social contract" and on to Marx's notion of "community" as all somewhat complicit in a totalizing terror that we will later explicate. Nancy's program, especially in *Being Singular Plural* (2000) and the *Experience of Freedom* (1993a) is "to think being-in-common as distinct from community" (Nancy, 2000, p. 24). We will return later to both the theory and practice of "being-in-common" toward the end of this chapter. Meanwhile, Nancy has an apt summary of such spacing: "But what is written, and what is to be read, is that which has not preceded its own habituation; it is the mêlée of the traces of meaning that get lost in looking for itself and inventing itself" (2000, p. 158).

Thus, we can argue that just as land and sea stand within and without each other, distinct and inseparable, so, too, do the epistemological and ontological traces that invisibly write the relation of the always unwritten story between two stories, in what Deleuze and Guattari (1988) often call "lines of flight" (p. 9). Like land and sea, they also stand in a relation of "fix" (epistemology's destiny) and "flux" (ontology's demand), forever rewriting the other, as indeed do tides, erosion, flood, etc., in the original analogy. That recalls Perec's "continuous ribbon of text" between land and sea, as well as Nancy's explosion of *nothing*" (emphasis in the original): "It is the explosion of *nothing* (emphasis added), in fact, it is the spacing of meaning, spacing *as* (emphasis in the original) meaning and circulation" (Nancy, 2000, p. 3).

And Now, a Mid-Air High Theory Collision between Jean-Luc Nancy and Friedrich Von Hayek

Let's rehearse this trip of ours, before it becomes more complicated and devious. Earlier, I cited Nash on the need for a "new vocabulary" for a changing world that could no longer be wholly described in old and familiar ways. This is no revolutionary call, because things have long been thus. Both "modernism" and "postmodernism" appeared as invocations of the unfamiliar, and the process continues.[18] Our endemic problem of meaning is that words are inherently conservative, dated, inert, so that the task of meaning is always a belated and half-conscious catching-up on ourselves that word-crashes and semantic collisions perform. Our problem is never the one of thinking something new, but disinterring the new of something whose novelty is as yet unacknowledged. (It's a pantomime epistemology: "Look behind you!")

In considering word-crashes, we entertained the possibility that they were "symptomatic" of nondialectical, asynthetic assemblages that said more than intended about new ways of making meaning.[19] Similarly, semantic collisions were read as necessary oxymorons of contemporary meaning, whereas the distance between stories, as "near-miss narratives," was posited as a kind of unacknowledged chiasmus, reflecting the ineluctable crossing-over of meaning, the inherent and generative instability of a story *with* another story. In sum, a proliferation of "co-possibilities," to return to the language of Nancy once more ("l'un avec l'autre," as he frequently invokes the founding relation): "The outside is inside; it is the spacing of the dis-position of the world; it is our disposition and co-appearance" (Nancy, 2000, p. 13).

Taken together, we might see these discursive phenomena as unstable triangulations of a contemporary dilemma in understanding the emergent, and the next step in this excursion is to look at how Nancy-Hayek (a "with" rather than "against" encounter) might help tease out additional implications for how values relate to such instabilities of meaning.[20] In so doing, the intention is to rehearse the chiasmus, *to make theory enact a performance of sense.*

Like our two stories, Hayek and Nancy make opposites more readily than commonalities, yet it is a "with" reading on which we initially insist. Hayek is usually seen as a guru of the Right, of the neoconservative backlash. Famously, Margaret Thatcher is reported to have once pulled a Hayek book from her iconic handbag, brandished it in the air and declared, "This is our bible." Nancy, on the other hand, would certainly be placed on the Left, sometimes as a post-Marxist or even anarchist, sometimes as a Derridean disciple. Of course, one may invoke more than one of each, but the parameters of the debate here rely on certain Hayek texts (*Road to Serfdom* [1944], *Law, Legislation and Liberty* [1952], and the *Counter-Revolution in Science* [1976]) and on a similarly selective Nancy (mainly *Being Singular Plural* [2000], *Experience of Freedom* [1993a], and *Birth to Presence* [1993b]).[21]

There are some interesting cross-overs between Hayek and Nancy in relation to a cluster of ideas concerning the relations between liberty, justice, freedom, and equality, and the association of these terms with the others. Hayek would prioritize liberty *against* a notion of justice, just as freedom stands in some contradiction to equality, following Adam Smith (Desai, 2002, p. 26). Crudely, Hayek argues that liberty, defined in terms of formal properties, requires a certain license for a degree of injustice in the form of generated inequalities and unintended consequences, both favorable and otherwise. These inequalities may be regretted, but they are the necessary price of freedom.

Marx and Engels anticipate such individualism as "the icy water of egotistical calculation" against which they posit a state calculation of "equality," but also and in contradiction, "an association in which the free development of each" would be "the condition for the free development of all"—an idea to which we return (Marx & Engels, 2005 [1848], pp. 184, 222).[22] Nancy, on the other hand, sees freedom as a "surprise," "event," "leap," "happening" that places us at liberty to do good or evil (Nancy, 1993a, p. 8, 2000, pp. 159–172).[23] Freedom, for Nancy, is *beyond* good or evil, being "without content or ethical norms" (Nancy, 1993a, p. 132). If there was a way of condensing Nancy to a phrase, that phrase would be, in all its ambiguity, "Freedom is a start" [surprise, event, beginning, discovery, incompletion, point of origin].

At any rate, both resist the usual "jigsawing" together of these terms (e.g., "No freedom without justice," "No justice without equality," etc.) in favor of a certain paradoxical indeterminacy.[24] As Nancy puts it, "equality will never do justice to singularity" (2000, p. 24).[25] That indeterminacy, or unpredictability is taken by both to be inevitable and as a kind of enabling risk that leads to generative contradictions:

Hayek says: "If we knew how our present knowledge is conditioned and determined, it would no longer be our present knowledge" (1952, p. 89). Such "super-rationalism" (p. 90), he argues, can only be superstition, and precludes what he takes to be the "positive" indeterminacy of any free, open, or "great society" (Hayek, 1976, p. 39). His is a liberty defended by "abstract rules," (1976, p. 11), formal rather than substantive guarantees, but which nevertheless relies on uncertainty and ignorance of the future to leave space for the operation of freedom in particular circumstances: "Indeed, what will certainly be dead in the long run if we concentrate on immediate results is freedom" (1976, p. 29). Such openness, which he latterly came to call the "catallaxy" (1976, p. 107) of part-chance, part-skill, is the positive serendipity of the social:

> Most of the knowledge on which we rely in the pursuit of our ends is the unintended by-product of others exploring the world in different directions from those we pursue ourselves because they are impelled by different aims; it would never have become available to us if only those ends were pursued which we regarded as desirable. (1976, p. 111)

For Nancy, there is a distinct echo of Derrida when he writes: "Decision, or freedom, is the *ethos* at the groundless ground of every ethics. We have to decide on laws, exceptions, cases, negotiations: but there is neither law or exception for decision" (Nancy, 1993a, p. 163; emphasis in the original). Here decision is necessary, decisive in "its strike and cut" (Nancy, 1993a, p. 142) and yet indeterminate—a kind of indecisive decision, according to the paradoxical planes of the concept. It "inscribes the uninscribable in inscription itself, it *excribes*" in ways that the section on "near-miss narratives" tried to simulate (Nancy 1993b, p. 299; emphasis in the original).

We could sum up both sets of belief by saying that in different ways each philosopher seeks to think reason, within reason. In such a rethinking there is a recognition of "the inadequacy of equality *as in and of itself* an ideal" (Bholat, 2008, p. 18; emphasis in the original). There are elements of the unknowable in every situation, and of course, we would want to add Polanyi's point about the tacit nature of knowledge that we have, performatively but not representationally (Polanyi, 1962; see also Sennett, 2008). Beyond that, there is also the knowledge and values that we don't hold but that hold us.

It follows that such multi-layered indeterminacy leads both authors to undermine a conventional understanding of "social justice" and "educational equality" in particular. They refuse to define or measure it. Hayek's argument is that such definition and measurement leads to well-intended but eventually coercive and transcendent attempts by the state to legislate for these values through what can only be positivistic strategies and recurrent forms of "scientism" (1944, p. 15). In a sense, his prediction comes true in the Kazakhstan story—a collectivism "totalitarian in the true sense of this new word" (p. 42), and in the absurd forms of social arithmetic that accompany our own current regimes of "audit" and "improvement," whose public results quantify "quality" in educational discourses. To extend this argument against measurement regimes, Hayek, writing in the 1940s, points to "120 years" of recurrent positivism, which he defines as the "uncritical transfer to the problems of society of [...] the habits of thought of the natural scientist and the engineer" (1944, p. 15). Such aping of science "has contributed scarcely anything to our understanding of social phenomena" and yet "demands for further attempts in this direction are still presented to us [this in 1941–44] as the latest revolutionary innovations, which, if adopted, will secure rapid undreamed of progress" (Hayek, 1952, p. 14). Ring any bells?[26] The result is social engineering that promotes itself in the parallel language of plans, blueprints, and targets.[27] Hayek sees Britain in the early 1940s as well down that road to collective oppression via a "conservative socialism" (1944, p. 134), but his main target is the Stalinist five-year planning system, with its monstrous cruelties as well as its absurdities.[28]

Such absurdity also helps us make sense of certain strands in the history of Western modernity. The notion that society can be so engineered for social ends begins with Fourier and St. Simon, early socialists. By the 1830s, we have the emergence of that unacknowledged contradiction, "scientific socialism" (where the nonsense was in the "science" rather than the "socialism"). The great "pioneering example" is, without a doubt, the *Communist Manifesto* (Jones, 2002, p. 20).

Current Western states, finding themselves bereft of economic leverage in a global economy,[29] have compensated by inventing what we might call paracapitalist discourse within which to express the "knowledge economy." It is full of economistic measures and terms (targets, value-added, best practice, evidence-based performance), as well as borrowings from business (private sector takeovers of state action in education and health, Total Quality Management [TQM], all forms of quality assurance, trademarks, logos, even legislation that sounds like business product slogans—Every Child Matters in the United Kingdom and No Child Left Behind in the United States. Each of these pieces of legislation cries out for an exclamation mark, though not unfortunately in the manner of a lighthouse!). What has emerged in the United Kingdom is a discourse that is nostalgic for the economic power that the state once exercised through a national and imperial capitalism, and that therefore expresses a cargo-cult kind of enthusiasm for aping the "efficient" and "effective" as capitalism's dividend to civil society.[30] Thus we have the ignoble dream of a 19th-century "scientific socialism" replaced by the parallel absurdity of a 21st-century "scientific capitalism."[31]

This state/market relation can usefully be dubbed "market Stalinism," although not in the original sense that Graeber used the term (2002, p. 62).[32] Market Stalinism, as I see it, cedes the market to the global and organizes the local as a coercive paracapitalist simulacrum, evoking the notion of cargo cult.[33] It is perhaps also significant that Fourier and St. Simon's dreams ended in the establishment of religious cults. Stalin was certainly subject to cult worship and fear, and perhaps it is no coincidence that Hobsbawm refers to current economic theory as "neoliberal theology" (Hobsbawm, 1994a, p. 414), and "ultra-liberal economic theologians" (Hobsbawm, 1994b, p. 409). When Science tries too hard to be true, it becomes Religion.[34] And then it is a short hop to absurdity:

> Springfield, Ill. (AP) The State Senate of Illinois yesterday disbanded its Committee on Efficiency and Economy for reasons of efficiency and economy. (*Des Moines Tribune*, February 6, 1955; reported in Bryson 2007)

And Finally Getting "With" It

Both Hayek and Nancy are interested in what the former refers to as the "interindividual process" (Hayek, 1952, p. 86) but it is here that we need to make a radical distinction between them because Nancy's notions of "Mitsein," "co-ipseity," and "being-with" are not at all founded on the individual, but on the singularities and pluralities that make up and mistake the making up of each of us. His account is a rejection of the "Capitalized Other" in preference for "the lower case other" (Nancy, 2000, pp. 11, 13), and if we return to the ideals of the French revolution, we might infer that for Nancy the principle of *fraternity* has priority. Where is fraternity in any account of égaliberté? That, perhaps, is a more postmodernist question.[35]

At any rate, there is no fraternity in Hayek. His Collective Individual is the autonomous, self-interested "merchant," rather than the engineer and scientist. His "body without organs" is the "spontaneous order" of the market (Hayek, 1976, p. 3), which he sees, implausibly, as equalizing wealth in its tendencies.[36] Thus, although Nancy would share some of his critique of collectivism, he certainly sees the cult of individualism as just as dangerous:

> In the first case [collectivism], the singular becomes a particular within a totality, where it is no longer singular or plural; in the second case [individualism], the singular exists only on its own and, therefore, as a totality—and there too it is neither singular nor plural. In either case, *murder is on the horizon.* (Nancy, 2000, p. 92; emphasis added)

Khazhikstan and Berwickstan enact something of these collectivist and individualist fates. But the "murder" Nancy has in mind is expressed by the moral fulcrum of Auschwitz in the ethical story of the West, a barbarity written into the core rather than the periphery, and one that echoes through a series of subsequent catastrophes, from Rwanda and the Congo (Stronach, 2006) through the Balkans to Iraq. We must acknowledge that "our" 20th century managed to combine the excesses of individualism and collectivism in uniquely murderous ways. Milosz offers an illustration of that excess, from his experience in Auschwitz, an anecdote that perhaps marks out the strange (but really it is familiar) and perverse (but really it is normal) nature of such an individual/collective nightmare. He watched a transport arrive. Mothers with children were to go straight to the gas chamber, and a mother ran away from her child and joined the group of the young and single who were waiting to be taken to the labor camp. The child ran after her, crying "Mummy," alerting the guards. A Russian capo seized her in disgust and threw her and her child onto the truck going to the gas chamber. An SS guard congratulated him: "*Gut gemacht*. That's how one should punish unnatural mothers" (Milosz, 1990, pp. 120–121).

But it's not just then, it's now. Said offers a contemporary version of the nightmare of that certain combination of "moral" individualism and collective atrocity: "Some Israelis will never forgive [...] the Palestinians for what the Israelis have done to them" (Said, 2005, p. xix).

That would be to end on a note of horror, and it is certain that the pathologies of individualism as well as collectivism need to be carefully weighed. But the notion of being-with, of rewriting the individual/collective in terms of the singular-plural, is worth some further illustration, for it may not be just another in a series of utopian fantasies that characterize our thinking just as much as that series of horrors (Stronach, 2006). Certainly "co-ipseity" can be, and ought to be seen, as a form of utopianism, but there may be signs scattered here and there both in the local and in the global that promise a realization in practice rather than just in theory.[37] There may also be some practice to set alongside the theory: "Communities are not identified negatively against one another; they serve as venues of sharing in which singularity finds sense accessible according to priorities that require connections and intersections" (Hutchens, 2005, p. 145).

So, The Workers United Will Never Be Repeated?

A theme in this account has been the failure of coincidence to remain innocent, and its insistence on forming narrative bridges, "continuous ribbons of text." Shortly before the theoretical exploration of "co-ipseity," a colleague and I undertook empirical research into Summerhill School, a "child democracy" (Piper & Stronach, 2008; Stronach & Piper, 2008). It was striking how pupils dealt with association within that community. Despite the range of ages, abilities, ethnicities, etc., there was an absence of stereotyping and bullying. The democratic "Meeting" (one person one vote, whether pupil of any age or staff) dealt with cases rather than persons, and moral learning seemed to accumulate through a singular, case-based cumulative internalization of values such as fairness, respect, and responsibility. On the one hand, pupils expected to "be themselves" in often stark contrast with their experiences at conventional schools. On the other hand, they took that to go hand in hand with the right of others to do the same. The Meeting, we felt, was a "working dystopia" (Stronach & Piper, 2008, p. 24) for the settlement of disputes and the establishment of rules and their exceptions.

The school, we argued, was a "benign panopticon" (Stronach & Piper, 2008, p. 13) where all felt that there were hardly any secrets, and no one felt the need to pretend who they were or to feign obedience. The data showed the unusual ways in which pupils envisaged the "Other," both in their own thinking, and in their thinking about others.[38] There was a neutrality (Stronach & Piper, 2008, p. 22), almost an indifference—the very opposite of the kind of romantic interpretation that such schools sometimes get. (Is the key to difference indifference?) At any rate, we concluded that the school as a community acted as a kind of moral laboratory that had powerful therapeutic effects.

It is hard, now, to reread our Summerhill research without beginning to rethink it in terms of Nancy's "co-ipseity." The pupils learned a kind of cultural metonymic of self-other relations, characterized by "dispassion" and a separation of persons and cases (Stronach & Piper, 2008, p. 19). In theoretical terms, we might regard this as a "sociability" not prefaced on utopian constructs like "neighbor" or "fellow citizen"—or indeed "brother" or "sister"— but "constituted by a process of imaginary identification" (Balibar, 1998, p. 87). They learned to be "singular," to be unequal together. Perhaps Nancy best catches the "shifting pronouns" of such a community when he writes: "'Self' defines the element in which 'me' and 'you,' and 'we,' and 'they' can take place"[39] (2000, p. 95).

It is interesting that such a school spent decades as a target for closure from various inspecting bodies in the United Kingdom, whose practices of assessment were predominantly "paracapitalist" in that they addressed education with questions such as: "Are the outcomes robust?" "Is the school 'fit for purpose'?" "What's the added value?" It may also be significant that these forms of association came to be described by us (in "grounded" rather than in theoretical terms) in terms of unacknowledged semantic collisions, and in playing with educational theories by inverting them and presenting them as paradoxes. Again, the theme of catch-up comes to mind.

The first place we might look for a broader politics/philosophy of "co-ipseity" is the Zapastista movement. Its utopian appeal to the West has been entertainingly mocked by that individualist collectivist, Slavoj Žižek (2008), but there are features that reflect Nancy's themes rather well. First of all, it is a political and socialist association that has abandoned the notion of the "vanguard," throughout the 20th century the means toward a correct and scientific grasp of political situations. With it, too, goes the notion of a "scientific socialism," and its positivist paraphernalia of planning, targets, and direction. Personality cult is another key avoidance; it is, allegedly at least, a Marcos of the "non-self" (Klein, 2005, p. 212). Instead, a much more horizontal and negotiative Marxism engages with—by listening rather than telling— peasants and workers. Theoretically, at least, this is a reorientation toward understanding fraternity in new ways, ways which are not national, but both local and global through networks like the World Social Forum.[40]

There is no space here to elaborate the micro- and macropossibilities for "co-ipseity" and "being singular plural." I conclude that there is a "new language" of an emergent epistemology, expressed in words, concepts, and spaces between narratives and theories. That language is demarcated in ways that this chapter has tried to display, although there are many other possibilities for some kind of Derridean "New International" that could be explored. These new ways of making sense out of epistemological and ontological necessity have to be performed rather than represented. The "new" in this world cannot be envisaged without such stratagems. They extend the reach of postmodernism, putting it to new work with reimaginings of a (un)certain Marx, and in particular with notions of an embryonic and reoriented notion of fraternity, a neglected member of the French Enlightenment trio. In so doing, it has to be recognized that dystopian search for utopian certainty has been one of the deepest moral and political pitfalls of the 20th century. The virtues of an unpredictable, uncertain, indeterminate future, Derrida's "democracy to come" (1997, p. 104) are positive, generative, and the spacing whence many freedoms and fraternities may come. In that spirit, we may sense the possibilities of a future that is already happening: "What will become of our world is something we cannot know, and we can no longer believe in being able to predict or command it. But we can act in a way that this world is a world able to open itself up to its own uncertainty as such" (Nancy, 1997, p. 158).

Notes

1. A version of this chapter was delivered as a keynote address to the 4th International Congress of Qualitative Inquiry, at the University of Illinois, Champaign-Urbana, May 5–8, 2008.

2. The newness of the "global" is contested, especially by those who feel that the world was just as global in the age of empires, in the late 19th century. But the postimperial neoimperial hegemony is an interestingly different development, creating as it does relationships that are not state centred in the ways that the old empires were. As for the status of the postmodern, I argue elsewhere the case for thinking of a postmodern discourse, fueled by overarching ideologies of accountability and improvement (Stronach & MacLure, 1997).

3. There are those who misperceive postmodernism as a flight from the political and who are forever content to demolish that straw man (nihilistic, relativistic, apolitical, amoral, clever-clever, merely playful, endlessly permissive, etc.). This note is not to counter their impressions, merely to say hello to them once again. In terms of the "flight" noted above, at least it can be claimed that this strange plane/plain has a right wing and a left wing, and I will be trying very hard to avoid any Third Way connotations in relation to the fuselage, for which I have more anarchic ambitions.

4. Marxists have concerned themselves with life "after dialectics," but with a "certain defiant humility" that as yet lacks conviction (Therborn, 2007, p. 1). Negri points to its universalizing fantasy—"the falsity of the dialectic is that of a key that would open all doors, while ethics on the other hand is a key adequate to singularity" (2004, p. 4). De Sousa Santos rejects old notions of "synthesis" in calling for "*depolarized pluralities*" (2006, p. 166; emphasis in the original).

5. "Liberal interventionism" is another favorite of U.K. politicians such as Blair and Ashdown. (Cable, 2008). "Liberal" refers to what "we" are and do; "intervention" is what "they" get and deserve, whether they are free to choose or not.

6. Carver proposes "a mild form of postmodernism" but the dose is so small as to be positively homeopathic (to echo Mark Twain's joke in *Roughing It*) (1998, p. 2).

7. I point to my own word-crashes and semantic collisions not because they are particularly significant—they are not—but because of that property of happening behind our backs. Such word-smithing is partly unconscious, a doing that is not a viewing. But once you start looking, you can't stop finding, as our recent account of Summerhill School indicates (Piper & Stronach, 2008). There, we claimed that conventional theories and concepts failed to grasp the peculiarities of the school, which we described as a "benevolent panopticon" whose democratic meeting acted as a "working dystopia" for the settlement of complaints and the establishment of revocable rules (Stronach & Piper, 2008, pp. 13, 24). A final example: Nairn argues that contemporary politics can be characterized as "the gymnastics of sincere deceit" (2000, 66).

8. If such an emphasis on the contradictory should seem merely academic, consider research on Toyota reported in the *Harvard Business Review*: The company's organization is depicted as "stable and paranoid, systematic and experimental, formal and frank" (Heller, 2008).

9. These words themselves are familiar enough neologisms, but it is important to read them as *invocations* of the un-nameable in-between. Otherwise they very rapidly become a new definitional language of difference, addressing itself by simultaneously dismissing itself. "Applied" deconstruction is the result—a reduction of deconstruction to methodology. These words are more akin to "spells" than they are to concepts; they "spell out" a secular spirituality rather than to a material relationship. They divine rather than define.

10. As a heuristic, I offer a visualization of this kind of process of thinking:

> Imagine an apple. Inside a worm. The worm feeds. So both are inside each other. Contradiction, but not impossibility. Together, a worm-in-the-apple in the apple-in-the-worm etc. [...] A woman. She ate the apple. Inside, the worm. Which eats her as she eats it. Concepts—metaphors of words and writing—that are *voracious* rather than *veracious*. This is a postmodernist Adam and Eve story. (Stronach, 2002, p. 297; emphasis in the original)

11. In the United Kingdom, the anti-airport expansion group known as "Plane Stupid" is a good example. They argue against the impotence of parliamentary "democracy" and consider that "[c]ivil disobedience is going to be the next big political wave" (Aitkenhead, 2008).

12. There is an unfortunate tendency to regard both Stalinism and fascism as historical aberrations in European history. The argument cannot be made here, but the position taken is that it is more plausible to see them as moments inherent to the modernist project.

13. The Nazis extended such reach via the concept of "Freizeitgestaltung" policy, which Hayek glosses as "literally: the shaping of the use made of people's free time" (1944, p. 75, note).

14. There is a Scottish Parliament with control over limited areas of government, far less than the state/federal dispensation in the United States.

15. The good people of Berwick have played this game before. At the end of the 19th century, they remembered their roots and applied to join the Scottish rather than the English Football League.

16. And many others. Miller cites a leading anthropologist of "identity," Kapferer: "Identity has started to attain an aura of self-constructed plurality which escapes the documentation of institutional growth" (Miller, 1995, p. 10).

17. About here, in such arguments the Moebius strip sometimes gets invoked. I won't because I don't know what it is. But of course I have. This game can go on in the smallest of arenas, in toenotes rather than footnotes, even. This is the "Do not read me" double-bind (Nancy, 1997, p. 53).

18. Augé develops, for example, the notion of "non-spaces" to describe the new sorts of cultural spaces that contrast motorway and shopping malls with, say, markets and cathedrals, arguing that we need a new terminology and indeed a new sociology to account for the unusual un-belonging of the impersonal and universal spaces of the postmodern (although he prefers "supermodernity") (1995, p. 31). The current controversy over the novelty of the "global" is part of just such an adjustment (Hobsbawm, Friedman, Castells, Wallerstein, etc.).

19. Deleuze: "Dialectic thrives on oppositions because it is unaware of far more subtle and subterranean differential mechanisms: topological displacements, typological variations" (1983, p. 157).

20. This is important because the argument usually goes that such instabilities of meaning lead inevitably to parallel uncertainties of value. This is the postmodernist "black hole" of morality and politics that critics so enthusiastically invoke. If we cannot know with certainty, then we cannot value with any warrant to belief. The strategy here will be to turn that argument on its head: It is only in uncertainty that values like justice can be realized, mainly following the Derrida of "Force of Law" and Nancy's *Experience of Freedom*.

21. In the light of the argument in the "near-miss narratives," I ask myself, "What already reads across that gap?" and the answer, at the limit of my reflexivity, would have to involve a tacit as well as explicit engagement with Derrida and Deleuze.

22. Derrida offers the incalculable virtue of an uncertain equality: "What would an equality be, what would an equity be, which would no longer calculate this equivalence? Which would, quite simply, no longer calculate at all" (1997, p. 64).

23. "Freedom is the leap into existence in which existence is discovered as such, and this discovery is thinking" (Nancy, 1993a, p. 58; see also Hutchens, 2005, p. 82). But it is not an autonomous leap. Instead, it is a "withdrawal of the properness of self" (Nancy, 1993a, p. 70), a "sharing of being" (Nancy, 1993a, p. 75), a "back and forth" presence (Nancy, 1993a, p. 5), a "passion," "jouissance" "ecstasy"(Hutchens, 2005, p. 3; Nancy, 1993b, pp. 6, 18) as the very condition for meaning, and as such a "*fact* of reason" as he puts it (Nancy, 1993b, p. 21; emphasis in the original).

24. "Thinking, undoubtedly, is for us what is most free. But freedom is this fact which less than any other can be reduced to thinking" (Nancy, 1993a, p. 172). In other words, words fail us before the "event" of freedom. Another way of looking at this kind of jigsawing might be to contrast two statements: Justice is freedom universalized (made law-like, regulated); and justice is freedom personified (in the instance, for the person). E. O. Wright perhaps best illustrates the jigsaw effect, in calling for "a *radical democratic egalitarian* understanding of justice" (Wright, 2006, p. 2; emphasis in the original). It is interesting that he rejects the notion of "blueprints" (see Hayek's criticisms) but remains firmly within positivistic assumptions about the possibility of a "scientifically grounded" approach to a "robust, socialist economy" (pp. 6, 13). Sounds like another bag of sugar to me.

25. Such a "singularity" is not an individuality, indeed, it is in direct opposition to it. Perhaps best located in the sorts of singularity that Deleuze and Guattari propose, that is, an "ensemble of entities able to articulate needs, wants, desires, fantasies, aspirations" (Tormey, 2003, p. 360).

26. One last ring of the bell: "The methods which scientists or men fascinated by the natural sciences have so often tried to force upon the social sciences were not always necessarily those which the scientists followed in their own field, but rather those which they believed they employed" (Hayek, 1952, p. 14). He takes an obsession with "quantification" and its "blind transfer

to the social arena as responsible for "the worst aberrations and absurdities" (p. 51). However, not all such "scientistic" fantasies are quantitative. It was Freud who dreamed that he was creating a "science of the singular" (Freud 2006 [1899]). It would be fascinating to try to work out what makes such a recursive, collective, insistent forgetting possible within the western modernist project, from the follies of Condorcet, through Comte and the early socialists to psychometrics in the early 20th century, and up to the current obsessions in the United States and the United Kingdom, in particular, not just to advance positivist quantification, but to stamp out qualitative research or isolate it in subordinate ghettos (called case studies). Positivism makes as many comebacks as God, possibly for related reasons. Earlier, we called it "zombie positivism" (Stronach, Frankham, & Stark, 2007, p. xx). Both offer certain Universal Knowledge. Equally, it would be useful to trace and explain the failure of its many demolitions and "deaths" (e.g., recently "scientism is spent" [Margolis, 2003, p. 17]).

27. Hayek even defined "civilisation" as necessarily accompanied by "a steady diminution of the sphere in which individual actions are bound by fixed rules" (1944, p. 43). Russell, too, argued against this kind of positivism and pseudo-science around the same time: "A scientific oligarchy is bound to become what is called 'totalitarian,' that is to say, all important forms of power will become a monopoly of the State" (1968 [1952], p. 56; see also Kolakowski on Soviet positivism as a kind of "philosophical suicide" (2005 [1976], p. 552).

28. The analogy between Britain and Stalinist Soviet Union should not be over-drawn, of course. But it is significant that the criticisms that Skidelsky makes of that latter system—"the quantum which the indicator measured became the principal purpose of production"; the distortion of one-dimensional targets; a quantitative emphasis that inhibited creativity; "the fruitless quest for rationality through the computer"; the "planning cult" (Skidelsky, 1995, pp. 81–108)—can equally be made against the U.K. government's education and health regimes. And current moves toward "greater managerial autonomy" (p. 107) place Blair/Brown alongside Krushchev/Kosygin. Oddly, on such quantification of virtue, Marx is prescient, citing Aristotle as the source of the positivist fantasy: "There can be no exchange without equality, no equality without cummensurability" (Bholat, 2008, p. 19).

29. Gray (1999) refers to this "hollowing-out" of the state. The current U.K. economic crisis is a fine illustration of the "butterfly wings" principle. It originated in the U.S. subprime mortgage market.

30. It is not implied that such nostalgia is merely incidental. It is also a cover-up in ways illustrated elsewhere (Stronach, Hallsall, & Hustler, 2002). Nostalgia is the form of expression of a more deliberate structure.

31. Gray: "Global democratic capitalism is as unrealisable a condition as world-wide communism" (1999, p. 21). Such a paracapitalist discourse relies on quantitative measures because it needs a language of comparison in order to

express notions of effectiveness and improvement. In the United Kingdom, this resulted in a kind of "one-club" thinking in which Random Controlled Trials(RCTs) represented a perceived gold standard of accurate appraisal. Laurence Sterne long ago demolished this kind of monocular thinking: "My father, whose way was to force every event in nature into a hypothesis, by which means never man crucified TRUTH at the rate he did" (2003 [1759], p. 586). In the essay "Human excess," Nancy regards such quantification as "all of it science and truth for fools" (2000, p. 178). The effect is considerable. As Miller comments in regard to contemporary anthropology, "Ethnography is becoming an island of open research in a sea of closed "hypothesis testing" surveys" (1995, p. 20). There is nothing new in this for Marx, who cites Aristotle: "There can be no exchange without equality, and no equality without commensurability" (Bholat, 2008, p. 19).

32. Graeber writing in *New Left Review*, treats neoliberalism itself as "a kind of fundamentalism—or, better, market Stalinism" (2002, p. 62). As a more fruitful semantic collision, I refer to the linked practices of the state as well as the habits of the market, although this account would certainly be sympathetic to his call for a "new anarchism" of evolving democratic spaces and practices, both locally and globally.

33. Cargo cults emerged after World War II. Melanesian islanders, nostalgic for the wealth that military bases had briefly brought to their lands, organized reminiscent cults designed to bring back those prosperous days. The element of mimicry is certainly part of the paracapitalist antics of the U.K. state, perhaps most obviously in relation to higher education and the so-called knowledge economy (White Paper, 2003). In the 1980s, I recall mocking the creeping vocationalism of secondary education, noting in its spread across the age range; "the vocational crèche is just round the corner" (Stronach, 1987, p. xx). When satire becomes successful prediction, it is time to get scared. The relation of the local to the global is enormously controversial, but the position taken here is skeptical of the notion of "flows" on the sorts of grounds that Ekholm-Friedman and Friedman argue—better to consider "positioned practices such as assimilation, encompassment and integration" in identifying "the relation between container and contained in the sense of the variable forms of incorporation of the products of the global field of interaction into the practice of local strategies" (Ekholm-Friedman & Friedman, 1995, p. 136).

34. Marx and Engels noted the combination of a "search for a social science" and a faith in a "new Social Gospel" (2005 [1848], pp. 254–255). They failed to hear, however, the rattle of their own tamborine.

35. The term is used despite its gender connotation. I intend a mosaic sense of human solidarity, as a "singular plural" relation rather than its erstwhile connections to collectivity (Critchley, 1998). In keeping with the spirit of this chapter, the emphasis on "fraternity" has both Left and Right connotations in the United Kingdom. Derrida: "the very work of the political: the properly

political act or operation amounts to creating (to producing, to making, etc.) the most friendship possible" (1997, p. 8). Indeed, Cruddas and Rutherford (2008) argue for the need for the Left to "reclaim fraternity" from a new conservative position that argues that New Labour has failed because "it has abandoned the fraternity of ethical socialism."

36. There are other serious criticisms that can be made of Hayek's assumptions. Overall, it seems that Hayek thinks capitalism in terms of the game "Monopoly," where equal rules and chance lead to unequal outcomes through part-chance (the fall of the dice), part-skill (decisions to invest). He forgets, or does not want to acknowledge, that the *real* game of "Monopoly" called capitalism or "Free Enterprise" as he would prefer, always starts in the middle, never at some "equal" beginning, is never "free," and for the majority is already ended. But our overall concern here is with a certain overlap or collision between some of Hayek's and some of Nancy's ideas.

37. It is not possible here to fully explicate Nancy's attempt to rewrite the relations of individual and collective in terms of a singular-plural formula. Indeed, as he recognizes, the task has only begun. His aim, however, is to treat philosophy/politics as a "disjunctive exposition" (2000, p. 23) and, as such, his proposal is congruent with the tenor of this chapter.

38. This was marked in the data by what we came to call the "shifting pronouns" with which pupils and sometimes staff talked about moral dilemmas:

> The Meeting teaches the anti-social that they "can't get away with this stuff because everyone thinks I'm a right twit now and I have to calm down and build relationships [...] the more they go to the Meeting [ie are "brought up" for a misdemeanour] the more fed up and vocal the meeting gets [...] so it [the problem situation] gets sorted out" ; "so you really have to use your head and think oh can I do this like if you were going to carve your name in a wall, you'd think oh do I think I can do this, no, I probably can't. (Stronach & Piper, 2008, p. 15)

39. In earlier writing, the "Meyousthem" was posited (Stronach, 2002) and subsequently developed in an article on reflexivity as the "survol" of a reflexive "signature" (Stronach et al., 2006). It was startling to see the conceptual strategy of "semantic collisions" much involved in that theorizing, because there were no conscious connections at the time between Nancy's work and the collection of data on Summerhill. I seem to spend a lot of time here catching up with myselves.

40. It would be seriously wrong to see "fraternity" as some sort of "let's agree to differ"—the parodic "postmodern politics" that Žižek rightly argues offers an apparent end to politics (1998, p. 1007). His question is a good one, even if his answer is obscure: "Will we be able to invent a new mode of repoliticization questioning the undisputed reign of a global capital?" (p. 1009).

References

Aitkenhead, D. (2008). Life in prison? Bring it on. *Guardian*, May 31. Available online at http://www.guardian.co.uk/environment/2008/may/31/activists.prisonsandprobation (accessed February 20, 2009).

Augé, M. (1995). *Non-places. Introduction to an anthropology of supermodernity* (trans. J. House). London: Verso.

Badiou, A. (2005). The adventure of French philosophy. *New Left Review* 35(Sept.–Oct.). Available online at www.newleftreview.org/?page=article. view=2580 (accessed March 15, 2008).

Balibar, E. (1998). *Spinoza and politics* (trans. P. Snowdon). London: Verso.

Baudrillard, J. (1996). *Cool memories II, 1987–1990* (trans. C. Turner). London: Polity.

Bholat, D. (2008). Beyond freedom and equality. Department of Anthropology, University of Chicago.

Bryson, B. (2007). *The life and times of the Thunderbolt Kid. Travels through my childhood*. London: Black Swan/Transworld.

Burbach, R. (2001). *Globalization and postmodern politics. From Zapatistas to high-tech robber barons*. London: Pluto Press.

Cable, V. (2008). The new terror. *Guardian*, May 31. Available online at http://www.guardian.co.uk/books/2008/may/31/politicalbooks.politics (accessed February 20, 2009).

Carver, T. (1998). *The postmodern Marx*. Manchester, UK: Manchester University Press.

Critchley, S. (1998). The other's decision in me (what are the politics of friendship?). *European Journal of Social Theory*, 1(2), 259–279.

Cruddas, J. & Rutherford, J. (2008). Out-thought by the Tories. *Guardian*, May 10. Available online at http://www.guardian.co.uk/commentis-free/2008/may/10/labour.conservatives (accessed February 20, 2009).

Deleuze, G. (1983 [1962]). *Nietzsche and philosophy* (trans. H. Tomlinson). London: Athlone.

Deleuze, G. (1994). *Difference and repetition* (trans. P. Patton). London: Athlone Press.

Deleuze, G. & Guattari, F. (1988). *A thousand plateaus* (trans. B. Massumi). London: Athlone Press.

Derrida, J. (1997). *Politics of friendship* (trans. G. Collins). London: Verso.

Derrida, J. (2001). What is a "relevant" translation? *Critical Inquiry*, 27(2), 174–200.

Derrida, J. (2005). *Paper machine* (trans. R. Bowlby). Stanford, CA: Stanford University Press.

Desai, M. (2002). *Marx's revenge. The resurgence of capitalism and the death of state socialism*. London: Verso.

De Sousa Santos, B. (2006). *The rise of the global left. The World Social Forum and beyond*. London: Zed.

Droogers, A. (1980). *The dangerous journey. Symbolic aspects of boys' initiation among the Wagenia of Kisangani, Zaire*. The Hague: Mouton.

Ekholm-Friedman, K. & Friedman, J. (1995). Global complexity and the simplicity of everyday life. In D. Miller (Ed.), *Worlds apart. Modernity through the prism of the local*, pp. 134–168. London: Routledge.

Ferguson, N. (2005). *Colossus. The rise and fall of the American empire*. London: Penguin.

Figes, O. (2007). *The whisperers. Private life in Stalin's Russia*. London: Allen Lane.

Freud, S. (2006 [1899]). *Interpreting dreams* (trans. J. Underwood). London: Penguin.

Friedman, T. (2006). *The world is flat. The globalized world of the 21st century*. London: Penguin.

Fukuyama, F. (2007). *After the neocons. America at the crossroads*. London: Profile Books.

Graeber, D. (2002). The new anarchists. *New Left Review*, 13(Jan.–Feb.), 61–73.

Gray, J. (1999). *False dawn. The delusions of global capitalism*. London: Granta.

Gunn, C. (2008). Scots plan to capture 20 miles of England. *Sunday Post*, February 10, p. 3.

Hayek, F. (1944). *The road to serfdom*. London: Routledge.

Hayek, F. (1952). *The counter-revolution of science. Studies in the abuse of reason*. Glencoe, IL: The Free Press.

Hayek, F. (1976). *Law, legislation and liberty. A new statement of the liberal principles of justice and political economy. Vol. 2: The mirage of social justice*. London: RKP.

Heller, R. (2008). No mavericks lie in the sub-prime graveyard. *Guardian* (*Observer*), June 1. Available online at http://www.guardian.co.uk/business/2008/jun/01/investing.subprimecrisis (accessed February 20, 2009).

Higgins, N. (2004). *Understanding the Chiapas rebellion. Modernist visions and the invisible Indian*. Austin: University of Texas Press.

Hobsbawm, E. (1994a). *Globalisation, democracy and terrorism*. London: Little Brown.

Hobsbawm, E. (1994b). *The age of extremes. The short 20th century, 1914–1991*. London: Michael Joseph.

Hutchens, B. (2005). *Jean-Luc Nancy and the future of philosophy.* Chesham, Bucks, UK: Acumen.

Jameson, F. 2008 [1999]. Marx's purloined letter. In J. Derrida, T. Eagleton, F. Jameson, A. Negri et al., eds., *Ghostly demarcations. A symposium on Jacques Derrida's "Specters of Marx,"* pp. 26–67. London: Verso.

Jones, G. (2005 [1848]). *Preface. The Communist Manifesto. Karl Marx and Friedrich Engels.* London: Penguin.

Klein, N. (2005). *Fences and windows. Dispatches from the front lines of the globalisation Debate,* 2nd ed. London: Harper.

Kolakowski, L. (2005 [1976]). *Main currents of Marxism. The founders. The Golden Age. The breakdown* (trans. P. Falla). New York: W.W. Norton.

Marcos, Subcomandante Insurgente. (2000). Oxymoron! (The intellectual right and liberal fascism) Available online at http://flag.blackened.net/revolt/mexico/ezln/2001/marcos/oxymoran_may.html (accessed February 15, 2008).

Margolis, J. (2003). *The unravelling of scientism. American philosophy at the end of the 20th century.* Ithaca, NY: Cornell University Press.

Marx, K. & Engels, F. (2005 [1848]). *The Communist manifesto. Karl Marx and Friedrich Engels.* London: Penguin.

Miller, D. (1995). *Worlds apart. Modernity through the prism of the local.* London: Routledge.

Milosz, C. (1990) *The captive mind* (trans. J. Zielenko). New York: Random House.

Nairn, T. (2000). *After Britain. New Labour and the return of Scotland.* London: Granta.

Nairn, T. (2007). Union on the rocks? *New Left Review,* 43(Jan.–Feb.). Available online at http://www.newleftreview.org/?view=2654 (accessed April 23, 2008).

Nancy, J-L. (1993a). *The experience of freedom* (trans. B. McDonald). Stanford, CA: Stanford University Press.

Nancy, J-L. (1993b). *The birth to presence* (trans. B. Holmes). Stanford, CA: Stanford University Press.

Nancy, J-L. (1996). The Deleuzian fold of thought. In P. Patton (Ed.), *Deleuze. A critical Reader,* pp. 32–51. Oxford: Blackwell.

Nancy, J-L. (1997). The free voice of man. In S. Sparks (Ed.), *Retreating the political. Phillipe Lacoue-Labarthe, Jean-Luc Nancy,* Pp. 107–113. London: Routledge.

Nancy, J-L (2000). *Being singular plural.* Stanford, CA: Stanford University Press.

Nash, J. (2001) *Mayan visions. The quest for autonomy in an age of globalisation.* New York: Routledge.

Negri, A. (2004). *Subversive Spinoza: (Un)contemporary variations* (ed. T. Murphy; trans. T. Murphy, M. Hardt, T. Stolze, & C. Wolfe). Manchester, UK: Manchester University Press.

Perec, G. (1999 [1974]). *Species of spaces and other pieces* (trans. and ed. J. Sturrock). London: Penguin.

Piper, H. & Stronach, I. (2008). *Don't touch! The educational story of a panic.* London: Routledge.

Polanyi, M. (1962). *Personal knowledge. Towards a post-critical philosophy.* New York: Harper.

Rus, J., Castillo, R., & Mattiace (Eds.). (2003). Maya lives, Mayan utopias. *The indigenous peoples of Chiapas: The Zapatista rebellion.* New York: Rowman & Littlefield.

Russell, B. (1968 [1952]). The impact of science on society. London: Unwin.

Said, E. (2005). *From Oslo to the roadmap.* London: Bloosbury.

Sennett, R. (2008). *The craftsman.* London: Allen Lane.

Skidelsky, R. (1995). *The world after Communism. A polemic for our times.* London: Macmillan.

Sterne, L. (2003 [1759]). *The life and opinions of Tristram Shandy, Gentleman.* London: Penguin.

Stronach, I. (1987). Ten years on. *Forum*, 29(3), 64–69.

Stronach, I. (2002). This space is not yet blank: Anthropologies for a future action research, *Educational Action Research*, 10(2), 291–307.

Stronach, I. (2006). Enlightenment and the heart of darkness: (Neo)imperialism in the Congo, and elsewhere. *International Journal of Qualitative Studies in Education*, 19(6), 757–768.

Stronach, I. (2007). On promoting rigour in educational research: The example of the RAE? *Journal of Education Policy*, 22(3), 343–352.

Stronach, I., Frankham, J., & Stark, S. (2007). Sex, science and educational research: The unholy trinity. *Journal of Education Policy*, 22(2), 215–235.

Stronach, I., Garratt, D., Pearce, C., & Piper, H. (2006). Reflexivity, the picturing of selves, the forging of method. *Qualitative Inquiry*, 12(6), 1–25.

Stronach, I., Halsall, R., & Hustler, D. (2002). Future imperfect: Evaluation in dystopian times. In K. Ryan & T. Schwandt (Eds.), *Exploring evaluator role and identity*, pp. 167–192. Greenwich, CT: Information Age Publishing.

Stronach, I. & MacLure, M. (1997). *Educational research undone: The postmodern embrace.* London: Open University Press.

Stronach, I. & Morris, B. (1994). Polemical notes on educational evaluation in the age of "policy hysteria." *Evaluation & Research in Education*, 8(1/2), 5–19.

Stronach, I. & Piper, H. (2008). Can liberal education make a comeback? The case of "relational touch" at Summerhill School. *American Educational Research Journal*, 45(1), 6–37.

Therborn, G. (2007). After dialectics. Radical social theory in a post-communist world. *New Left Review*, 43(Jan.–Feb, pp. 63–114. Available online at www.newleftreview.org/?view=2653 (accessed April 23, 2008).

Tormey, S. (2003). Review of "From Bakunin to Lacan: Anti-authoritarianism and the dislocation of power." *Contemporary Political Theory*, 2, 359–361.

White Paper. (2003). *The future of Higher Education*. London: HMSO.

Wilk, R. (1995). Learning to be local in Belize: Global systems of common difference. In D. Miller (Ed.), *Worlds apart. Modernity through the prism of the local*, pp. 110–132. London: Routledge.Wright, E. (2006). Compass points. Towards a socialist alternative. *New Left Review*, 41(Sept.–Oct.). Available online at www.newleftreview.org/?view=2638 (accessed April 23, 2008).

Žižek, S. (1998). A leftist plea for "Eurocentrism." *Critical Inquiry*, 24, 988–1009.

Žižek, S. (2008a). The political and its disavowals. Available online at www.generation-online.org/p/fpzizek6.htm (accessed May 13, 2008).

Žižek, S (2008b). Invited keynote address to the Discourse, Power, Resistance conference, Manchester Metropolitan University, March.

Coda
Mentoring Relationships
Creating a Future for Qualitative Inquiry

Carolyn Ellis
University of South Florida

Tony E. Adams
Northeastern Illinois University

Laura L. Ellingson
Santa Clara University

Arthur P. Bochner
University of South Florida

Norman K. Denzin
University of Illinois, Urbana-Champaign

Aisha S. Durham
Texas A&M University

D. Soyini Madison
Northwestern University

Renee Alexander Craft
University of North Carolina, Chapel Hill

Ronald J. Pelias
Southern IllinoisUniversity

Nicole Defenbaugh
Bloomsburg University

Laurel Richardson
The Ohio State University

Carolyn Ellis: Welcome to our panel on "Mentoring Relationships: Creating a Future for Qualitative Inquiry." If we want the current qualitative movement to continue to flourish after the current generation retires, then it is important to pay attention to the mentoring of graduate students. Every time we give workshops and presentations, participants ask many questions about mentoring. In this panel, we will talk about some of our experiences, tensions, and turning points in mentoring relationships between professors and graduate students during graduate school and after students receive their Ph.D.

We are fortunate today to have five mentoring pairs, plus Laurel Richardson as a discussant. The first pair is made up of Ron Pelias from Southern Illinois University and his mentoring partner, Nicole Defenbaugh, an assistant professor at Bloomsburg University. The second pair consists of Art Bochner and Tony Adams from the University of South Florida. Tony will soon be a faculty member at Northeastern Illinois University. Third, we have me, Carolyn Ellis from the University of South Florida, and my mentoring partner, Laura Ellingson, an associate professor at Santa Clara University. Fourth, we have Soyini Madison from Northwestern University and her mentee, Renee Alexander Craft, an instructor at University of North Carolina. Fifth, we have Norman Denzin from the University of Illinois and his mentoring partner, Aisha Durham, a visiting assistant professor at the University of Georgia, who soon will be a faculty member at Texas A&M.

I gave the panelists a number of questions in advance, which we will divide into only two rounds in order to give you, our audience members, an opportunity to ask questions and tell your stories. We plan this as an informal, dialogic session, where the mentor and the mentee will address these questions together.

The first round: Describe your mentor-mentee relationship prior to finishing the Ph.D. degree. How did you negotiate the tensions inherent in the relationship, for example, on the dimensions of independence-dependence, supervision and friendship, personal and professional, emotional support and academic standards? Each pair should tell us the story of your mentoring relationship, the phases or stages you've passed through, and give an example. From your experience, what are the most difficult phases and why, and, again, give an example if possible. Each pair should limit themselves to five minutes for this round.

The second round: Since several pairs will include mentees who are now faculty members, I am also interested in how the mentoring relationship evolves after the Ph.D. is awarded and the student moves on to the first academic position. What do you see as the norms and expectations regarding mentoring relationships after the dissertation and awarding of the degree?

Nicole Defenbaugh and Ron Pelias make up our first pair. [Carolyn sits down and looks out over the forty or so people in attendance, many of whom are graduate students. There is a feeling of excitement and anticipation in the air as Ron and Nicole move to the front of the room. They stand side-by-side, so that they are facing both each other and the audience.]

Ron Pelias: Do you want me to start?

Nicole Defenbaugh: Sure.

Ron: I thought you were going to start.

Nicole: I was going to start.

Ron: Okay, start.
[Laughter]

Nicole: And that's our relationship. Thank you for coming.
[Laughter.]

Nicole: Our relationship as a mentor-mentee was very much like that. We took turns discussing our ideas. We negotiated the mentor-mentee relationship very well. The best metaphor that I can use would be the ebb and flow of the ocean tide with its high and low moments. It just works. This was one of the best mentoring relationships I've ever had. We appreciated each other's voice. Ron listened to what I had to say and respected my ideas and words. This was especially important since my work is primarily autoethnographic. Our relationship was not easily definable; yet, somehow, it organically defined itself.

Ron: When we were talking earlier, we recognized that our relationship moved through the traditional friendship stages, from initial getting acquainted to a fully developed relationship. The interpersonal literature describes this movement as initiating, experimenting, intensifying, integrating, and bonding. We moved through all of these stages.

Nicole: They even say in most relationships you get to a point where you finish each other's sentences. There was a point when I was writing my dissertation that I would stop at a sentence and say, "Oh, yeah. Ron wouldn't like that." I began to anticipate what he would say and what revisions he'd request. It was very much like the stages of interpersonal development, as Ron mentioned. We even had the coming apart stages because I left SIU [Southern Illinois University] for my new job. We went through deterioration stages. We didn't talk much anymore. It felt like the mentoring relationship just ended. And that was difficult because I didn't leave on a bad note—as is the case when most relationships end. I simply got a job and moved away. That part of the relationship has been a bit hard for me.

Ron: Talk about the tension you mentioned to me before this session started.

Nicole: One of the tensions we had was during the prospectus. It was a big mess. The reason it was a big mess was because I handed my work to Ron and said: "Here you go. Could you read this?" He read it assuming it was my final draft and that I had made all of the appropriate revisions before handing it to him. After my prospectus was defended, we sat down and talked about the process. I remember saying, "The first draft I handed you was my rough draft." And he responded, "Oh, really? Is that what that was? Good, because I didn't know." From then on, we understood where the other was coming from. Again, it was very dialogic. We had to discuss what was happening, how we were understanding each other's ideas, and how we were interpreting each other's work.

Ron: I wanted Nicole to tell this story because when I was trying to think about tensions, I couldn't think of any. For me, that incident was simply gone. I had jotted in my own notes for this panel that our working relationship was conflict- and tension-free. I thought this was so because Nicole was very good about letting me know what she needed. How I remembered the issue about her rough drafts was that she told me what kind of reader she wanted me to be: "I want you to look at a rough draft. Don't worry about editing. This is just a really rough draft. I want you to tell me if you think the parts are in the right place. I'll go back and tighten it later."

[Nicole and Ron sit down and Tony Adams and Art Bochner move to the front of the room.]

Tony Adams: There are three things I want to say about my relationship with Art. The first thing has to do with my relationship with my father. When I started at the University of South Florida, I hated my father. I thought he was a mean, hateful man. I didn't want anything to do with him. Then I met Art who encouraged me to say to myself, "Hey, step back a minute. Be reflexive. See what role you play in your relationship, how you and your father work *together* to make problems." He encouraged me to reframe the relationship I had with my father. And this reframing helped my relationship in positive, beneficial ways. Now, every time I interact with my father I feel as though Art is sitting on my shoulder saying, "Do this. Don't do that. Think about yourself in relation to him, consider how the two of you are working together and influencing each other."

The second thing about Art is that he encourages me to take risks while, simultaneously, he acts as my safety net. For instance, I have a biological grandfather who is, for the most part, a family secret. Art never explicitly said, "Go contact him," but I felt as though Art would be my support system in case I wanted to seek him out. So with this support, I contacted my grandfather. The contact was, and has been, very meaningful. I now have a relationship with a man who once was a family secret, but who I am coming to know. I am learning who he is and what he likes and I get to hear his stories about the family. I can't thank Art enough for giving me the push to make contact, and, again, for helping me find ways of trying to better my relationships.

The third thing is that I enjoy the togetherness Art and I have. I know he cares about me. He places just as much importance on how I'm doing as on what and how much I've done. He makes me want to be a better person and a humane scholar. I appreciate him. I appreciate *us*.

Art Bochner: When I reflect on my mentoring relationship with Tony, and other students as well, I see that my perspective on mentoring is that it is a full-blooded relationship. As Tony indicated, it is not just a relationship on doing your dissertation and getting through the program, but it is about you as a whole person and your life and what's between us. It's a relationship. Too often, we faculty assume that within the academy our most important conversations are going to be with our colleagues. But when I look back over my forty years of teaching college, I must say that my best conversations now, and really in the history of my life in the university, have been with my students. The best conversation I had at this conference, and I had many wonderful conversations, but the best one was the two hours I spent with Tony yesterday. I wish we would've taped that and played a part of that here. We went through a whole metacommunication of our life together over the past four years, focusing on his dissertation work and on our relationship—what was helpful, what we learned from each other. So I see it as a very full-blooded relationship, and a wonderful conversation. With conversations, there is no predicting where it will go, and that's what it's been like.

What else do I want to say? In terms of the demands that I make—if you want to call them demands—I start from the beginning to establish the framework for a lasting relationship. One of the first conversations I have with students is about how this is going to be a life-long relationship, one that involves both caring and criticism. In a way, I guess it is like a parental relationship. Negotiating the relationship, like Ron and Nicole mentioned, can be difficult at times, but it is usually fine because it is set against the backdrop of "I'm on your side, you can trust me." If there is not trust from the beginning, then I don't think a mentor-mentee relationship will work. It is very much like any good relationship in that way.

My relationship with Tony is particularly special because his dissertation project on "coming out" narratives, and his own theoretical work in relation to sexual identity, has taught me so much. When I think of all the students I've had over these many years, I am grateful for how much I've learned from them. Sometimes we think of the mentoring as a top-down relationship in which you're giving but not receiving, but I do expect to receive from every student. And I've learned so much from Tony.

[Art and Tony sit down and Laura Ellingson and Carolyn Ellis walk to the front of the room.]

Laura Ellingson: Carolyn and I started with drama and emotion, of course. I was trying to visually perform being credible, and wanting her to like me and be proud of me, and we weren't even working together yet. It was my first semester in the Ph.D. program [at the University of South Florida], and I was taking Carolyn's qualitative research methods class. I had an appointment with her to talk about my project for the class. Before our meeting, I had a doctor's appointment that was a disaster. It was a really painful and horrible experience, and I left it sobbing, sobbing, and sobbing, all the while trying to get myself together for Carolyn, trying to get myself to perform "person you'd want to work with." I really tried hard. I walked into Carolyn's office and two other graduate students were sitting there, and Carolyn said:

Carolyn: "Oh, there you are!"

Laura: And I went "Waaaahhhhhh!" And Carolyn, not missing a beat, gave me a hug.

Carolyn: And we hugged and hugged.

Laura: Yes we did! And I cried and cried and cried. And Leigh [Berger] and Judy [Perry], who were there, just watched me. It was Carolyn's office, so who knew what was going to happen next. Judy and Leigh got up and left quietly, and Carolyn shut the door and held me until I stopped crying. And, of course, Carolyn was terrified because …

Carolyn: I knew Laura previously had cancer, bone cancer. And I thought, "Oh my, the cancer has come back."

Laura: Actually, the doctor's appointment had been about another issue, but the doctor was incredibly insensitive. I was hurt by the communication in a very painful way. After I calmed down, Carolyn and I started talking about the project, specifically that I really had to use my experience. "This experience has to be part of your project," she said. "You're a cancer survivor. You want to study health communication. We have to build on that." And I said, "I've been trying to get up the nerve to ask you if you'd like to be my advisor." And she said ...

Carolyn: "I would love to be your advisor!"

Laura: And I said, "Art was assigned my advisor, and I'm afraid to tell him that I want to work with you." And she said ...

Carolyn: "Do not worry. I can take care of Art."

Laura: So out of this wonderful, emotional, painful time, Carolyn was there. I didn't need her to literally be my mom, but I needed to know that when I came into her office and burst out crying that it was going to go okay. We built this amazing intellectual partnership out of what was initially a very emotional connection.

Carolyn: Since most of my students have elements of autoethnography in their dissertations, I think that part of my responsibility as a mentor is to be there for them emotionally. Sometimes it can get complicated because you're their emotional support and their friend, but also their teacher and guide. How do you negotiate all of those roles? It is interesting because with Laura I really never felt a lot of tension among these roles. We could move from one to the other so easily. I have to say, she was just an extraordinary student. She was motivated and talented, and that part of the relationship went so well. I like to think about how relationships evolve with students. I always tell them that initially it is like the "falling in love" stage, you're perfect and they're perfect, and then, of course, eventually each finds out that the other is not perfect and neither is your relationship. I tell my students that at some point you're going to hate me. And at some point I'm going to be real frustrated with you. And it is going to be okay, we'll get through it. But I have to say, I don't think Laura and I ever got to that point.

Laura: Before my meeting with Carolyn, I had been in love with her for two years.

Carolyn: You mean you aren't now? [Laughter]

Laura: I'm back in love. The first bump in the love—I mean we never really had a terrible tension—but the first bump was when she said, "You can't do all of that in the dissertation." And I said, "Oh, yes, I can." She was secure about my talents, but she said, "You just can't do *all* of that."

Carolyn: To me, the hardest problem for students is narrowing down the topic. Laura had three different approaches and three different writing styles ...

Laura: And five topics. I was like "no problem!" The amazing thing about this tension, and Art participated in the tension too because he was part of my committee, is that I had to sell what I wanted to do to them. I had to explain how this was going to work. The end result was a compromise: I kept the multi-method, multi-genre part that is so important to me, but I drastically narrowed the topic to do that. Carolyn was right. You can't do everything. So I really narrowed the focus of that study so that I could have all of the perspectives that I wanted. I am in the process now of publishing a book on multi-genre crystallization and how important that work is to me in terms of presenting work in multi-modalities.

Carolyn: And in the last phase—and Laura reminded me that it was actually the second year of our relationship—we actually decided to write an article together. This was the first time I published with a student. She quickly became a colleague and we easily moved among all of those roles, because she took at least equal responsibility for the article.

[Carolyn and Laura sit down and Renee Alexander Craft and Soyini Madison move to the front of the room.]

Renee Alexander Craft: "What do you want your legacy to be?" In 1991, Michelle Thomas, then a college junior and president of a campus organization dedicated to social justice and activism, addressed that question to me just three days into my undergraduate experience at UNC [University of North Carolina]. Her teacher and mentor, Dr. Sonja Hanes Stone, had raised a similar question with her years prior and so, with acute focus and attention, she asked the same of me. "Wow!" I thought. "*I could have a legacy?*" It's a powerful dose of agency and accountability to give a freshman. Three linked thoughts followed on the heels of the first: that Michelle had a mentor, that she was part of her mentor's legacy, and that she was mentoring me. When I think of how to begin a story about my relationship with *my* teacher and mentor, Dr. D. Soyini Madison, I realize how much that question frames, contextualizes, and animates it. I want to offer three concise stories that point to the type of ever-evolving mentor/mentee/mother/sister/friend/colleague relationship we share.

In the spring of my freshman year, I founded an African American literary magazine to address what I saw as a void on campus. By then, I had heard quite a bit about Dr. Madison. She was one of the faculty members that students raved about. What drew me to her were the ways students talked about how she nurtured their creativity, presented them with productive challenges, and gave them the tools they needed to address them. It didn't hurt that they also talked about how much fun they had in the process. As an English/journalism double-major, I found it difficult to enroll in classes outside of my departments, but I hoped that Dr. Madison would join the editorial board of the magazine to help shape its mission and vision. Several faculty members declined my invitation. One, in particular, doubted the project would ever get off the ground. He had been approached too often, he said, by students with impressive ideas but poor follow through. Soyini, on the other hand, took a leap of faith with me and helped see the project through its infancy and development. I was not a student in her department and had never set foot in one of her classes, but she took the time to nurture, encourage, and empower me. So our mentor-relationship began with her willingness to "see" me, believe in my vision, and help me accomplish it.

Years after I graduated, began my dream-career, abandoned it as a nightmare, and returned to UNC as a staff member. Soyini spotted me on campus and asked what I was up to. By then, I knew I wanted to go back to school and, as a poet, assumed an MFA would be the most logical choice for me. Soyini smiled and said, "Why don't you come up to my office?" I was happy to comply. After welcoming me in and offering me a chair, Soyini sat down, rested her bangled wrists on her desk, clasped her fingers, and said:

"I know you. Tell me if I'm wrong, but I think you want to do embodied work, you want to engage critical theory. You're not just going to want to write about your own work, you're going to want to engage it theoretically, and you're going to want to engage it through your body."

"Yea!" I said.

"You can't do that in an MFA program," Soyini replied.

Before the corners of my lips sank below neutral, she continued, "You can do that in Communication Studies, and you can do that through performance."

She then offered to give me feedback on my application materials and help me understand the process, should I choose to apply. She pointed the way, sat back, and gave me room to make my own decision. Because Soyini had been consistent in both her concern for me and her willingness to be a resource and advocate, I trusted the vision she articulated.

Once I entered the program, she offered me the opportunity to serve as her teaching assistant, met with me as often as I needed, asked me productive questions to help me define my research project, and gave me suggestions consistent with my interests. She challenged me when she thought my field of vision was too narrow; was stern with me when she thought my work slipped below my potential; and helped me find the will, energy, and resources (financial, emotional, social) to move forward when I might have faltered.

By the time I announced to Soyini that I wanted to pursue my doctorate and a teaching career in higher education, we had established a relationship of trust. Like our initial conversation about graduate school, we differed in our approach as to how I should proceed. My slate of schools was admittedly shallow. I had lived in New York previously and had gotten very cold and quite lonely. So, I narrowed my search to temperate climates close to my networks of family and friends. I wanted to be in an excellent program, but I wanted more to be warm and comfortable. Again, Soyini offered me a vision for the type of work she knew

I wanted to pursue and the type of environment that would challenge me and help me continue to grow as an artist, scholar, and individual. She said, "Northwestern would be the best place for you right now." She had introduced me to Dwight Conquergood's work in her critical/performance ethnography class and knew that I was interested in deepening my understanding of critical ethnographic theories and methods. Evanston was not temperate (most of the year) nor was it close to any of my networks. I was nervous and mildly resistant, but I trusted Soyini. I knew that Dwight had been her mentor and that she loved him. Just as I knew something of Sonja Haynes Stone through the work of Michelle Thomas, I knew something of Dwight through my relationship with Soyini and my engagement with his research. So, trusting Soyini, I trusted Dwight too, even before we interacted. As I have said elsewhere, when your mentor sends you to her mentor, you don't ask questions; you go.

I consider Soyini a mentor-sister-friend. She is a part of my family. She has been present in word, deed, or flesh for most of the critical moments of my life over the past eighteen years. Her mentorship, like her pedagogy, research, and activism, comes out of a praxis of social justice. We have differed over the years, but we have not had great friction or tension, in my opinion, because we've established a relationship built on trust, accountability, consistency, and love. That is the type of legacy I am proud to follow and one I hope to recreate.

[Soyini and Renee sit down and Aisha Durham and Norman Denzin move to the front of the room.]

Aisha Durham: You want to go?

Norman Denzin: You start.

Aisha: Are you sure?

Norman: Positive.

Aisha: So this is very improv. We talked earlier and I told him that I was going to talk about home because that is a part of my research, and in moving from Virginia and Georgia to Illinois, there was a sense of displacement. But I'm going to change that and talk about the mentor-mentee relationship and use the saturated metaphor of a circus. I am going to use the metaphor, not in terms of organized chaos, but in terms of imaginative possibilities. That metaphor has so many sensory elements for me, as did walking into Denzin's interpretive methods class. On the first day, Denzin came in and gave us a project. The project wasn't about research, but about reimagining our worlds. [Aisha begins to cry ...]

I came to this program not because of the name of ICR [Institute of Communication Research]—I didn't even know what ICR was—but I came because of that commitment to larger projects of emancipatory democracy. I didn't know how my work was going to look, and Denzin didn't know how it was going to look. In that space, everybody had their own talent. He outlined the project, and he had a grab bag of methodologies and ways to represent and honor your own voice. Nobody knew what was going on because he would come into class, tell us what we were going to do, give us the information, and sit in the back of the classroom and listen, and watch. Some of us had cheap tricks, for example, to make you cry. Some of us, in terms of being real intellectual acrobats and being on the tightrope, knew that we had the safety net there to be able to leap, to be able to try, to be able to explore different ways of being and representing ourselves in that one moment.

So my difficulty was being in that space, that space where everybody was seen as freakish—because that is what ICRers are—and then stepping outside of our department. Outside of that space, people are asking, "What are you doing? How are you using poetry? Are you really using film? Are you doing somatic work? What are you all doing over there?" But in that one space everybody's unique talent is celebrated and unique voice is heard. So I felt like if I left this circus-this space of imaginative possibilities— I would shut down, and in some ways be retrained to re-think in new ways. But it was because of the mentorship of Denzin, whom I cannot call by his first name, that I am able to engage with other students as a professor in the same way he engaged with us. I can step back and honor someone else's voice, that moment of what someone is doing, while still having that ringleader idea, and sense of coming together in terms of that community.

Norman: [Decides not to add anything.]
[Aisha and Norman sit down.]

Carolyn: The second set of questions is about the relationship that evolved after the Ph. D. is achieved, though you should feel free to talk about whatever you want.

[Nicole and Ron once again move to the front of the room and assume their initial positions.]

Nicole: I want to add that our relationship worked so well because it was based on trust. I had Ron as a professor in a few classes and every time I started a paper and approached him about it, he would encourage me to talk more about my experiences. Every time I went in and explained, "I'm interested in theory," he would say, "Continue with that, but also think about how your writing makes you feel? How do you understand that? How do you embody that?" Like many of the mentees here, I would come in crying. Ron was very similar to the other mentors here in that he was a colleague, counselor, and friend. He allowed me to speak my voice, my ill voice. He nurtured me, embraced me, and was intellectually rigorous. All of that together really made this work. I found somebody who trusted what I had to say, and allowed me to find my voice. That was what I was looking for in a mentor.

Our relationship now? I don't know how to answer that. I live 800 miles away from Ron. Every time in the past when I needed to talk with Ron, I would knock on his door and I'd do this kind of comedic gesture: I'd lean in, and he'd wave. I saw Ron every day. Though Ron was often too busy to see me every day, he always made the time. Sometimes—he doesn't know this—I would go in his office just to chat. I'd come up with some dissertation idea just to get through the door, and quickly divert into, "Okay, so, I'm having some issues with my doctor right now." I wanted to talk to him about everything. Now our communication is via technology. We had just begun to develop wonderful dialogic conversations, open communication face-to-face, but now we're forced to speak via e-mail. It has created some tension for me because I no longer get this long, beautiful Ron answer to my questions. Instead I get brief "Okay, fine" e-mail responses. Now I think, "Wait, where's the rest of it that I used to get." So technology has enabled me to talk with him, but it also complicated the style of communication we have.

Ron: Some wonderful things have carried over from our mentoring relationship. Mentoring relationships often function as a teacher-student apprenticeship. That is not my favorite model. Nicole and I quickly emerged into a colleague-colleague dynamic. As colleagues, we have permission to work with each other in certain ways. Nicole's topic required deep disclosure. One day she said to me, "I'm telling you all of this about me. What about you?" I answered, "Well, I like to have a bowl of ice cream at night." Now she'll e-mail and say, "Enjoy your ice cream tonight." We enjoyed, and continue to enjoy, a kind of teasing relationship with each other that has been great fun. Often when she would give me dissertation pages, I would say, "You really want me to read this crap?" After a session we might have, she would give me a grade: "I think this talk was about a 'C.'" I don't think I ever got an "A." [Laughter.] Playfulness and enjoyment around the hard work not only helps to get the job done but also to build an enduring relationship.

[Nicole and Ron sit down. Tony and Art move to the front of the room.]

Tony: Art pushes me to do meaningful work. He motivates me to attend to important, politicized human affairs. I never did this before our relationship. I was doing work for work's sake, to produce to meet deadlines and mundane requirements. I didn't care about what my work did, or why it was important. Art, however, pushed me to make my work matter, make our work as scholars matter.

Art also taught me about the importance of self-respect. One of his mentoring goals is to allow his mentees to leave the graduate program with self-respect. With me, he was, and is, successful. He has taught me ways to love myself, and ways to continue to love myself and others. [Tony begins to cry] Now you talk … [Tony points to Art.]

Art Bochner: When I reflect on my mentoring relationship with

Tony, and other students as well, I see that my perspective on mentoring is that it is a full-blooded relationship. As Tony indicated, it is not just a relationship about doing your dissertation and getting through the program, but it is about you as a whole person and your life and what's between us. It's a relationship. Too often, we faculty assume that within the academy our most important conversations are going to be with our colleagues. But when I look back over my forty years of teaching college, I must say that my best conversations now, and really in the history of my life in the university, have been with my students. The best conversation I had at this conference—and I had many wonderful ones, but the best one was the two hours I spent with Tony yesterday. I wish we would've taped that and played a part of that here. We went through a whole metacommunication of our life together over the past four years, focusing on his dissertation work and on our relationship—what was helpful, what we learned from each other. So I see it as a very full-blooded relationship, and a wonderful conversation. With conversations, there is no predicting where it will go, and that's what it's been like.

What else do I want to say? In terms of the demands that I make, if you want to call them demands, well I start from the beginning to establish the framework for a lasting relationship. One of the first conversations I have with students is that this is going to be a life-long relationship, one that involves both caring and criticism. In a way, I guess it is like a parental relationship. Negotiating the relationship, like Ron and Nicole mentioned, can be difficult at times, but is usually fine because it is set against the backdrop of "I'm on your side. You can trust me." If there is not trust from the beginning, then I don't think a mentor-mentee relationship will work. It is very much like any good relationship in that way.

My relationship with Tony is particularly special because his dissertation project on coming out narratives, and his own theoretical work in relation to sexual identity, has taught me so much. And when I think of all the students that I've had over these many years, I am grateful for how much I've learned from them. Sometimes we think of the mentoring as a top-down relationship in which you're giving but not receiving, but I do expect to receive from every student. And I've learned so much from Tony.

[Art and Tony sit down and Carolyn and Laura take their positions at the front of the room.]

Carolyn: I want to go back to the love fest. I was really taken by what Aisha had to say. It made me think about how very important these relationships are and how intimate they can be, how really sweet they can be, and how important they can be. My best friends are my students and former students. But it is an interesting relationship because they're friends, but they're also colleagues, and they're also like my children, so it is an amalgamation of different kinds of relationships. Sometimes I think they know me better than maybe anybody, other than Art. They're the people who I come to with my work, who help me think through what I'm doing, because we've been in that same head space for so long. And we've also shared emotional lives and traumas. So they're just really incredible relationships and it is hard for me to let them go. I'm really sad right now because Tony's going to go miles away from us, and he's such an important part of our life. Even though we don't see each other every day now, we know we can see each other every day, if we want.

But what is gratifying about former students, such as Laura, is that we continue to be in touch all of the time over e-mail. We make plans to see each other at conferences and other times, whenever possible. So the relationship continues, and it is really nice to look forward to the times we're able to get together.

Laura: It is. I live in California. That is about as far away as I can get from Florida. But I didn't have the experience that Nicole has had—maybe Carolyn's a little more chatty that Ron is. I've gotten the two-word e-mails that say, "Sounds good," but I've also gotten some amazing e-mails that have made me feel like this connection is going to continue forever. This connection has been a really important part of my life—it really does feel like going home when I go back to talking about something with Carolyn. We stay in touch quite often over e-mail. One of the things I've been able to do that I think is really important, that I wanted to share and have Carolyn share her response, is this: I've done pretty well. I got tenure. I'm writing my third book. But I can still go back to Carolyn and say "help!" And I did—I typed an email and the subject line was "Help!" I explained to her that my editor, in his infinite wisdom, had commissioned six reviews of my book manuscript, and the reviewers wanted six different things, most of which were diametrically opposed. I had six weeks to turn the manuscript around from all of these reviews. So I said, "Help, I just don't think I can do this. I am so overwhelmed. I'm so freaked out. It's just, I can't." And Carolyn said …

Carolyn: Let me tell you what I thought first. I thought, "Why is she insecure? This woman is so successful and talented. She is absolutely the best person to be writing this book. So how do I respond here?" But then I thought, "Okay, I know Laura. I know how she is. She is so confident and so together as she moves through the world, and then, all of a sudden, she'll just get nervous about whether she can accomplish something. What she needs is somebody to say to her: 'This is who you are. I have confidence in you. I know you can do this.' When you do, then she is up and running again. So that is what I did. I wrote her an email saying, "You are the best person to do this book. Look at your successes" and so on, sentiments that I firmly believe. Immediately she was up and running. You learn each other's needs, each other's cycles. I might not act that way with every student because I think at some point it's good to kick them out of the nest and let them move on. You don't want to enable them to feel helpless, but that wasn't at all what was going on here.

Laura: No, I was having a really bad moment. It helps to know that I can go back to Carolyn, that she won't think I'm incompetent or that there is something wrong with me needing to come back to her. It helps to have that moment where she says "You really can do this." I print her emails out and save them. She writes the most amazing pep talk emails. And then I get back to work. The funny thing is that this email brought us first circle, because the book we were talking about is about multi-genre representation in qualitative research. The very little tension we've ever had in our relationship was over how I was going to get all these different perspectives into my dissertation. I have a wonderful and supportive partner, and I have good friends and colleagues, but there was literally no one else I wanted to go to besides Carolyn to hear her say, "You really can do it" and to not think any less of me—quite the contrary. I knew that if she just got me back up and running, then I could do it. And I did. I printed the reviews and I went back to typing.

Carolyn: This is not a one-way street. Laura also responds to my work. We continue to publish together. I turn to her often for resources and ideas and moral support.

Laura: It's wonderful. [Carolyn nods in agreement.]

[Laura and Carolyn sit down and Soyini and Renee walk to the front of the room.]

Soyini: I am happy that you invited me to be on this panel because I never really considered, in a formal organized manner, what mentoring means and what actually constitutes my method or actions as a mentor until now. After giving it more concentrated thought, I realized that first and foremost it is to love being a member of this community—this academic community—of which we live and labor. It begins with believing that academic and intellectual work should matter in the world, because there is such great potential, in the reach of our work, to affect the kind of world, far and near, that we hope for. I think this is where I begin as a mentor.

It has been my experience that mentoring also requires genuine commitment and sometimes it requires sacrifice, a sacrifice of your time and energy when you have worked so hard and you are so overburdened by academic responsibilities that you feel you have no time or energy left to give. But you still mentor, because you know it is the right thing to do, and it is what educators must do, but you mentor also because you are committed to the person. They have potential and they are worthy. They will make a contribution to the lives of others and they will also become mentors. To observe Renee as a teacher, scholar, and ethnographer, and to witness how others benefit from her labor is a joy beyond measure.

Through the years, I have become more and more convinced that being a mentor is fundamentally about being an agent of generosity. There is such jealousy, resentment, and competition in the academy. Sometimes it is hidden, unintended, and unconscious, and sometimes it is flagrant, mean, and very bad for your health. As mentors we must guide our mentees to fight the inclination at every turn to demean or resent the success of others or to be dismissive of the rewards and acclaim of others. Mentors must serve as models demonstrating sincere support and generosity, in deep and abiding ways, when colleagues achieve success. One common example is when a colleague gives a presentation or a public talk. We must encourage our mentees to always provide encouraging and complimentary comments or supportive, constructive feedback. It is rude and insensitive to not acknowledge, or to ignore and say nothing after a friend or colleague has given a presentation. This brand of "silence" happens all the time in academia and as mentors it is just as important to teach and nurture generosity, as it is to teach and nurture career success. We should not be stingy with sincere, deserved, and heartfelt praise. We all want, and need, and welcome praise. It substantiates what we do. If we cannot praise honestly, we must teach generosity in the act of engaged, thoughtful, and supportive suggestions and critique. We all want and need responses to our work; we want to be taken seriously, and to be given suggestions that enrich our work and expand our thinking beyond our own limitations. Being a mentor is encouraging community, camaraderie, and generosity of spirit.

Finally, being a mentor is captured in the way Tony so wonderfully talked about the influence of creation and art relative to social justice. I do believe that when we are working toward a socially just world that we must begin with honoring the labor of our academic community and carrying forth acts of generosity. Mentoring is to foster this labor of love and integrity, but to what end? We know that if the world isn't working right and we don't have clean water and we don't have clean air and if warfare carries us along paths of greater destruction, the work that we do counts for very little if positioned outside of these realities. On the contrary, it should be more urgent because of them. I think this is the added challenge of being a mentor, that is, being un-apologetic about teaching and encouraging the urgent. I have come to realize that mentoring for me forms a kind of trajectory. It starts with believing that this labor is valuable, it is almost divine. Then carrying this labor of love forth to being an agent of generosity that constitutes a level of integrity—that is ultimately about love also. And, finally, leading to and reckoning with politics, survival, and well being that is made of and in a world, both near and far, that we engage, critique, and contribute to a body politic.

[Soyini and Renee sit down and Norman and Aisha move to the front of the room.]

Norman: It started with a phone call to Aisha in Athens, about eight years ago. The voice on the other end of the line connected to this graduate application: "I want to come to Illinois, and I want to do black feminist hip-hop, and I want to do critical ethnography." She has sent an outstanding application. I had to put a voice to the application and encourage her to come to Illinois. I nominated her for a three-year distinguished Illinois fellowship, which she got. And that was the beginning of the end. And that's the story. [Laughter.]

There are so many good things that have been said here, and I agree with all of them. It all happens in this seminar room, 336 Gregory, in this seminar I have been teaching for forty years which continues to evolve. But since 9/11/01 it has evolved in a particular fashion, which is to locate our performances and our subjectivities and our experiences in this post-9/11 world that suddenly overnight became a neofascist state that located all of us in these competitions with each other over race, class, and identity. What we do in that room is about how we're going to enter into that space and contest it, and resist it, and if you don't want to be in that space, don't come to 336 Gregory. This room is a safe space. This will be a sacred site where we will take risks to explore and to resist and to contest these formations that are impinging on us. We will have the courage to make ourselves vulnerable to each other, and the vulnerability starts with me. So the only performance of the first class is always me, making myself vulnerable. If you're willing to be part of that space, and to share in my vulnerability, then I'll share in yours, and I'll make sure this room is safe for all of us. And then you let go. Everybody has spoken about this willingness to let go in that space, and to sit in the corner and let each person come forth and take their own risks and to just be on the margins. It's all about authority, and authority figures in our lives. Are we as faculty and colleagues going to let go of authority invested in us in a way that no longer makes that important? We're trying to create an empowering community within this atrocious academy and this disastrous historical moment, this neoliberal state, which is pressing in on all of us and making us be accountable to all sorts of systems. We're trying to create in this room that sacred space that can go anywhere, in what Aisha calls home. If I can be comfortable in this home-space, if I can create that space myself, and for her, and for Claudio, and for everybody else, then they can take that home anywhere. When we talked on Tuesday, Aisha talked about going back to Athens, and now she's going to College Station and she feels fine. Because home is where she is today. That is what we're trying to do in 336 Gregory.

Aisha: I'm going to cry. I just want to add that there's a component in terms of mentorship with Denzin that allows you to be able to have your own voice. There are a lot of mentor-mentee relationships that when you walk away you become a ventriloquist. Everything you say is something like, "Oh, this must be your advisor. This must be your mentor." But in some ways, what Denzin does is to provide you with the tools and then you're wondering the whole time, trying to figure out what it is that you are supposed to say. It is an entire project on how you're going to contribute to changing and having that commitment to social justice. What are you going to do with your own voice? I think that has been the most significant and the most important dynamic in our relationship because I never thought that I didn't have a voice and I never thought I was silenced in that particular way, it's just that I didn't think anybody was listening to what I said. I not only had financial support by literally working in the office with Denzin and hearing the stories, but I also had institutional support and emotional support when I had those moments. "I'm this black feminist scholar" and I'm always having to have these double identities, you know, being *the* black woman who is angry all of the time, but now understanding why I'm so angry about the world. I just want to say that in all of that organized chaos that I talked about there's that point of imaginative possibilities with being able to hear your own voice, speak your own voice, and even after that spotlight is not on you, you continue because the moment when you're going to be called, as the keynoter from last year asked [nodding to Soyini Madison], what will be your answer?

[Aisha and Norman sit down, and Laurel Richardson stands.]

Laurel: I've been thinking about how these mentors, mentor mentors, mentor you who are also mentors, and all of the different ways there are of mentoring and the different sets of directions one might take one's mentoring. I've also been hearing, as I know you all did too, how different the voices were. So you're true to your own voice and your own way of mentoring. Some mentors are comfortable with a total life enmeshment and other mentors might be much happier with a cooler relationship with their mentees. The important thing is staying true to who you are because you want to model your truths to your students as they progress.

The second thing I want to say, the thing that is important to me in my mentoring relationship, is the production of siblings, and the panel touched on that. The students are friends with each other, they become each other's eternal colleagues into the future once they're gone. It's really important, as a mentor, to create relationships between those persons that are noncompetitive, highly cooperative, friendly, loving, supportive, and open to all those possibilities. The panel identified those characteristics as important. In my mentoring, I have tried to make sure students are supportive to each other because this is going to be their community forever. So, in addition to mentoring relationships, sibling relationships also are important.

[After discussion with the audience in which some hint at mentoring relationships that are not ideal, Laurel summarizes.]

Laurel: In my sense of the universe, there are no accidents. Like now. Usually I take conference notes on the conference program, but because I left the program in my room, I've taken a notepad out of my book bag. Who knows how long the notepad has been secreted there? I don't remember acquiring it. Across the top of the notepad page is this aphorism: *Leave a trail of genius.*

Leave a trail of genius, indeed.

Ironically, a mentee both leaves and leads a trail of genius, teaching mentors about topic, process, commitment and letting-go—and, then, *voila,* mentees become mentors, make new trails, produce new generations—"academic grandchildren," who, if they are lucky will have adoring "aunts and uncles" and a host of "cousins."

Mentoring can take many different forms—be "full-blooded," and "full-time"—or not. I would be remiss if I didn't touch upon that "or not." Some of you in this room may have had neutral functional role-relationship with your mentor. Some cultures prefer limiting these relationships, and some people are happier with maintaining distance, separation between their private and professional lives. These are legitimate choices that we must also honor, rather than falling into a kind of American ethnocentrism. There are many ways—many trails—of genius.

Some of you have had disastrous relationships with your mentor. I imagine that for me listening to the "love fest" up here might be disheartening and disturbing. You might even feel jealous, angry, deprived. I am as sorry for your pain and loss as I am excited by the potential you bring to your students. What you have learned through the turmoil and travail can be the impetus for a mentoring style that abhors denigration, models integrity. In some ways, you come to the mentoring role with greater strength, determination, and compassion than those who have had it "easy." You have much to pass on. [Many in the audience nod.]

Leave a trail of genius. Create the future for qualitative inquiry.

Index

About the Authors

Editors

Norman K. Denzin is Distinguished Professor of Communications, College of Media Scholar, and Research Professor of Communications, Sociology, and Humanities at the University of Illinois, Urbana-Champaign. One of the world's foremost authorities on qualitative research and cultural criticism, Denzin is the author or editor of more than two dozen books, including *Performance Ethnography, Reading Race, Interpretive Ethnography, The Cinematic Society, Images of Postmodern Society, The Recovering Alcoholic, The Alcoholic Self,* and *Searching for Yellowstone.* He is past editor of *The Sociological Quarterly,* coeditor of the landmark *Handbook of Qualitative Research* (1st, 2nd, and 3rd editions, Sage Publications, with Yvonna S. Lincoln), and coeditor of the *Handbook of Critical & Indigenous Methodologies* (Sage, 2008, with Yvonna S. Lincoln and Linda Tuhiwai Smith). With Michael D. Giardina, he is coeditor of *Contesting Empire/Globalizing Dissent: Cultural Studies after 9/11* (Paradigm, 2006) and a series of books on qualitative inquiry published by Left Coast Press: *Qualitative Inquiry and the Conservative Challenge: Confronting Methodological Fundamentalism* (2006); *Ethical Futures in Qualitative Research: Decolonizing the Politics of Knowledge* (2007); and *Qualitative Inquiry and the Politics of Evidence* (2008). He is also the editor of the journal *Qualitative Inquiry* (with Yvonna S. Lincoln), founding editor of *Cultural Studies/Critical Methodologies,* series editor of *Studies in Symbolic Interaction,* and *Cultural Critique* series editor for Peter Lang Publishing. He is the founding president of the International Association for Qualitative Inquiry and the director of the International Congress of Qualitative Inquiry.

Michael D. Giardina is visiting assistant professor of advertising and affiliate faculty of cultural studies and interpretive research at the University of Illinois, Urbana-Champaign. He is the author of *From Soccer Moms to NASCAR Dads: Sport, Culture, and Politics since 9/11* (Paradigm, forthcoming) and *Sporting Pedagogies: Performing Culture & Identity in the Global Arena* (Peter Lang, 2005), which received the 2006 "Most Outstanding Book" award from the North American Society for the Sociology of Sport. In addition to a series of books edited with Norman K. Denzin on qualitative inquiry, he is the editor of *Youth Culture & Sport: Identity, Power, and Politics* (Routledge, 2007, with Michele K. Donnelly) and *Globalizing Cultural Studies: Methodological Interventions in Theory, Method and Policy* (Peter Lang, 2007, with Cameron McCarthy, Aisha Durham, Laura Engel, Alice Filmer, and Miguel Malagreca). He is also the associate editor of the *Sociology of Sport Journal*, and sits on the editorial board of *Cultural Studies/Critical Methodologies*. With Joshua I. Newman, he is currently completing a book titled *Consuming NASCAR Nation: Sport, Spectacle, and the Politics of Neoliberalism*.

Contributors

Tony E. Adams is an assistant professor in the Department of Communication, Media & Theatre at Northeastern Illinois University (Chicago). He teaches courses on relationships, gender, persuasion, identity, and communication theory. His work has appeared in journals such as *Qualitative Inquiry, Soundings, Cultural Studies/Critical Methodologies*, and *The Review of Communication*.

Arthur P. Bochner is professor of communication and co-director of the Institute for Human Interpretive Studies at the University of South Florida. He has written extensively on ethnography, autoethnography, and narrative inquiry, and has published such books as *Ethnographically Speaking: Autoethnography, Literature, and Aesthetics* (AltaMira, 2002, with Caroyln Ellis), *Composing Ethnography: Alternative Forms of Qualitative Writing* (AltaMira, 1996, with Carolyn Ellis), and *Understanding Family Communication* (Gorsuch, 1995 [1990], with Janet Yerby and Nancy Buerkele-Rothfuss). His work has also appeared in journals such as *Qualitative Inquiry, Journal of Contemporary Ethnography, Communication Theory,* and *Studies in Symbolic Interaction.*

Gaile S. Cannella is Research Professor of Critical and Qualitative Research Methodologies, Freeman School of Business, at Tulane University. She is the author of *Childhood and (Post)coloniza- tion: Power, Education, and Contemporary Practice* (Routledge, 2004, with Radhika Viruru) and *Deconstructing Early Childhood Education: Social Justice and Revolution* (Peter Lang, 1997) and editor of *Kidworld: Childhood Studies, Globalization, and Education* (Peter Lang, 2002, with Joe L. Kincheloe) and *Embracing Identities in Early Childhood Education: Diversity and Possibilities* (Teachers College Press, 2001, with Susan Y. Grieshaber).

Renee Alexander Craft is an assistant professor of communications at the University of North Carolina, Chapel Hill. Her research focuses on black identity, cultural performance, and nationalism(s) in the Americas. Based on six years of critical ethnographic and historical research with the Congo community of Portobelo, Panama, including a sustained one-year experience supported by a Fulbright Full Grant, she is completing a manuscript entitled *When the Devil Knocks: The Congo Tradition and Politics of Black Identity in Panama.*

Nicole Defenbaugh is an assistant professor of communications at Bloomsburg University, Bloomsburg, Pennsylvania. Her research includes multimethodological inquiries into the construction of illness identity, especially inflammatory bowel disease (IBD) and the influence of gender discourse in chronic illness through a per- formative lens. She is the author of a forthcoming book, entitled *Sites of Discovery: A Narrative Journey of the IBD Body.* She was the recipient of the 2008 Illinois Distinguished Dissertation Award, given by the International Association of Qualitative Inquiry.

Cynthia B. Dillard is a professor of multicultural education in the School of Teaching and Learning at The Ohio State University. Her major research interests include critical multicultural education, spirituality in teaching and learning, epistemological concerns in research and African/African American feminist studies. Most recently, her research has focused in Ghana, West Africa, where she established a preschool and was enstooled as Nana Mansa II, Queen Mother of Development, in the village of Mpeasem, Ghana, West Africa.

Aisha S. Durham is an assistant professor of communications and African studies at Texas A&M University. Her general research areas include performance ethnography and interpretive methods, black feminist cultural criticism, and media and popular culture. Recent work about race, class and gender representations, and lived experience extends her research on hip hop feminism and is featured in *Meridians: Feminism, Race, Transnationalism* and *Qualitative Inquiry*, as well as her coedited anthology, *Home Girls, Make Some Noise!* (Parker Publishing, 2007, with Gwendolyn Pough, Elaine Richardson, and Rachel Raimist).

Laura L. Ellingson is associate professor of communication at Santa Clara University. Her primary interests are in patient-physician communication and communication among interdisciplinary healthcare team members. Her research uses primarily feminist interviewing and feminist ethnographic methods. She is the author of *Communicating in the Clinic: Negotiating Frontstage and Backstage Teamwork* (Hampton Press, 2005).

Carolyn Ellis is professor of communication and codirector of the Institute for Human Interpretive Studies at the University of South Florida. She is the author of many books, including *The Ethnographic I: A Methodological Novel about Autoethnography* (AltaMira, 2004), *Composing Ethnography: Alternative Forms of Qualitative Writing* (AltaMira, 1996, with Arthur P. Bochner), and *Final Negotiations: A Story of Love, Loss and Chronic Illness* (Temple University Press, 1995). Her current research projects investigate autoethnograpy, narrative writing, and issues of illness and loss.

Frederick Erickson is professor of social research methodology and director of CONNECT: A Center for Research and Innovation in Elementary Education, at the University of California, Los Angeles and Seeds University Elementary School. He is the author of many books, including most recently *Arts, Humanities, and Sciences in Educational Research—and Social Engineering in Federal Education Policy* (Teachers College Record, in press) and *Talk and Social Theory: Ecologies of Speaking and Listening in Everyday Life* (Polity Press, 2004).

H. L. (Bud) Goodall, Jr. is professor and director of the Hugh Downs School of Human Communication at Arizona State University. He has written many books, including most recently *Writing the New Ethnography* (AltaMira, 2000), *Weapons of Mass Persuasion: Strategic Communication to Combat Violent Extremism* (Peter Lang, 2008, with Steven R. Corman and Angela Tretheway), *Writing Qualitative Inquiry: Self, Stories, and Academic Life* (Left Coast Press, 2008), and *A Need to Know: The Clandestine History of a CIA Family* (Left Coast Press, 2006).

Jean Halley is an assistant professor of sociology and anthropology at Wagner College, Staten Island, New York. She is the author of *Boundaries of Touch: Parenting and Adult-Child Intimacy* (University of Illinois Press, 2007) and editor of *The Affective Turn: Theorizing the Social* (Duke University Press, 2007, with Patricia Ticineto Clough).

Aaron Hess is a postdoctoral research fellow in wellness and health promotion at Arizona State University. His research interests include rhetoric, ethnography, new media, and alcohol and other drugs prevention.

Gloria Ladson-Billings is the Kellner Family Chair in Urban Education and professor of curriculum and instruction and educational policy studies at the University of Wisconsin-Madison. She is the author of numerous books, including *Dreamkeepers: Successful Teachers of African American Children* (Jossey-Bass, 1994); *Beyond the Big House: African American Educators on Teacher Education* (Teachers College Press, 2005); and *Crossing over to Canaan: The Journey of New Teachers in Diverse Classrooms* (Jossey-Bass, 2001).

She is also the editor of such books as *Education Research in the Public Interest: Social Justice, Action, and Policy* (Teachers College Press, 2006, with William F. Tate) and *City Kids, City Schools: More Reports from the Front Row* (New Press, 2007, with William Ayers, Gregory Michie, and Pedro Noguera). She has also served as president of the American Educational Research Association.

Yvonna S. Lincoln is professor of higher education and human resource development at Texas A&M University, where she holds the Ruth Harrington Chair of Educational Leadership and University Distinguished Professor of Higher Education. She is the coauthor of *Effective Evaluation* (Jossey Bass, 1992, with Egon Guba), *Naturalistic Inquiry* (Sage, 1985, with Egon Guba), and *Fourth Generation Evaluation* (Sage, 1989, with Egon Guba), the editor of *Organizational Theory and Inquiry* (Sage, 1985), and coeditor (with Norman K. Denzin) of *The Handbook of Qualitative Research* (1st, 2nd, and 3rd editions, Sage) and the journal *Qualitative Inquiry*.

D. Soyini Madison is a full professor at Northwestern University in the Department of Performance Studies. Professor Madison also holds appointments in the Department of African American Studies and the Department of Anthropology. She is the author of *Critical Ethnography: Methods, Ethics, and Performance*, coeditor of *The Sage Handbook of Performance Studies* (2006, with Judith Hamera), and editor of *The Woman That I Am: The Literature and Culture of Contemporary Women of Color* (PalgraveMacMillan, 1993). Madison lived and worked in Ghana, West Africa, as a senior Fulbright scholar conducting field research on the interconnections between traditional religion, political economy, and indigenous performance tactics. She received a Rockefeller Foundation Fellowship in Bellagio, Italy (2003) for her current book project, Acts of Activism: Human Rights and Radical Performance, based on fieldwork in Ghana.

Joseph A. Maxwell is professor in the Graduate School of Education, College of Education and Human Development, at George Mason University. He is the author most recently of *Qualitative Research Design: An Interactive Approach* (2nd edition,

Sage, 2005). He has also published widely on qualitative research and evaluation methods; combining qualitative and quantitative methods; medical education; Native American society and culture; and cultural and social theory. His present research interests focus primarily on the philosophy and logic of research methodology; he also pursues investigations in cultural theory, diversity in educational settings, and how people learn to do qualitative research.

Michele McIntosh, RN, MN, is a doctoral candidate in the Faculty of Nursing, University of Alberta and a lecturer in the School of Nursing, York University, Toronto, Canada. Her doctoral research is investigating participants' perspectives of risk, benefit or harm resulting from participation in unstructured qualitative interviews.

Janice M. Morse, Ph.D. (Nursing), Ph.D. (Anthropology), FAAN (Fellow of the American Academy of Nursing) is a professor and Presidential Endowed Chair at the University of Utah College of Nursing, and Professor Emeritus, University of Alberta, Canada. She was the founding director and scientific director of the International Institute for Qualitative Methodology, University of Alberta, founding editor of the *International Journal of Qualitative Methods,* and presently serves as the founding editor for *Qualitative Health Research.* From 1998–2007, she was the editor for the *Qual Press* and is currently editor for the series Developing Qualitative Inquiry, The Basics of Qualitative Inquiry (Left Coast Press) and Research Programs in Nursing (Springer). She is the author of 350 articles and fifteen books on qualitative research methods, suffering, comforting, and patient falls.

Ronald J. Pelias is professor and director of graduate studies in the Department of Speech Communications at Southern Illinois University, Carbondale. He is the author of numerous books on performance studies and performance methodologies, including most recently *Performance Studies: The Interpretation of Aesthetic Texts* (St. Martin's Press, 1992); *Writing Performance: Poeticizing the Researcher's Body* (Southern Illinois University Press, 1999); and *A Methodology of the Heart: Evoking Academic and Daily Life*

(AltaMira, 2004). In 2000, he received the Lilla A. Heston Award for Outstanding Scholarship in Interpretation and Performance Studies and the Distinguished Service Award, both from the National Communication Association.

Michelle S. Perez is a Ph.D. candidate at Arizona State University in the Department of Curriculum and Instruction, Early Childhood Education. She is currently conducting her dissertation research in New Orleans, Louisiana, examining discourses of power surrounding young children, charter schools, and the privatization of public education in New Orleans post-Katrina. Other research interests include using marginalized feminist, critical, postmodern, and poststructural philosophies to examine structures of power that exist socially and institutionally and oppress/privilege/"other" individuals and groups based on constructions/representations of race, class, gender, sexuality, age, and ability.

Laurel Richardson is Professor Emeritus of Sociology at The Ohio State University. She is an international leader in qualitative research, gender, and the sociology of knowledge. She has written many groundbreaking books, including the landmark *Fields of Play: Constructing an Academic Life* (Rutgers University Press, 1997), which received the 1998 Charles Cooley award from the Society for the Study Symbolic Interaction. Other publications include *Travels with Ernest: Crossing the Literary/Sociology Divide* (AltaMira, 2004, with Ernest Lockridge); *Writing Strategies: Reaching Diverse Audiences* (Sage, 1990); *Feminist Frontiers* (1st–7th editions) (McGraw-Hill, 2003, with Verta Taylor and Nancy Whittier); *The New Other Woman: Contemporary Single Women in Affairs with Married Men* (Macmillan, 1985); and, most recently, *Last Writes: A Daybook for a Dying Friend* (Left Coast Press, 2007).

Karen A. Stewart is a doctoral candidate in the Hugh Downs School of Human Communication at Arizona State University. Her research in visual communication focuses on public art, protest art, experimental cultures, and virtual communities.

Ian Stronach is Research Professor of Education at Liverpool John Moores University, England. His research spans a range of qualitative approaches to educational research—teacher research, action research, illuminative evaluation, deconstruction of the same, research methodology, and theory from a post-structuralist/postmodernist point of view. He is an editor of the *British Educational Research Journal* and a member of the British Educational Research Association Council.

Sarah J. Tracy is associate professor and director of The Project for Wellness and Work-Life in The Hugh Downs School of Human Communication at Arizona State University. Her organizational qualitative research focuses on identity, care work, emotion labor, workplace bullying, work-life balance, stress, and burnout. Her scholarship can be found in journals including *Management Communication Quarterly*, *Communication Monographs*, *Qualitative Inquiry*, and *Journal of Applied Communication Research*, among others.

Laura H. Vaughan, MSPT, is a physical therapist and independent scholar. She is interested in the intersection of religion, politics, and everyday life in contemporary America.